PASTORALISM AND THE TRIBESMAN OF MOUNTAIN

PASTORALISM AND THE TRIBESMAN OF MOUNTAIN

The Arung Zet Sa of Kanaor

Raghubir Singh Pirta

SHIPRA

ISBN: 978-81-7541-440-2

First Published in India in 2009

Pastoralism and the Tribesman of Mountain

Published by:
SHIPRA PUBLICATIONS
115-A, Vikas Marg, Shakarpur, Delhi-110092, INDIA
Phone: 91-11-65277210, 91-11-22500954
Fax: 91-11-22458662
E-mail: info@shiprapublications.com
www.shiprapublications.com

Affectionately

to

Kala

Foreword

In this timely book, Professor R.S. Pirta deals with the life and profession of the pastoralists in general, and of a western Himalayan pastoral community, known as *arung zet sa*, in particular. These pastoralists are natives of Kanaor, a District to which I belong. I appreciate his endeavor in this regard and also thank him for using original historical name of Kinnaur as *Kanaor* in this book which may not be known to many. Dr. R.S. Pirta, professor of psychology in Himachal Pradesh University, Shimla, specialises in the experimental and comparative psychology branches of this discipline. The latter area synthesises knowledge from biology, ecology and brain sciences to enrich our understanding of behavior and mental processes. The emphasis is particularly to develop insights from laboratory and naturalistic observations on variety of animals. This is probably the single most important distinction of this book by Dr. Pirta, that he is trained in conducting naturalistic observations on animal behavior, and therefore, competent to give an appropriate perspective to transhumant system of pastoralism, the *arung zet* system as it is known in Kanaor. Besides this, his association with Gandhians like Sunderlal Bahuguna was instrumental in the incorporation of the humanistic dimension to the issues of pastoralists.

I happened to meet him during a visit to my native village Nako somewhere in 1994, when he was leading a team from Italy who were either pastoralists themselves or were connected with this profession. We all stayed together in my village house which had minimal comfort and modern facilities. However, Dr. Pirta had no complaint for the material inconveniences; rather he felt joy and happiness in living and sharing the primordial truth. He is a very humble human being, full of humility, kindness and intellect. He is compassionate, caring and concerned about the feelings of others.

In this book Prof. Pirta focuses on the importance of man and animal relationship which is embedded in the phenomenon of interdependence. He follows holistic approach to understand the problems, relevance and future of the pastoral community, the *arung zet sa* of Kanaor. There is commendable effort to see local issues in context of global scenario. As per the practice prevalent in Kanaor, he has divided the pastoralists in two types – first, most prevalent of the day is agro-pastoral profession known as *kim zet sa*, to which I am exposed to and have direct experience, where the animals like sheep and goats are domesticated and the products thereof such as milk, wool, meat are used for human consumption and animal waste is used to manure the agricultural and horticultural fields, and second, the pastoralists now shrinking in their number, solely engaged in the rearing of sheep and goats and are always on the move from one place to another for search of pastures. They are known as *arung zet sa.* This profession is certainly on the verge of disintegration and the number of persons practicing this profession has substantially reduced because of many difficulties. Noticing and moved by the disintegration of the profession, Prof. Pirta has taken up all these issues and visualizes a future for these pastoralists, the *arung zet sa* of Kanaor in his book.

He has also analysed the views of various renowned scholars, intellectuals, and important persons about Kanaor. In some instances the views of some scholars are contradicted and proven wrong with the presentation of the ground reality, based more on the facts as he had gathered from the places and persons directly, where this profession had been prevalent and is still continuing, though in small numbers. This book is thus, certainly going to be a significant contribution on his part to the pastoralist in general and the *arung zet sa* of Kanaor in particular. This is a significant attempt from the psychological viewpoint on the pastoralists, where the behavior of the animals is explored to discover the nature of sheep and goats for the benefit of the human beings, but above all it has intrinsic value. He underlines the interdependent nature of phenomenal existence and to learn and adopt certain positive behavioral patterns even from the animals. These are the basic tenets of the natural phenomena. The truth needs no qualification as the same is always reflected and prevalent; however, to get to know the truth one needs right perception and knowledge. Prof. Pirta with his due diligence and understanding argues that every human being has potential of knowing the truth, even the pastoralists who are very humble, simple and poor but with their experience and inborn human potential are masters in their own field. Therefore, he emphasises the involvement of these pastoralists in the preservation and development of this profession. His visualization of a future of transhumance is commendable and certainly going to be beneficial in augmenting any concerted and constructive programme of development and preservation, initiated either at government level or privately through voluntary social organisations. It can be a guide in this respect, of course, and it would certainly be a record and source for generating new insights among the interested scholars.

To summarize, the first five chapters of the book succinctly deals with important aspects of pastoralism that are on the one hand local, but on the other hand raise important global issues. The remaining three chapters introduce the reader to other dimensions that has relevance to pastoral profession. In this venture Dr. Pirta has elicited the cooperation of a native pastoralist and distinguished linguist of Bhoti, and three young researchers from Himachal Pradesh University. These contributions form Part II of the book. Shri V.S. Negi describes the ethnology of the *arung zet* system; Chhaya Pirta and Sonia Pakhretia incorporate the biological information on pastoralism; and Dr. R.S. Ranta narrates the socio-cultural aspects of these communities.

On the whole, in my opinion this book not only gives theoretical account of pastoralism for the academicians but it suggests practical measures for understanding the complexities of human and animal relationship, and for the development and conservation of culture of the natives engaged in pastoralism at the global level.

10-10-2008

H.C. Negi (I.R.S.)
Commissioner (A) XIV Income Tax,
501, Earnest House,
Nariman Point
Mumbai

Preface

The society in Himachal Pradesh has many scenarios. While life in the palaces of small princely states had a Victorian flavour, the pastoralists moved under the open sky. The latter mode of subsistence is transhumance where a community is partly sedentary but some of its members are always on the move with the herds of sheep and goats. For some they may represent the early stage of human evolution, the volume explores pastoralism from the humanistic perspective.

There are two related issues that have significance in decision making about some sensitive issues related to the profession of pastoralism. The first issue is the deification of a political category by the behavioural scientists. For example, the people in a certain area declared as tribal or backward are then assumed to be lacking in some cognitive abilities. Another issue involves the dialogue between tradition and science, a policy decision neglecting one or the other knowledge system may have to bear associated costs. In this volume these issues have been analysed after critical evaluation of some important studies on pastoralism, in particular, and the social and cognitive issues in general.

A review of the available reports of the Food and Agriculture Organisation (FAO) since independence, made in this volume, has significance for the researchers in animal husbandry. It highlights that in scientist's lure for exotic species the local diversity of sheep and goats was neglected, as noted by the FAO experts as early as in the nineteen sixties. They also pointed out a fallacy in the experimental designs employed by the breeding scientists in India. For example, in making comparative assessments, groups of exotic (e.g. Polwarth) and indigenous (e.g. Rampur Bushair) sheep were not kept under identical conditions. Little or no attempt was made to incorporate the elements of collective traditional knowledge of pastoral communities in developing modern breeding farms.

Although, institutional input in research and technical know-how since the independence is substantial, its impact on the lives of pastoralists is invisible. These people, traditionally capable of rearing large herds of sheep and goats, are presently driven to unlearn these animal husbandry skills. Instead efforts should have been to revolutionise pastoralism as an industry by providing necessary research and development input, and thereby improving the pastoral services to society. Moreover, the proud owners of large herds in the wild, the *arung zet sa*, would not have to develop an alien identity of a poor 'tribal'. The two aspects of man-animal relationship, the first one signifying the human need for food, and the second indicating the curiosity of early man, respectively, parallel the present day molecular gene farming and the passionate accounts of animal world by the evolutionary psychologists.

The pastoral societies in the high altitude areas from Ladakh to Arunanchal Pradesh have enriched their lives by adopting the Wheel of Life. Perhaps transhumance was instrumental in this development. Of particular significance is the doctrine of the interdependent origination (*pratityasamutpada*). This concept is analogous to the basic ecological relationships among the living and non-living objects. Although it is a difficult task, while on the one side is the realm of spiritualism, whereas on the other side is the realm of science. In this volume the attempt is to achieve integration where the 'cognized models' of people based on their interactions within the ecosystem are important units in planning and development. This approach would, for example, be crucial to explore the interdependence between the transhumance and the ecosystem in the Himalayan region. Specifically, it is holistic attempt to explore two interrelated issues, to understand the impact of pastoralism on environment in a fragile ecosystem, and to assess the mediation of religion and culture in this relationship.

The volume consists of eight chapters. The first five deal with the preceding issues, namely, the global and regional scenarios of pastoralism; the Himalayan dilemma; harmony and conflict over resource use; resilience of social bonds; and, lessons from the naturalistic life of animals. The other three chapters deal with the neglected issues of pastoralism as mentioned in the report of the FAO in 2001. To fulfill these neglected aspects help of experts were solicited. They include: an insider's story of the transhumant pastoralist, the *arung zet sa*, the biological aspects of pastoralism, and the traditional institutions of pastoral well-being.

To live in an inhospitable environment and to deal with diverse social groups, pastoral households have evolved patterns of adjustment varying in nature from material to non-material. They have developed complex institutions, usually ignored by the investigators. Largely, the contribution of transhumance is simply measured as an economic activity; the present volume is an appreciation of the deeper psyche of the pastoral folk mind.

Behaviour is a key to understand the life of animals, particularly the migratory herds of sheep and goats. Though domesticated by man, they live under natural conditions. For the management of migratory herds of sheep and goats scientific studies on the behaviour of these animals is as much important as are physiological and anatomical studies. For example, the survival of lamb or kid is considerably related to mother-infant affectionate relationship taking place during early phases of development. There also occur interactions between physiological states and behavioural states. Moreover it is during this period that the infant becomes a part of social organization where different patterns of behaviour, innate or learned, are needed for normal social relationships. These patterns are important during interactions with mates of like age or adult members of the group. Some of them help an individual to escape from predators. It is through these behaviour patterns that the effective heterosexual relationships develop among adults during the mating season.

If local communities, for example the people of Himachal Pradesh, remain aloof from global issues, the cost may be very high. Not only that, there is the fear of the colonization of minds of people. The chances of combating any such colonization, in particular, and avoidance of subjugation in general, are likely to increase if people of Himachal Pradesh participate actively in the global cognitive revolution. But participation in global cognitive revolution, which is likely to benefit the people of this State as well as the entire humanity, further depends on choosing between the two options. The first option is to leave behind the traditional cultural base and adopt the western individualistic ideology (selfish model), having its associated losses and gains. The alternative option is to build upon the existing traditional base (altruistic) and incorporate and assimilate the new information according to contextual elements for the well-being of community.

The process of globalization by its very nature overlooks the local cultural complexities and advocates universal approach. On the other hand, social scientists suspect the universal approach to understand local problems. It is however the mental uniqueness, evolving along biological, cultural and divine pathways, on which the humanity prospers. Cognitive uniqueness of human species has a quality of immense diversity. This diversity becomes manifold as the mental state interacts with the physical. All this is possible due to the shaping of minds in specific ecological settings, for example, the development of a child in a pastoral community in the Himalayas.

Acknowledgements

The plan to undertake this study has a long history and overlaps my research on monkey behaviour in the western Himalaya, where I met pastoralists in the mountains touching the Tibetan plateau in summer to the Sivalik hills during winter. The insights into the problems of pastoralists, however, developed slowly from participation in the foot marches of Chipko, spearheaded by Gandhian social workers in the Himalayas. The thoughts of Shrimati Vimla Bahuguna and Shri Sunderlal Bahuguna went deep down in the recesses of my mind, yet the goal, *one sheep, one tree*, is far away.

The field work was accomplished by eliciting the cooperation of pastoralists, with whom I stayed, roamed, and fed my belly. The pastoralists voluntarily shared their experiences, therefore, these people really deserve the copyright of this volume. A proud transhumant pastoralist, Shri Vidya Sagar Negi, patiently listened to my verbalizations, and then began a study on the pastoralists of Kanaor. The results have been published in the volume entitled: *The Nomadic Shepherds of North-West Himalayas*. An Italian pastoralist Mr. Antonio Viglietti accompanied me in a transverse walk from Nako village near Tibetan border to the Chood Dhar in the mid Himalayan range. He also sent several old reports on pastoralism from FAO, Rome.

A meeting with the well known pastoral leader Shri Thakur Singh Bharmourie, the Chief Parliamentary Secretary, Himachal Pradesh, and the brain-storming session with more than twenty officials, all Gaddis, provided further insights into the issues of transhumance. Even more rewarding was the field study on the behaviour of sheep and goats by Sonia Pakhretia, a research scholar of Psychology Department.

For an early draft of this volume, a small financial grant was received from the Institute of Integrated Himalayan Studies, H.P. University. For this, I am thankful to the Vice Chancellor Professor S.K. Gupta, and the past and present directors of IIHS, Professor Yoginder Verma and Professor Vidya Sharda, respectively. The encouragement received from Professor Suresh Kumar is unforgettable.

The research of Professor Madhav Gadgil at the Center for Ecological Sciences, I.I.Sc. Bangalore, on pastoralism and his quest for evolution of behaviour were instrumental for the present study. Long, and at times disagreeable, conversations with Professor Chetan Singh helped to go deeper into problems. The studies of Professor L.S. Thakur on the temples and monasteries, and the company of Professors A.C. Pal, O. P. Chauhan, and M.L. Jharta, have been simply invigorating.

The intimate social-network of my joint family has always been an asset for the acquisition of information, and, at the same time a secure base for new initiatives. Comments of Shri D. Kumar, Shipra Publications, were crucial for shaping this volume.

Contents

List of Boxes, Figures and Tables

List of Boxes

List of Figures

List of Tables

1

Global and Regional Scenarios

The animal drawings on the walls of the pre-historic caves documented human curiosity in these creatures as early as thirty thousand years ago. Strangely enough, it took another twenty thousand years to secure the company of these animals. The invention was, however, a turning point in the cultural and biological evolution of our species (Diamond, 1989; Protsch & Berger, 1973). These animals were a great relief to the group tired of its predatory forays. Killing other animals required tremendous effort, and there was always the fear of being killed. Taming animals met both these needs. It is noteworthy that this old invention of satisfying human needs prevails even today in one or the other form among all societies of the world. However, one wonders about the meaning of these works of art that predates taming. For these primitive artists their subjects were perhaps more than merely prominent feature of their culture (Waters, 1964), whereas the post-modernist visualizes these works of rock art as the expressions of mundane as well as supernatural that do not follow time and space (Malik, 1999).

These two aspects of early man-animal relationship, the first one signifying the secure supply of food, and the second indicating the curiosity about the fellow creatures, respectively, parallel the present day molecular gene farming and the passionate accounts of animal world. While the former is more obvious and visible, the latter is apparently less convincing and has remained largely obscure from planners, public and the users. It has taken a long time to realise that the curiosity about the nature of animals is more fundamental than the refinement of techniques in livestock management and development.

The present volume aims to draw attention to this hidden aspect of man-animal relationship. Primarily it satisfies human curiosity, but its greater role for the enrichment of man-animal relationship deserves recognition. Though the migratory herds of sheep and goats served the poorest of the poor by transporting essential items like salt to the remote villages of the Himalayas, they also catered the elite classes with the finest *pashmina* wool. There is however need to move from a purely selfish goal, benefiting only man, to one that is at least reciprocal, if not altruistic, where interdependence guides our behaviour with the herds of sheep and goats. Such humanistic orientation would reduce various social conflicts that pastoral communities face. This is necessary for man as well as animal, and above all for the love of life (Wilson, 2006).

The human curiosity about animals is visible in various disciplines of knowledge. Be the artists, poets, and writers, on the one extreme, and the observers of fine details of animal behaviour, on the other. The latter comprises of comparative psychologists, ethologists, socio-biologists and the evolutionary psychologists. On the basis of archaeological evidence historians speculate that people practiced pastoralism in Gujrat about 3,000 years ago (Varma, 1991). At this time also, pastoralism is the important mode of subsistence in Gujrat. The Bharvads and Rabaris specialize in breeding and herding of cattle, sheep, goats and camels. In the State of Uttaranchal, in the Himalayas, the paintings in rock shelters of Megalith period show people, probably herders, with goat and bovine like animals. It indicates the prevalence of animal husbandry in north-west Himalayas almost at the same period as in Gujrat (Mathpal, 1992). Moreover, it is reasonable to assume that to rear the herds of sheep and goats complex social system was necessary, and thus it acted as catalyst for cultural complexity.

The Tibetan plateau and the adjacent Himalayan mountains of Asia are the largest alpine areas that serve as the breeding grounds for important fauna, including sheep and goats (Kendeigh, 1980). There are estimates that by 4,000 B.C. western Eurasia already had the 'big five' domestic livestock: sheep, goats, pigs, cows and horses (Diamond, 1989). The domestication of sheep and goats is indirectly an indicator of the efficient social system. Along with the pastoral system, the widespread stone and iron tool making, particularly in the mid-Himalayan ranges, may have facilitated a unique kind of cultural evolution in the region (Box 1.1).

The holistic understanding of pastoralism thus requires inputs from animal behaviour science and mental science for which evolutionary psychology is well equipped. This branch discards the reductionist stance of standard social science paradigm, and derives strength from collectivist social norms, sophisticated philosophy of mind, metaphor of reincarnation, deep cosmic sense, and anti-consumerist euphoria (Miller, 2006). We shall explore some of these issues in this section, not only because they are important for the well-being of pastoral communities, but also because

> **Box 1.1:** Over the Brua Pass: Retracing an Old Sheep Walk
>
> For long, wrote Deuster in 1939, the major wealth of Kanaoras consisted in their herds, mainly sheep and goats, which also found good use for the transport of goods. In summer they stayed in Tibet and in winter they came down in the lower parts of Himalayas. He estimated that, at that time, around 72,000 sheep and goats were in Kanaor. Sheep provided wool that was largely sold at Rampur, whereas the goats were reared for more costly fine quality fibre, the *pasham*.
>
> However the traffic of trade above the passes of Dhaula Dhar range, for example, the Brua Pass was hardly more than of local importance. At that time, Deuster (1939) noted "*The salt is brought from Kinnaur to Rohru or Chaila, as this is also called, the Kinnauris bring grains from there, of which they have scarcity mainly rice which is not grown in their region.*" (p. 67)
>
> Today, besides delicious varieties of apples, the people of Kanaor grow seasonal vegetables. Now the seasonal crop of peas is carried in lorries to market as far as New Delhi. And the farmer of Kanaor returns either with cash or a mobile set, a means of telecommunication. The essential goods are available everywhere in Kanaor. These days the sheep and goats cross the 13,000 feet Brua Pass only for grazing in the summer pastures.

they may enlighten us about the myths created by the academicians about these people.

Cognitive and Social Responses

For cognitive scientists, comments Wilson (2006), the mind is not just an entity, the brain at work, but more specifically as a flood of scenarios. Whether it is set in the past, present or future, whether based on reality or entirely fictive, mind processes them all. This conceptualisation underlies our approach to people engaged in pastoral activities. Taming herds of sheep and goats, and the other animals as well, may have needed various skills from the group. They are highly dynamic and have evolved tremendously upto the present times. The future scenarios are of molecular farming, rather than the ones we have chosen for the present study, those of men traversing various altitudinal zones with their flocks of sheep and goats. Yet the scenarios of latter had the importance. Not that they are still earthly, but because it may help in conceiving alternative ways of change in these societies.

A related important issue is, whether plant domestication started earlier, simultaneously with or later than the animal domestication. Today we find these three stages all over the world. The most common pattern is the practice of animal husbandry with agriculture of the other two patterns, only agriculture or animal rearing, are less common. How people use herds of sheep and goats to exploit the rugged Himalayan mountains, with few domesticated plants, for survival, is a key to understanding their social life and environmental adaptations. This in fact is the focus of the present study. The Gaddis and Kanaoras, moving with the herds of sheep and goats, exemplify such interdependence between man and animal. It also provides a contrast to understand the impact of modern agriculture and horticulture development in the fragile ecosystem of the Himalayas.

One view to look at the society is to study the relationships of the group, as a whole and through its individual units, with the living and non-living things. The ways of interaction differ from place to place, and varies over time. Though the non-living things like rivers, valleys, hills, clouds and clear sky appear as passive agents, they in fact induce significant changes in the lives of people. These changes relate to the rhythm of procuring daily needs through the melodious songs in praise of nature. At the very elementary level of the development of society one may try to understand the structuring of a social group with regard to utilization of resources.

Ecologists view social organisation from this perspective. In other words, the patterning of access to resources significantly contributes in the development of social organization (Gadgil, 1991). In the hunter-gatherer societies the access to natural resources is equitable. However, in the more developed hierarchical societies individual's access to resources is highly skewed or inequitable. In addition to that, the geographical features also influence the broad distribution of occupations in which people engage. According to People of India (POI) project of the Anthropological Survey of India there were 2,753 communities in 32 States. Himachal Pradesh has greater number of traits as well as communities as compared to its neighbouring States, the possible reason being wide disparity in its terrain.

From the analysis of POI project data, "*One expects pastoral nomads, i.e. shepherds, cowherds, etc. who move over large distances with their livestock primarily to occur in habitats where grazing resources are highly seasonal. This would be the case in regions of scanty rainfall or seasonal snowfall. Indeed while only 26 out of 3,954 (0.65%) communities in regions of high or medium rainfall practice nomadic pastoralism, as many as 9 out of 646 (1.5%) of communities in tracts of low rainfall, 4 out of 103 (4%) in tracts of scanty rainfall and 15 out of 196 (7.5%) in tracts of snowfall do so. Part of cultural diversity of the Indian subcontinent can thus be explained by the ecological setting.*" (Joshi, Gadgil & Patil, 1993)

Singh (1998) disagrees with Gadgil on the specialisation according to the utilisation of natural resources, and its (presumed) unaltered continuity over a period, changelessness of this sort was rare. Another historian Guha (1999) also questions Gadgil's thesis of resource specialisation. This misinterpretation is perhaps due to the use of reductionist approach by these historians. Gadgil in his holistic argument has even documented continuous interaction among adjacent groups, and also with the groups much farther in the urban centers, for example, in the case studies of pastoralists in North Kannara (Gadgil & Malhotra, 1981). For us, in the present study, it is more important to further probe Singh's argument, as it pertains to pastoral and agro-pastoral groups in Himachal Pradesh.

In the 'Epilogue' to his book, Singh (1998) summarises his argument about ecology and peasant life in the Western Himalayas from 1800-1950. It is not clear whether the smallness of scale of the resource use also assumes limited cognitive achievement or mental capacity, or not. For he writes "*Making fibre from wild nettle or cutting grass for hay from sun-scorched mountain slope did not have the impressive visual effect of a falling giant deodar, but it was 'insignificant' activities of the former kind that made existence in Himachal possible.*" (Page 234) Perhaps a strong view about this statement is, while the demise of British rule was being written, the author belittles the hill folk. That is, Singh seems to suggest that local people had limited cognitive development, forgetting that it was the failure of the colonial masters to inculcate new skills among its subjects, for over a century (Box 1.2).

Box 1.2: Kanam, a Village Proud of its Culture

About Huns, the nomadic pastoralists of the bygone era, writes Ammianus Marcellinus "*No one ever ploughs a field in their country, or touches a plough handle. They are ignorant of time, law or settled existence and they keep roaming from places in their wagons. If you ask one of their children where he comes from; he was conceived in one place, born far away and brought up still further off.*" (FAO, 2001)

In a foreword of a book by Hoon (1996) the transhumant Bhotias of Kumaon Himalaya, Tolia writes, not only that he was an administrator responsible for the development of this Himalayan region, but was also one of them. Very few show such self-confidence, when the community (the Bhotiyas) is the "tribe." He further noted, the Hungarian scholar-saint Csoma de Koros, "*set out in search of his roots, i.e., the Hoons, and ended up becoming the first Tibetologist the world knows of. It was Korosi who informed the rest of the world who these Monpas were, how they were geographically segregated and what their relations with the Huniyas were (people of gNagri Khorssum or western Tibet).*"

Csoma de Koros did this commendable work in a prestigious family, the Loktas of Kanam, in the Kanaor. They had a library of the Tibetan scriptures, 105 volumes of Kangŷur and 225 volumes of Tangyur (Gupta, 1998). He found there a congenial environment for the scholarly work, the foundations of which were laid down by Rin-chen-bZang-po in the 11th century. Csoma de Koros used the library at Kanam village from 1827 to 1830 to compile an authoritative Tibetan dictionary and grammar.

One may, however, commit a mistake in comprehending the meaning of this phrase, but the consecutive statement of the author does not leave scope for any such misunderstanding. As Singh concludes with greater firmness that the ordinary hill peasant could not comprehend the nature of the process into which he was being drawn. But it is unlikely that the human population in Himachal Pradesh is highly skewed towards negative side in mental ability. We, on the other hand, assume that like all other human beings, people in Himachal Pradesh are also distributed normally on mental ability—a large portion of normal individuals in the middle, and above and below it are individuals respectively with greater or smaller measure of the ability.

It is reasonable to assume that there is lack of written evidence reflecting the cognitive competence of the pastoral and agro-pastoral groups. As a result of which they were reasonably lower from the comparison group (the British). Though the intention of the author was to study the cognitive dimensions (see the introductory chapter of Singh's book) of the people of Himachal Pradesh, it is doubtful if he exhausted all the measures open to an historian. Yet, Singh makes last frantic attempt to make us believe that the progress that one may see (in Himachal) was the result of the innovations of the colonial rulers flourishing in the hands of sincere administrators. This exclusion of the masses, largely belonging to pastoral and agro-pastoral communities, in the peace and prosperity of Himachal Pradesh, leads to an improbable conclusion, which seems highly unlikely, that the complex 'innovations' can germinate in infertile minds.

It draws our attention towards a fallacy of historians, noticed by Goswamy (1975) in his work on Pahari portraits of 'ordinary people.' He pointed out that there was a trend to overlook the achievements of the common folk. The denial of the 'cognized models' of 'ordinary people,' be they be the beliefs in local deities classified under the little tradition (Verma, 2002) or systems of marriage not conforming Manu's prescriptions (Kapoor, 1993), would be a gross error in understanding these communities. It is depriving the global fraternity from the glimpse of the richness of cultural diversity. Even the 'operational models' one intends to impose upon these communities require a deeper understanding of 'cognized models' in the first instance (Rappaport, 1979). That there is considerable regional variety, for instance, of designs in various styles of traditional Hindu mandirs in Himachal Pradesh, as Chetwode (1975) stresses, strengthens the preceding argument to a considerable extent. Chetwode especially noted that the chalet style temples constructed in the Sutlej valley, particularly excels in their architectural richness. The valley is the home of proud *arung zet sa*, the transhumant pastoralists of Kanaor.

In an historical analysis, Ratnagar (1991) has suggested that the Jamuna basin in the vicinity of Mathura, was the legendary home of the pastoral Yadava rulers, the followers of the cowherd Krishna cult. These areas developed into suitable niches of pastoralism; though it is difficult to establish if these pastoralists had any linkages with the pastoral communities of the Himalayas, the legend of Krishna even today dominates their life.

One way to develop hypotheses about the evolution of pastoralism is to couch it in ecological determinism, a new trend in historical writings. For example, agro-pastoralism can prevail in zones, which cannot support successful agriculture or pastoralism (Ratnagar, 1991). As an alternative hypothesis, we may imagine evolution of different modes of livelihood (e.g. hunting and gathering, transhumance, sedentary agriculture, agro-pastoralism, etc.) at different places, not necessarily as an adaptation, but innovations of human mind. Later, they are used to adapt to different environments to maximize benefits. The sedentary agriculturists can thus maximize benefits by engaging in pastoral activities. Similarly, pastoralists may engage in some agricultural activity to supplement food and fodder. There is yet another possibility, irrespective of the previous two strategies, with some cognitive development, people may widen their activities and modify subsistence patterns or adopt other modes of living.

It is essential to keep these alternative scenarios in mind, they may either make the ecological hypothesis even stronger, or allow us to reject the hypothesis on reasonable grounds. It is quite possible that certain groups are relegated to the means of livelihood merely due to prevailing socio-cultural processes. This may happen even with the entire population. Therefore some investigators seriously question the adaptive nature of pastoralism. In pursuing this argument, Young (1991) asked whether pastoralism of Rashaayda 'Bedouin' was an adaptation to natural environment in Sudan? He wrote that it was not an adaptation because the territories the Rashaayda inhabited were not the 'natural pastures.' Those habitats, due to continuous grazing over a long period have lost their pristine condition. The plant distribution has drastically changed. It was falsely assumed that the same was probably true for the Rashaayda's ancestral homeland in Arabia from where they emigrated to Sudan.

However, this viewpoint narrates only one side of the story. It overlooks the other factors that might have precipitated in overgrazing of a certain habitat or emigration to other territories. With the increase in the diversification in the use of natural resources, some communities directly sell their products whereas the others transform it in different ways to increase its market value. Although some of these changes are based on developments in social relationships and patterns of resource use, but highly significant innovations are seldom possible without cognitive in put. Some examples are: a book written by an author after a journey of the Himalayas; a plant extracted from Himalayas for manufacturing drugs; or, multiple uses of hydroelectric power generated from the Himalayan rivers. All these processes may occur far away from the place where natural resources exist. It is an important characteristic of the modern society. The farther the two classes, the 'ecosystem people' and the 'elites' move from each other in the use of natural resource, the greater are the chances of conflict between them. Where it has been observed that the 'elite' was inducing the ecosystem people for greater and greater extraction of natural resources. The result was the development of big urban centres siphoning the natural resources from far away areas. In this way, by the end of pre-colonial period Murshidabad in Bengal became one of the largest urban centre of production of fine textiles (Gadgil, 1991).

The preceding observations, the one by Young and the other by Gadgil, are important for us in two ways. First, the science of ecology deals with live interactions between biotic and abiotic elements of an ecosystem. For the historian these relationships lie fossilized in the primary and secondary sources. Thus its recovery involves a large component of imagination where one must be ready to accept alternative explanations. Second, there is enormous scope for ecologists and historians to cooperate to develop a sound science of eco-history. For this they need not be unnecessarily wary towards each other. This is noticeable when Singh (1998) and Guha (1999) discard the ecologist's (Gadgil's) hypothesis about the organisation of society in India. Since, it appears later that ecological determinism is an important basis in their (Singh as well as Guha) explanations of agro-pastoralist and pastoral social systems, and also in understanding the relationships of these social systems with the larger power structures within which they work.

Nobody denies such dynamic interactions, still one finds groups that differ considerably in patterns of resource use, and, at different stages of development. Therefore a challenging problem is to explore why certain groups remain at particular stages of development whereas the others adopt new modes of life. This has significance, particularly for humanistic reasons, in the context of the transhumant populations in which we are interested here. Some possibilities are: entrapment in a terrain with limited options; socio-political constraints; intrinsic socio-cultural factors; and, lack of cognitive resources.

Scenarios of Pastoralism in Himachal Pradesh

Many factors lead to the enrichment of the human culture in particular regions. Those factors may be: assimilation from earlier, and surrounding, human cultures over time (historical); the individual's insatiable hunger to dominate the others (political); a social system where persons with special skills receive patronage (social); a system to generate surplus through differentiation (economic). However, a factor pervading all these factors, historic, political, social, and economic, has remained inconspicuous. It is the individual and collective cognition and behaviour of common people interacting with the artificial and natural components of ecosystem through cultural and biological evolutionary mechanisms. These common people hardly speak for themselves. Sometimes their tribal chiefs, the *gurs* (spokespersons of deities), poets and writers speak for them. It is very important to know the interactions of the common people with their biotic, abiotic and homotic (man-made) components of an ecosystem.

The study of pastoral communities introduces us to deeper levels of conflicts, cooperative and competitive, where social, religious and political identities form intricate web inside and outside the individual and his group. In evolutionary terms, they may be visualised as individual, group and interdemic selections. For example, the invasion of Aryan pastoralists is largely conceived by the historians responsible for the demise of Harappan civilisation in the North-West India. It is an example of interdemic selection, where one population, divided in several groups, supplants the other. However, when we look into the conflicts between sedentary and pastoral groups, there are elements of cooperation and competition that not only involve direct access to natural resources but the social and religious identities as well. The deities get divided, Rama is idealized as a hero by the sedentary agriculturalists, and the Krishna becomes the beloved and saviour of the pastoralists. At the regional level, the conflicts within an agro-pastoral group take different forms. In some unique case, an individual pastoralist of a socially deprived section with some charisma, emerges as deity after death, and thus we have Doom Devata and Baba Balak Nath Ji in Himachal Pradesh.

Though these deified heroes of agro-pastoral communities of the mid-Himalayan mountains have some meaning for the Gaddis and the Kanaoras, these pastoral groups also have deities of various complex patterns. In the same way a distant pastoral group like the Todas of Nilgiri has an entirely different cultural identity. But it also differs within the region, for example, consider the pastoral group that have different religious identity, for example the Muslim Gujars. Both these groups, the Todas and the Gujars, rear water buffaloes in the mountains, respectively, in the South and in the North. The Todas of Nilgiris in South India are a dying culture. These traditional dairy keeping people consider everything sacred around them including their buffaloes. However their culture do not receive much respect from the lovers of wildlife, the tea estate owners, and the town people. All of them have encroached upon the sacred land of Todas (Chhabra, 1994). The same is the story of Gujars in the Western Himalayas (Box 1.3). Gujars are the sturdy and handsome pastoralists of the Western Himalayas they move up and down with the herds of buffaloes. In winter one finds them in the *tarai* and *bhabar* forests of Punjab, Haryana, Uttaranchal and Uttar Pradesh frequenting the nearby towns to sell their milk and to procure necessary items of daily needs. But in summer they climb with their cattle to the beautiful pastures of the Himalayas. They speak local dialects of the areas where they go, besides their own that has influence of Urdu. They also worship Hindu gods and goddesses along with their Muslim traditions.

Box 1.3: The Rhythm in the Life of Gujars

Although Gujars do not have separate territory, they interact with wide variety of people, as their profession requires it, yet they have kept their cultural identity intact over a long period. The dress, the dialect, the look, the buffalo herd and the *kotha* or hut make a Gujar stand distinct in the Western Himalayas. The Gangi song of Gujar is popular on the lips of Himachali, Punjabi, Dogri and Kashmiri. His philosophy of life has the indelible imprint of the beauty of nature as expressed in the following lines (Bedi, 1991):

Uchra uchra rab bo, uchare assade passu bi bo,
jo dinde dudh bo, jiste assanu jiuna milda.
Per rab tan passuon bahut uchera, jo dinda unanu janam bo.

(God is great, but our herds are also great, for they provide milk, which fetches us, food to survive. But god is far greater than the herds, as He is their Creator.)

The reverence for other culture is part of the life of people who live close to nature, particularly those moving with the herds of sheep and goats. They learn to share. It is reflected in their use of natural resources. The modern civilised people behave curtly with them but pastoralists reciprocate with courtesy. For the planners of twenty-first century sheep and goat rearing is a paltry business. On the other hand the tradition is still reinforcing these systems. These communities contribute to the richness of the cultural diversity in these rugged mountains. The mountains that appear sleepy and sometimes devoid of human culture to a visitor pulsate with slow and steady rhythms of the pastoralists.

The sheep and goats are reared by almost all sections of society in Himachal Pradesh (Figure 1.1). In its political boundary of 55,673 square kilometers, known as Himachal Pradesh, according to the Livestock Census 2003 (conducted by the Department of Animal Husbandry, Government of Himachal Pradesh), there were about 9,06,027 sheep and 11,15,587 goats. The broad details of these two populations are presented here. Thus a comparison of sheep and goats in Himachal Pradesh indicates greater number of females, in sheep as well as goats (Figure 1.2).

From 1992 to 2003 there is noticeable decline in the number of sheep but the goat population is more or less same (Figure 1.3).

For over 60,77,900 persons in Himachal Pradesh (Census 2001), there are 149.06 sheep and 183.55 goats per thousand (Figure 1.4).

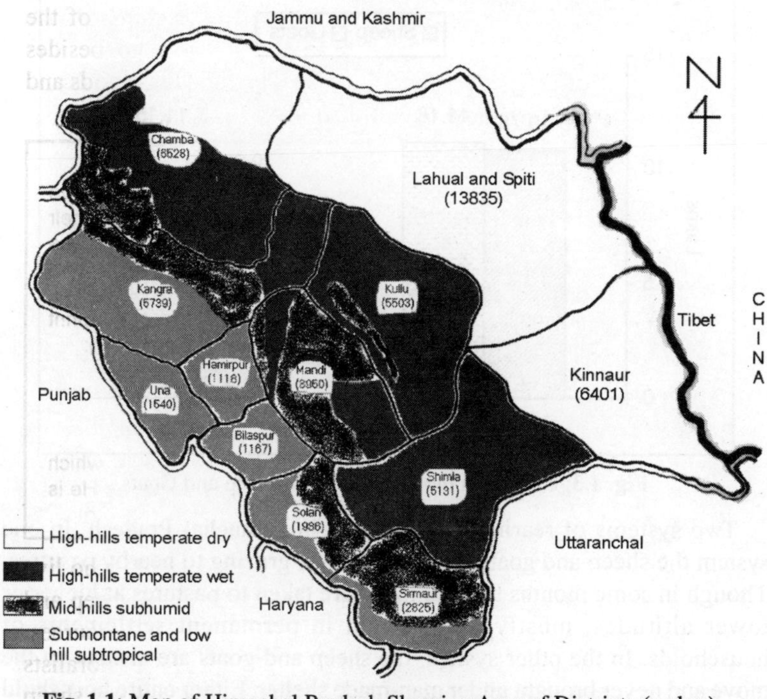

Fig. 1.1: Map of Himachal Pradesh Showing Area of Districts (sq km)

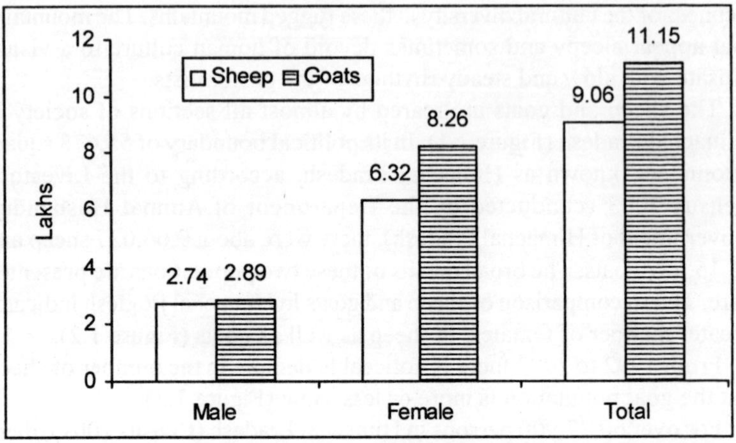

Fig. 1.2: Sheep and Goats in Himachal Pradesh (Livestock Census 2003)

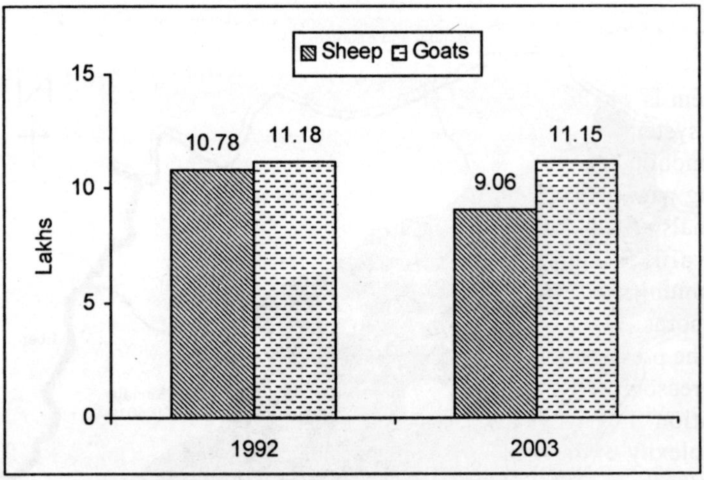

Fig. 1.3: Change in the Population of Sheep and Goats

Two systems of rearing are prevalent in Himachal Pradesh. In one system the sheep and goats are taken out for grazing to nearby pastures. Though in some months these animals are taken to pastures at higher or lower altitudes, mostly they remain in permanent settlements of households. In the other system, the sheep and goats are always on the move and never brought under man-made shelter. Either entire household or some member(s) of the family take care of these mobile herds. The agro-pastoral populations in most of the Himachal Pradesh adopt the

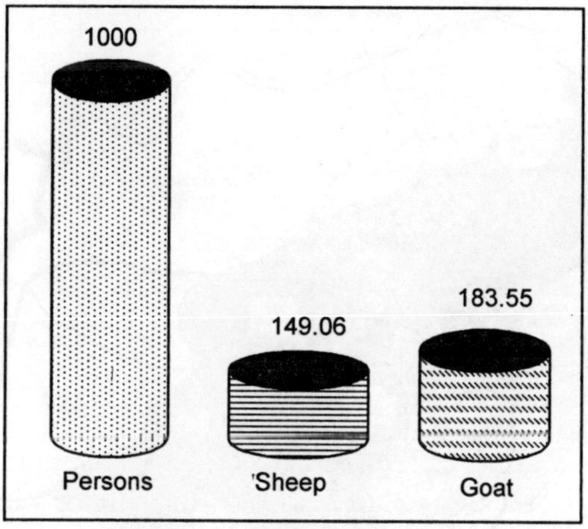

Fig. 1.4: Number of Sheep and Goats per Thousand Persons

first system of rearing sheep and goats. Though the herd size in this system is smaller, the total number of sheep and goats reared through this system are greater from the second system. In the second system, the mobile herds of sheep and goats always remain under the open sky along with their herders. In this system the herd size is larger, and the animals are taken to alpine pastures in the summer and to low altitude Shivalik hills in the winter. In Himachal Pradesh, mainly two communities follow the second system, they are the Gaddis and Kanaoras (Figure 1.5).

The present report shall confine to the pastoral system in Kanaor for two reasons. First, the people of Kanaor engage in both the systems, in addition they were also involved in trade with Tibet. Second, the complexity of the social systems that has developed in Kanaor has not been given much attention. Not only have they incorporated an element of Buddhism through pastoral trade, spanning from the Tibetan plateau to the Indian planes, they have also shown readiness to adopt the modern horticulture to supplement their livelihood. Therefore we shall follow the terminology used by the Kanaoras for these two systems. The sheep and goats reared under the first system are termed as **kim zet**, whereas the sheep and goats reared under the second (mobile) system are known as **arung zet**. Chapter 6 by Vidya Sagar Negi provides an elaborate introduction to these two systems, and has been reported for the first time according to our information (Figure 1.6).

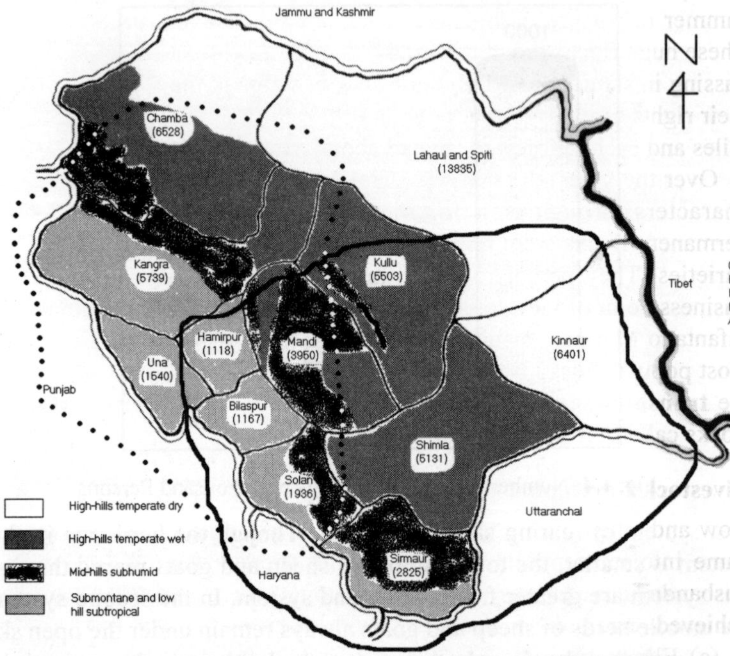

Fig. 1.5: The Territories used by Gaddis (dotted) and Kanaoras (solid)

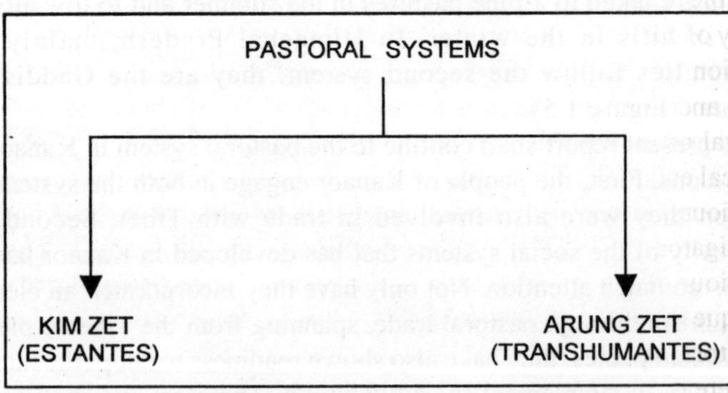

Fig. 1.6: The Two Pastoral Systems

Interestingly, we find that the terminology, some features of social system, and the yearly pastoral cycle of the Kanaoras appear similar to the system that prevailed in native Spain, some 500 hundred years ago. There were immense sheep walks and pastures, holdings as large as 30,000 or 40,000 sheep (merinos) existed. They were owned by the King and some principal nobles and clergy. These huge flocks were driven north in summer to pasture in mountains, and south at the approach of winter. These huge flocks did considerable damage to cultivated country while passing in summer and fall, but a special tribunal, the Mesta, protected their rights of passage. These great drives of flocks covered 200 to 400 miles and each journey consumed about six weeks.

Over the years, the merinos reared by the families acquired special characters through isolation and breeding by their owners. These permanent flocks were termed as cabanas and were equivalent to sub-varieties. They perhaps were more important for social prestige and business point of view, rather for their inherited traits. For example, the Infantado Merinos, owned by Duke of Infantado, were the largest and most popular flock. These large flocks of migratory sheep were termed the **transhumantes** and were distinguished from the small stationary flocks called the **estantes** (Vaughan, 1950).

Livestock Development and Research

How and when the traditional ways of isolation and restricted mating came into existence is not known. But these techniques of pioneer husbandman are familiar even today. Through these methods, the herders achieved remarkable success in

(a) Elimination of undesirable characteristics, (b) strengthening of desirable traits, and (c) production of novel attributes (Stone, 1964). The variety of domestic animals that we see today is the result of slow artificial selection for morphological and behavioural traits. Selection of traits in sheep and goats by the breeders depends on a number of factors: the survival of individuals in a particular terrain; the variety of fibers; the physical endurance for transportation; the quality of meat; and, above all behaviours conducive for taming. In general we find that the contemporary investigators in India are neither familiar with nor ready to consider behaviour of sheep and goats as an important factor. The present report is unique in drawing attention to this neglected aspect in the development of pastoralism.

There is a need to appreciate the experiences of herders in the selection of breeds. Noble (1987), a Scottish who followed Gaddis in the valleys and peaks of Dhauladhar in Chamba, Kangara and Kullu, narrates the reactions of a Gaddi about introducing the Merinos in his flock of sheep. While trying to persuade a Gaddi shepherd to improve his native stock and quality of wool by incorporating merinos, she only invited his scorn, "*All right, the wool is finer, but it's soft, not strong. At the winter clip there's nothing of it — it's all come off on the thorny bushes. And anyway, in autumn, when there is more of it, a merino fleece weighs less than one from our own sheep and we get the same price for a kilo of wool whatever it's like.*" In the following section we explore some selected reports of experts on this issue. Before that, the reader may glance at the work of Mira Behn, a Gandhian, on livestock development in the Himalayas (Box 1.4).

In 1956-57, Naerland, an expert from Food and Agriculture Organization of the United Nations visited northern India, including the Pashulok Farm established by Mira Behn in Rishikesh, to help the State Government of Uttar Pradesh in sheep and wool development in the hill areas. He observed that no precise figures were available but it was estimated that approximately one million sheep in the hill areas of Uttar Pradesh (now Uttaranchal) were struggling for bare existence at that time. The sedentary villagers kept some of them and the remaining were the migratory flocks of tribal people (the Bhotias). They were of mixed varieties, low yielding types, and had low reproduction rates. Undersized and weak lambs were born and heavy losses occurred during growing period. No fodder crops were grown and the sheep and goats grazed on poor hill pastures throughout the winter. However, the expert noted that many of the sheep were strong and hardy animals through natural selection, but exotic breeds died due to lack of veterinary facilities.

Besides several other observations, Naerland (1958) made a highly significant remark "*No sheep farm can be run successfully and profitably from an office desk and the knowledge of practical sheep husbandry and management in all its aspects cannot be acquired exclusively in a classroom but must be gained on a well-run sheep farm.*" New methods of sheep husbandry can be introduced among the flock owners in the hill areas only through practical demonstrations of beneficial results.

He recommended that there was need for strong research base and veterinary assistance. He suggested that assessment of conditions of hill pastures, carrying capacity, possibilities of grassland development, and re-forestation were immediately needed. He was not in favour of importing exotic varieties of sheep. Another significant noting in the report was for the scientists engaged in breeding experiments of different varieties. A mistake often repeated was, for making comparisons, groups of exotic (*Polwarth*) and indigenous (*Rampur Bushair's*) sheep were not kept under similar conditions. He advocated for the recruitment of hill people as shepherds, trainers, etc. in veterinaries and research centers.

Box 1.4: Pashulok: The Livestock Farm

After her release from the detention camp, Aga Khan Palace, Poona, in 1944, Mira Behn (Madeleine Slade) became interested in "Grow More Food" programme initiated by the government. Mira Behn's knowledge of agriculture and animal husbandry was impeccable, and well-known to leaders of India. By 1946 she became the Honorary Special Adviser of the government of United Province (now Uttar Pradesh). But her love for the Himalayas and Nature, prompted by changed political scenario in 1947, brought her closer to the destination. She searched a beautiful wild habitat by the side of the river Ganga near Rishikesh in the Virbhadra block. It was full of wild elephants, tigers, leopards, sambhar, spotted deer and all kinds of birds, and covered with tall *bhabar* grass. In 1948, a piece of 2146 acres of land was leased out to fulfill her dream—the livestock farm **Pashulok** (Gupta, 1993). In this wilderness, the dormant living force in her became alive. It also met her twin objectives, the upliftment of the man and the animal and the establishment of close bonds between the two. People in this area were poor and mostly Harijans, secondly the tending to cattle, sheep and goats was seen with indignity. Knowing the importance of cattle for agriculture and in day to day life of people, she had a strong belief that there was no other solution, but to improve the conditions of livestock.

Mira Behn had three objectives in her mind: improvements in the breeding stock, dissemination of knowledge among villagers, and taking care of the forests and pastures in the higher reaches of the Himalayas. In order to achieve these objectives she established cattle breeding farms in Garhwal, Himachal and Jammu. She was very particular about the varieties of livestock needed for the hills and even became curious about the cross-breeds of Yak and cow near the higher altitudinal zones of the Himalayas. Unfortunately, much of the work initiated by her was not followed up. The Pashulok, spread over 2146 acre was transferred to the Animal Husbandry Department of Uttar Pradesh in 1952-53, and 1048 acres of its land were given to Indian Drugs and Pharmaceutical Ltd. Even worst was the replacement of Pashulok by Central Sheep and Wool Research Centre. She lived in the Himalayan region from 1945 to 1958. In her later life in Europe, 1959 to 1982, she was in constant touch with the Gandhian social workers in the Himalayas and wrote about the disappearing oak forests of the Himalayas.

In a brief note about her lifetime work, she reiterated the need to improve pastoralism in the Himalayas. This, she thought was possible only by eliciting the cooperation of herders who live and die with their animals. Mira Behn showed rare affection for Gandhians saving the green cover of the Himalayas. When one such crusader, Sunderlal Bahuguna (1993), visited her in 1981, Mira Behn was in an oak forest in Austria. Sensing Bahuguna's frugal clothes in Alps, she made him comfortable with her *mirzai*, a special woolen coat of pastoralists in the Himalayas. She even kept her last piece of *mirzai* for Bahuguna as a parting gift in 1982, when she left for her heavenly abode. For Bahuguna, it was a gift of *mamata*, where earthly maternal affection transcends to the spiritual one.

Another FAO expert, Warwick, visited the Indian Council of Agricultural Research during 1957-58, to study the working of sheep and wool research programmes sponsored by the Indian Council of Agricultural Research or promoted by the States themselves. His task was to suggest improvements in the programmes considering the prevailing nutritional (including grazing), environmental and economic conditions. A startling observation in Warwick's report is, that he also found a fallacy in the crossbreeding experiments being conducted at various centers in India. The fallacy was the lack of control group in the experiments without which it was difficult to derive any conclusion when indigenous breed was crossed with exotic breed for better quality. It is not surprising that the researchers in India even these days were apathetic about the desirability of an appropriate control group in experiments and comparative studies, a point elaborated in the fourth chapter in this book. Warwick (1959) writes "*In the study of crosses of indigenous types of sheep with other breeds, a control group of indigenous ewes to be bread to rams of the same indigenous type should be included. This is to (a) measure improvement in production, if any, by the crossbreeds, and (b) to measure the potential improvement possible in the indigenous stock without crossing.*" The expert has described in detail how to select the control group, and what precautions were to be taken.

Another interesting suggestion was, the government flocks in the Himalayan region (e.g., Garsa in Himachal Pradesh) be taken to winter pastures also. In the Himalayan hills the government flocks are taken to high alpine pastures for grazing in summer season. He found that in winter the flocks returned to their headquarters' pasture located at lower altitudes in the hills. However, these flocks were not moved to the plains for grazing. The expert noted that the winter vegetation at the headquarters' pasture in the hills was inadequate in quality for the optimum nutrition of the breeding flock. These observations support that the *arung zet* system of sheep and goat rearing has evolved to take care of the nutritional requirements of the flocks during winter.

Consider a third report, under the FAO assistance programme when the Animal Production Officer Dolling visited Central Sheep and Wool Research Institute, Malpura, Rajasthan and its two regional centres in Kodaikanal, Tamil Nadu and Garsa, Himachal Pradesh, during 1967-68. During his assignment he reviewed the experimental work concerning sheep and wool, suggested future research possibilities, and gave practical suggestions on sheep and wool production. At the very outset, in his report, he makes it explicit that research and management were inseparable.

Dolling (1968) observed that the evidence on such primary subject as the best lambing season, if any, was lacking. It was also not known that the lambing of ewes at one time was any more productive than the shepherds' practice of lambing throughout the year.

The emphasis of these FAO experts was that the research efforts must be directed to find out the best way of improving the local sheep. Since in India the shepherds, who had small flocks, represented the industry hence the objective of sheep breeding in India rested on two things: the shepherds and the sheep products. In other words a research worker may aim at breeding sheep keeping in view the needs of the shepherds of a particular area, i.e. the sheep that can adapt to the high altitude areas of Himalayas. On the other hand the aim of a breeding programme can be to select sheep for good production of apparel wool, meat and lambs. An improved variety of sheep may not necessarily give good results if taken to an environment that does not suit the animal or that is poor in nutrition. Dolling (1968) emphatically noted that the point of interest was whether sheep selected and tested in the laboratory of the Institute will prove to be those best suited to shepherds' flock conditions. In statistical terms, whether there was a significant breed type X environment interaction. This observation is important, as the aims of a center at Garsa were (a) To determine the best method of producing a sheep, growing good quality apparel wool, which will thrive under existing management conditions of Himachal Pradesh. The wool produced here need not necessarily be a long staple combing wool, but may be a shorter, mushiar type suitable for carding and knitting. (b) To raise the level of productivity of the mountain pasture. Garsa is located in Himachal Pradesh where the sheep are mostly migratory, under the *arung zet* system.

In a report of FAO, Acharya (1982) has described the breeds of sheep and goat in India. In addition he has also given some evolutionary aspects of the domestication of the sheep and goats. The wild goat *(Capra hircus)*, the chief ancestral stock from which the various breeds of domestic goats have been derived, was the earliest ruminant to be domesticated. The two seals from Mohanjo-daro show a wild boar goat with enormous curled horns, and a bearded domestic male goat with side-spreading horns. The Gaddi goat, which greatly resembles the ancestral wild goat, has been used as a beast of burden in the mountains. There were many wild varieties of sheep *(Ovis orientalis vignei)*. The archaeologists tell us that the inhabitants of Mohanjo-daro and Harappa already possessed domesticated sheep. They provided milk, meat and clothing for the inhabitants of the cold north.

A recent report on pastoralism in the new millennium (FAO, 2001) observes that there are extensive pastoral production systems that cover some 25 percent of the world's land area and produces 10 percent of the meat used for human consumption, while supporting some 20 million pastoral households. These pastoral systems are split between the extensive enclosed systems of North America, Australia and parts of South America, and the open access systems of Africa, the Andes, Asia and Siberia, which are "traditional" producers. The rangelands exploited by pastoralists often cannot be used by conventional agriculture, although as technical advances spread cultivation into remoter regions, pastoralists would be forced to live under more inhospitable conditions. Although spontaneous settlement is quite common on the fringes of the pastoral domain, national governments were also hostile to pastoralists. Many countries were enforcing policies of sedentarization for the welfare of those they aim to settle. But they were based on political considerations and were unlikely to meet with long-term success.

Therefore it was almost certain that the future of pastoralism would depend heavily on political decisions made by national governments in countries with extensive grasslands. It was also a fact that the conditions for existing pastoralists were likely to become more difficult as both farmers and the wildlife lobby expropriates land. Thus the report has recommended for a more sympathetic understanding of pastoral production systems to protect their ways of life and to enhance their capacity to produce protein on otherwise marginal land. Largely these systems involved migratory herds of sheep and goats, the transhumant system, where regular movement of herds among fixed points in order to exploit the seasonal availability of pastures was required. But the settled pastoralists who cultivated sufficient areas to feed their families from their own crop production constituted the agro-pastoral system. Some important suggestions of the FAO included: production of niche products, either unusual species and breeds or meat and milk that are free from contaminants; the effective use of pastoral outputs in mixed farming; conservation of wild fauna and flora with pastoral production; the adoption of ecologically sensitive low-volume tourism through their indigenous knowledge.

In a comprehensive report on the transhumant grazing systems in temperate Asia, Suttie and Reynolds (2003) have discussed various features of this dominant system of pastoralism that involve migratory herds of sheep and goats as well as other animals. They found that transhumant stock rearing was very common throughout the Himalayas, and Gujars, Bakarwals and Gaddis followed such systems. This comprehensive volume includes a report on Himachal Pradesh by Bimal, which has described transhumance in Gaddis. Their native land, the Gadheran, is situated on both sides of the Dhauladhar ranges. They followed high altitude pastoral systems that were integral to natural resource utilization, management and production in the Himalayas. In Bimal's report, the main emphasis was on the biomass production, the grass or herbaceous vegetation. If management of grazing land was to be improved, more information was required for both planning of work and monitoring vegetation trends. The report by Bimal has clearly stated that the transhumant systems were potentially less damaging than sedentary ones because they exploit the herbage at fixed seasons, and leave it to recover for the remainder of the growing season. While many herders would prefer a more settled life, and many governments would like to settle nomads, alternative employment would have to be found. In the cold semi-arid zone, extensive herding apparently was the only practical way of earning a living from the land. The author believes that transhumant herding would yet continue for many years.

In general, besides the research on cross breeding or improving the indigenous breeds, it is important to collect vital statistics on shepherds' flocks. The accurate data on the number of sheep can be accumulated by tagging all sheep in a flock and by regular roll call of all sheep. Good field observations are prerequisite to good sheep management. Since India has now good expertise in the area of animal behaviour but there is need for coordination between the scientists engaged in animal husbandry and researchers conducting studies on animal behaviour.

For past several decades a conflict has ensued between wildlife conservationists and the pastoralists. It is strange that instead of helping the animal husbandry, which is mainstay of masses in the countryside, the enthusiasts of wildlife consider flocks of sheep and goats enemies to their conservation efforts. This conflict needs an amicable resolution. In addition, the Forest Department and the Department of Animal Husbandry have little interaction with each other. While for the livestock management grazing pastures are shrinking and deteriorating, the Forest Department adds to its woes by bringing more and more areas in the fold of national parks and sanctuaries. If one assumes that pastoralism is going to die, he may be mistaken. As it caters to our basic needs, and moreover, an important component of the economy; even in the deserts of Rajasthan. The Raikas (Rebari or Desawi), who are mainly concentrated in the western districts of Rajasthan migrate to Haryana, Uttar Pradesh in *dangs*

— the corporate social units of migration (Agrawal, 1992). Each *dang* has shepherds, cooks, sheep, goats, camel and dogs. A leader, the *nambardar*, guides the day-to-day activities of the *dang*. Agrawal observed that the changing environmental conditions adversely affecting the life of Raikas included, the earmarking of more area to wildlife sanctuaries and the expansion of the irrigated agriculture.

New Perspectives on Pastoral Life

Man has been moving with the herds of sheep and goats for a very long period. This phenomenon raises several questions, which may appear trivial like the sight of a herder struggling with his flock on a busy national highway. There are however, questions of immense academic significance as they have association with various pursuits of knowledge. These first of all relate to provision of the food and clothing. The rise of secondary social needs from these basic needs led to the development of two independent industries and also to the proliferation of the institutions for the inculcation of skills associated with them. The fine art of cooking and weaving flourished along with it.

Ultimately, these institutions of art and industrial empires acquire the status of the measurement of the complexity of our culture. At the same time, lack of food and clothing indicates impoverishment and undernourishment. But entirely different kinds of complexities arise from the modes of production for the artefacts used in our measures. For example, the process of production of the *pashmina shawl* largely involves human hands whereas the production of suiting from the mohair has largely been taken over by the computerized machines. Here the ideologies of human labour, processes of modernization, and above all, our finer qualities characterizing post-modernism, interact in an extra-ordinary fashion to affect the thoughts originating in the deeper recesses of mind. These thoughts may vary in nature. For instance, a thought may arise in the mind of a Gaddi pastoralist of the Himalayas to propitiate his deity by sacrificing a ram for the well-being of the herd of sheep and goats; but on the other hand is the origin of thought in the mind of an advertiser, where the aim is to increase the sale of a suiting through subliminal (perceptual) technique, for alluring the masses.

Although the thought of the Gaddi appear closer to post-modernism, it is possible that the advertiser uses a myth having greater identification with post-modernism, for example, the Heer-Ranjha scene with the background from a pastoral landscape. These cognitions involve shades of human thought embedded in the past. In the latter case, finer sensibilities are aroused, through bodily figures, postures, clothing, colour and landscape. The holistic impact is the creation of the intended effect. Whether we fall prey to the trap depends upon the fine balance of the elements in creating the holistic impact for subliminal allurement. Broadly they involve elements of man's evolutionary and cultural past catering to his essential needs. These are some complex issues, related to behaviours and cognitions, that evolutionary psychologist intend to study in human societies. In this endeavour, the shepherd's deity is as much an important subject of inquiry in this endeavour as is the 'subliminal' material of the advertiser. They enrich the knowledge base of society, increase public awareness and even increase the sale of the pastoral product. The society cannot afford to neglect these elements, and they are related to the well being of pastoralists.

The questions may be of generic nature, for example, how long the *Homo sapiens* has been moving with their herds of sheep and goats. This temporal sequence of pastoralism is important for evolutionary biologists, archaeologists and historians. Of equal or even greater significance is our inquisitiveness about the parts of the globe inhabited by pastoral groups. In fact, we need to understand, the processes of proliferation and extinction of pastoralism at global and regional level. It is equally important to know to what extent the pastoralist can afford an increase in the size of its flock without hampering regeneration of plant resources. In the recent past, it has aroused academic debates such as 'pastoralism has contributed to the expansion of deserts' and 'pastoralism is prone to the tragedy of commons.' For behavioural ecology the important problem is to ascertain whether pastoralism thrives as a niche phenomenon or sheep and goats thrive in all major habitats.

Conservation and biodiversity issues are significant but need quantification of field data and collection of unbiased historical evidence. For example, pastoralists alone could not have denuded the dense vegetation along the Shivalik hills, from the famous pilgrimage center of Hindus at one end on the banks of Ganges, the Haridwar in the east, and in the far west, near Pathankot. The whole area has been the winter pasture for the sheep and goats of pastoralists. Historical records of the Nurpur state (1058-89) tell us that there was a dense forest, *Mauwa da ban*, between Pathankot and Nurpur. This jungle reportedly "*abounded with elephants of enormous size*," noted Hutchison and Vogel (1982). Elephants were now confined to the forests near Haridwar, the Rajaji National Park. These large mammals now seldom cross the Yamuna river near Paonta

Sahib. An earlier report about the impenetrable jungle around Haridwar (Williams, 1874), appears only a case of imagination.

The other aspects are specific, for example, the development of a particular pastoral community living in the Western Himalayas. Though some of their problems may be general, such as skills related to animal husbandry—diseases, breeding, weaving and trade. There are, however, significant social and ecological factors which are extremely specific in nature, and crucial for their survival in high altitude cold desert. In this context, the major issue that has remained almost obscure is the exploration of the cognitive contribution of the pastoral communities in the area of cognition. This has become rather necessary at the stage of society when it categorizes such communities as backward and primitive. Moreover, administrators and planners even consider them as hindrance in the process of development.

The challenge therefore is to explore the diverse ways of pastoralism in order to develop an alternative way of life for these communities who still move with the herds of sheep and goats, which is commensurate with the global scale. This would be a view as closely endorsed by the humanistic values, and it intends to enrich pastoralism from the knowledge of various academic disciplines. In the early half of twentieth century the profession of livestock has benefited from the knowledge of biologists about breeding, diseases and anatomy, customs and traditions among different pastoral groups gathered by the anthropologists, and, techniques of training evolved by the comparative psychologists. The pastoralists and their flocks now need, and may in turn contribute to, the advanced disciplines of cross-cultural psychology, ethology, socio-ecology and evolutionary psychology. It would also require advanced techniques of biological sciences.

Though this may appear as an exclusively academically oriented utilitarian enterprise, the endeavour is to go deeper into it. For this we need cross-cultural, ecological, evolutionary and folk psychology paradigms to discover the hidden cognitive aspects of pastoral life. In turn, our conscious effort would be to contribute to the life of pastoralists, its flocks, and their ways of life. This enterprise is a reminder, that the society owes its daily provision of milk, meat and clothing to these communities.

Earlier, classical conditioning principles enriched the stores of human knowledge in the areas of learning and memory by using dogs, sheep and goats as the experimental subjects. There was little change in these principles, much over the last century or so, rather they provide tools for current neurological and behavioural research in memory, learning and behaviour therapy. Along with this, naturalistic studies (ethology) on the groups of various animals enriched our knowledge of the social organizations that radically altered our views of the evolution of human society. These foundations are laid on the affectional relationships originating from the mother-infant bond so conspicuous in sheep and goats, rather than the primordial group dependent on the 'sexual bond', which is shorter in duration and even disruptive to group life. These are questions, which form the foundations of human social organization essential for developing theories in social psychology and psychiatry.

One would argue from the love songs of pastoralists about the primacy of 'sex' as a 'glue' that binds society, however, he will be frustrated while explaining the sublimation of sex in the system of polyandry. The frustration would aggravate, when this investigator sees that there is even proliferation of asceticism, besides the polyandry system, in a pastoral community. For example, in Kanaor, the parents initiate their sons and daughters to monastic life to acquire the 'greater knowledge.' In contrast, these parents could have benefited by enlisting children's help for strengthening the household in two ways, in enlarging the flock size of sheep and goats, or in reaping the benefits of kin selection through sexual inputs. These two are highly significant losses to the parents. In addition, the acquisition of the "greater knowledge" is beneficial for the well being of all. The Freudian libidinal forces, that ruled the minds of the intelligentsia for a century (a pseudo-theory based on an imaginary primordial herd), the theory of group based on the affectional systems, has the sound basis of field and laboratory researches on social groups of rodents, sheep, goats, monkeys, apes and humans.

A matter of greater urgency is to know whether, or not, under the contemporary social, economic and political pressures, the pastoralists break the rules of the game and allow the tragedy of commons. We need to explore social mechanisms where it is hard for the pastoralist to step out of the territorial boundaries. These communities provide opportunity to understand how such cultural mechanisms have co-evolved with biological mechanisms of evolution. They, rather, reduce the scope of tragedy of commons.

The emergence of regional identities on the basis of language, material culture, food habits, folklore, ritual, local forms of religion, etc. are an important finding of the People of India (POI) project carried over from 1985 to 1990 by Anthropological Survey of India. These regional identities should not threaten us, because according to Srinivas (2002) they were the basis of unity. We learn to respect others. He considered it as a major 'cognitive shift' that needed further exploration. He also rejected the classification of certain communities, particularly tribal, as animists (followers of the little tradition) in contrast to the dominant greater tradition. Because, as Srinivas said, most of the Brahmins (followers of greater tradition) at a moment of crisis visited the witch doctor. At the same time the tribals also shared the upper caste cultural ideas. Moreover, if agriculture was practiced by all castes, the pastoralism was also a common practice of Brahmin, Kashatriya, Vaishya and Shudra. These minute aspects of relationship have greater significance, rather the four major Varna categories that pitted people against each other. Lastly, Srinivas has emphasized intensive studies on the tribal societies by Indians themselves by making the villages, towns and slums as their laboratories. The present volume also has such an ambitious objective.

The next chapter takes a closer look at these issues in order to clarify some myths that surround the tribal populations. This is essential since many times the narrow attitude of the investigator, about the socio-cultural systems of the pastoral communities and cognitive abilities of these people, becomes a major hurdle in understanding its richness and to initiate some developmental strategies.

2

The Himalayan Dilemma

The Food and Agriculture Organisation of the United Nations in its report *Pastoralism in the New Millennium* (FAO, 2001) has expressed deep concern about the plight of people engaged in rearing mobile herds of sheep, goats and cattle. Approximately twenty million households were engaged in it in the various parts of the world. These pastoralists met the basic needs of milk, meat and clothing of a large section of society to various degrees. Most of the time the pastoralists thrived under inhospitable terrains, and now they were being compelled to permanently settle in it. The most important drawback was not simply their archetypal existence the society was also indifferent towards their life and culture. The FAO report has underlined the rich and complex literature on pastoral development which was being effectively ignored. Even more conspicuous was the neglect of behavioural and biological research on these mobile herds of sheep and goats.

In their arm chair theorization, the social scientists see pastoralism as an inevitable stage in cultural and biological evolution. Historians describe them as uncivilised populations, largely contributing to territorial owners, and at times usurping them. The most significant element of pastoralism, their mobility, is seen by planners and humanists equally with indignity, for novelists it is a feature of romanticism. In these scenarios of civilized populations, the voice and vision of pastoralists is conveniently forgotten. This is because a large section of these communities are either nomadic or with little resources at their disposal. Perhaps, the pastoralists of Kanaor are a unique population in the Himalayas where it is possible to look for the complexity of culture and learn as to how pastoralism can survive and develop. And the tails of Gaddis may also unfold a similar story.

The FAO report has suggested four major policy orientations for the protection and support of pastoralism in the twenty-first century. In this ambitious project there is integration of pastoralism with the new world order in such a way that the supply of traditional needs of meat, milk and wool becomes secondary and certain other needs take precedence. Some of the essential ingredients of these new world order needs would be: (a) advertisements and sale of products produced in unique ecosystems, from unique species, and free from contaminants, (b) exploring new symbiotic relations with horticulture farming—the sheep and goats grazing in well-grown orchards where they reduce weeds, eat grass and provide manure fertilizer to the soil, (c) acceptance of the damage done to biodiversity as a challenge for active involvement in conservation activity, and (d) using the rich cultural complexity in various ways to ecologically sensitive, low volume but financially remunerative tourism. This volume was conceptualised keeping these ingredients of new world order in mind and to initiate the process at the regional level.

This requires familiarity with the new world order, preparation to meet its requirements, research on the uniqueness of each pastoral system, and finally development of necessary structure and social network for providing the essential elements of the new world order. In this chapter our attempt is to look into some of these elements to support such an endeavour and point out the lacunae in the material that exists.

Of Greater and Little Traditions

It may appear strange to start abruptly with a regional study, and that too on a pastoral group. But in fact a western Himalayan community provides the perfect integration of global and regional issues. This transhumant pastoral group, the Kanaoras of the Himachal Pradesh, have been a crucible for infinite social and cultural elements pouring from a vast region spanning from the north Indian plains to the Tibetan plateau. For various reasons, which will be clear to the reader later, we will begin with Sankrityayan's (1948/1957) *Kinner-Desh*, literally a country of Kanaoras, to initiate our analysis of pastoralism in Himachal Pradesh. Sankrityayan had a wishful thinking in the mind—to see the earthly "Kinners" become the celestial singers of the Vedic age fame. But at the same time he visualized affirmative change in these people towards atheism so that they advance to join the developed world at the dawn of the twenty-first century. Over a period of sixty years, this pastoral community, belying the wishful thinking of this *Mahapandit* (a great intellectual), has moved ahead in their own ways. They neither became atheist nor has there been much change in the continuation of the primitive pastoral life despite all the odds against it. Sankrityayan's work largely serves a symbolic purpose, for it is characteristic of several other academicians who worry about the pastoral communities on similar lines. In this volume, there is a suggestion to build an alternative self-concept where, for example, the use of "Kinner" for the individuals and "Kinnaur" for the country they inhabit is replaced with Kanaora for the individuals and Kanaor for their region. The latter term is free from a religious aura.

Though Sankrityayan was identified with the communist (*samyavadi*) ideologies of China and Russia, he was a Buddhist monk, too. Some of his general observations that bothered the inquisitive minds have significance for pastoralism in Greater Himalayas. Since he traversed the spaces across the entire Himalayas from Indian plains to the heart of the countries where institutions of communism were growing, Pathak (1994) has asked, why he kept quite about the expansionist moves of these regimes. As it is difficult to believe that he was innocent about these moves, the most conspicuous being the usurpation of Tibetan kingdom and later the attack on India by China. It had tremendous negative impact on the economy and spatial movement of pastoral communities across the entire range of the Himalayas from the west to the east, especially on the pastoral community of Kanaoras. But today the fact is that the collapse of Soviet Union opened the great Steppes of Central Asia to pastoralism. Even the greater surprise is that this vast terrain was presently supporting the unemployed urban workers adopting pastoralism due to closure of industries. Earlier than this, the roots of Afghan nomads, the *Pushto powanda*, traversing the long stretches between eastern Turkey and north India, were severed by international conflicts in this region (Balland, 1991). Among them were the familiar Kabuliwalas frequenting cities of north India in the winter.

Another issue is, on the one hand Sankrityayan spent time and energy to explore institutions of deities (particularly in Kanaor), on the other hand he outrightly discarded these institutions for their negative role in cognitive development (Yadav, 1998), as if they were black holes in the cosmos which devour energy instead of enlightening the spaces around them. If he intended to dissociate feelings and emotions from thinking, as several intellectuals still do, it is entirely an expression of denial or defence. Scientific evidence, in fact, strengthens the relationship of emotion and cognition. The close association of hypothalamic (centre of emotions) and cortical (cognitive center) associations in brain helps in the individual's survival. The fear of snake not only helps us to avoid a snake but we evolve novel ways of manipulating the life-threatening object. It would, rather, be more appropriate to say that the fear of death from diabetes led to the discovery of insulin injection as a remedy for it.

Unless pastoralists have ways and means to cope up with the

uncertainties that surround them, the institutions of deities would continue to solace them and thus help in their survival. They have enormous environmental uncertainties which require biological adaptations, the modern populations do live under an environment of uncertainties but those are largely man-made, for example, the computer viruses. Besides the contributions of the institutions of deities in the development of cultural artefacts, it is undeniably important in cognitive enrichment, especially for the advancing science of consciousness.

Consider a statement with which Sankrityayan starts his book on the Kanaora pastoral community:

> "Kinner or Kimpurush are celestial beings. The journey to their country is a visit to heaven. At this, the readers may have doubt on my journey. But one can also say, the country that once belonged to the deities, at a later stage, backward human beings occupied it, and this country of backward human beings, may again become heaven."
>
> (*Sankrityayan*, 1948/1957; Page 1)

The connection of "Kinners" with some communities mentioned in the Hindu scriptures has appeared repeatedly in the documents. For example, an administrator Sharma (1971) expresses similar views in a preface to the gazetteer on Kanaor. These are certainly conscious reproductions or inventions. The cognitive scientist has to understand whether it is an unpretentious cultural transmission, or not. Alternatively, one may get information from a source, which is then cognitively processed, yet may be finally transmitted as it was, with some implicit intention. In the latter case, a person first assimilates the information but transmits it only after some understanding and reasoning. Thus the person owes conscious responsibility about the statements he makes.

One very simple motive in the present case, to refer a particular pastoral group to some *pauranic* texts, is to prove its primitiveness, however, a sound argument needs much more than this. Sankrityayan did make such an endeavour, whereas others did not. He indeed initiated a very important work, but it needed perseverance, academic excellence, and sensitivity to native population. This was the excavation of the burials in Kanaor. Although it was extremely limited work, we may understand its importance from the following narrative from a distant continent—Australia. Here the two communities, the advanced sheep and goat herders of Europe and the aboriginals of Australian mountains along the river Murray, contested for space, where the defeat of the latter community was obvious.

Landscapes change, naturally and under man's footprints. Joseph Hawdon, the first European to see Lake Victoria, wrote "*To this splendid lake, of which I had the pleasure of being the first European discoverer, I gave the name of 'Lake Victoria' in honour of our most gracious Queen.*" This event occurred around the middle of nineteenth century, and ushered the era of new grazing pastures for European breeds of cattle, sheep and goat. Not only that, there ensued fierce territorial battle between aboriginals and Europeans. For the aboriginals Lake Victoria was not only sacred but a lifeline that fed the Murray river basin. The aboriginals could not defend their territory, as the letters dug deep on a plaque say (Leslie, 2005):

In remembrance of the Rufus River
Massacre on 27th August, 1841 and
The 2 tribes Barkindji/Maruara who
Occupied the Lake Victoria Area

How much was the attachment of these aboriginals to their territory, one can guess it from the events that took place nearly a century and a half later. Now Lake Victoria was under modern man's control, when in 1994 its waters were lowered around eleven feet for some repair work, a group of aboriginals sensed that there were burials around the lake, and they sought the help of an archaeologist Colin Pardue (he was exploring Aboriginal burials in Murray basin). It was later recorded that "*aboriginals lived at Lake Victoria for forty thousand years or longer, which would make it one of the longest continuously inhabited hunter-gatherer sites known to scholars anywhere in the world.*" (Leslie, 2005; Page 291) We find that no such work was followed by archaeologists and historians in Himachal Pradesh to ascertain the primitiveness of various communities designated as "tribes" or cultural displacements attributed to Aryan pastoralists.

After about one hundred and fifty years from these contests over the ownership of the territory, the Australia is facing another contest, now which is between the descendents of the Victorian empire, the modern agriculturalists and the modern pastoralists. In addition to space, the water is now the scarce resource. It was perhaps not possible for Sankrityayan to imagine that these resources, the space and water, would lead to severe contests in Kanaor. It is not due to belief in the religious institutions, but due to the non-sustainable use of the natural resources by the achievements of science—the most conspicuous being the insatiable hunger for hydroelectric energy. It has threatened the survival of the natives and the drowning of culture along with the fertile river valleys of the Himalayas. Though these gigantic projects are producing enormous energy, it hardly illuminates the huts of these natives, as a humanist would have imagined. We shall take this issue in Chapter 3.

Another significant point that needs attention is undermining the development of complex cognitive foundations among the people of pastoral communities. It is despite the fact that the Kanaoras were engaged in trade over long distances across the Himalayas, which definitely needed differentiation of cognitive skills—knowledge of weather and physical conditions of the landscape from Indian plains to deep valleys in the Tibetan plateau. These skills were to include: rearing sheep and goats, breeding them for special physical endurance, training them in several important skills, engagement with diverse communities and negotiating with them, and, finally assuming responsibilities required for the long-term trade relations (see Chapter 6). Moreover, it is not difficult to find that for the explorers who traversed the Himalayan mountains, besides the administrative support, pastoralists were crucial in these journeys, a fact seldom remembered. Sankrityayan was one of those intellectuals who frequented the pastoralist's (*Aj Pal*) trade routes (*Aj Path*) in the Himalayas. The word *Aj Path* literally refers to the routes of goats but in Europe sheep walks is a familiar term. The *Aj Path* is rather more appropriate for trade roots since the goats (instead of sheep) were largely used for carrying goods on these pathways. But it is largely ignored that the pastoralists might have played key role in the communication and dissemination of knowledge from one region to the other. Besides, it is entirely forgotten that they belonged to certain communities where important monasteries and temples came into existence.

Pastoral Identities

There is need to search alternative views on human competence (Segall, Dasen, Berry & Poortinga, 1999). This suggestion of cross-cultural psychologists based on long experience of field studies in almost all over the world need a careful follow-up. Because the criteria to evaluate competence seems biased, even with the development of the science of psychometry. These cross-cultural psychologists write, "*Europeans, from their earliest contacts with non-European societies, have felt a need to discover how non-Europeans think. They have long believed that 'they, the primitives' don't think quite as rationally as 'we, the civilized' do and that there is a form of thinking somehow adequately described as 'primitive'.*" (Segall *et al.*, 1999) Psychologists, no doubt, have devised tools to measure these differences between the 'civilized' and the 'primitive.' However, such claims of the superiority of the 'civilised' over the 'primitive' have been questioned by common wisdom and by the psychologists themselves.

In a popular write up, Goswamy (2007) re-discovers in Lord Macaulay, that there was a planned effort to undermine the high moral values, high caliber, and rich spiritual and cultural heritage of Indians, by imposing entirely an alien education system. A Gandhian, Dharampal (1983/1995) has collected good historical evidence, by exploring the Indian archives spread over the British Isles, that India had well-developed education system in its villages, at least in some parts of the country, before the Britishers came. But Goswamy cautions us that now we are learning a value system where our culture is increasingly marginalized. However, a greater tragedy is that our own system is indulged in Macaulay's tactics to homogenize the various sections of society who may be proud of their culture and traditions and the ways of living. These communities include the pastoral groups of Gaddis, Kanaoras and Gujars.

At times there is strange conscious search for the past, which leads us into a 'social trap.' This apparent glorious imagery makes people feel proud and they want to cling to it. But along with this, there is danger of getting associated with a socially non-prestigious past, for instance the indulgence in caste based pride and prejudice. And then to dissociate from it, and even deny the objective evidence of its prevalence. Perhaps evolutionary psychology has an answer for it. As the imagery of the glorious past would help us through various psychological mechanisms to increase our survival. These processes include conscious feelings such as, increase in self-esteem, feeling proud, demand for justice, and above all self-control over situation (Gazzaniga, 1994). But these mental mechanisms may also be used as tools of dominance by demolishing these feelings in others. The more 'developed' use such logic to discriminate themselves from the 'less developed.' Even when a better-placed person empathises with the destitute, he may use the logic of discrimination, one may think "*We must do something for the 'tribal'*." We need to understand this issue deeply because the pastoral populations we are studying comes under the 'tribal' category, though many others like them are left out from this categorization. For example, Roy Burman (1993) noted that falling in line of a dominant group, as is the case with accepting a 'tribal' category, may also lead to certain consequences that are psychological in nature.

In India, '*jan*' is used for tribal people or 'less developed' and the 'better placed' come under '*jati*.' According to the Census of India 2001, there are 8.2 percent Scheduled Tribes (ST) in India. In Himachal Pradesh the ST population is 4 percent of the total state population, and includes the two major transhumant pastoral groups, the Gaddis and the Kanaoras (Figure 2.1).

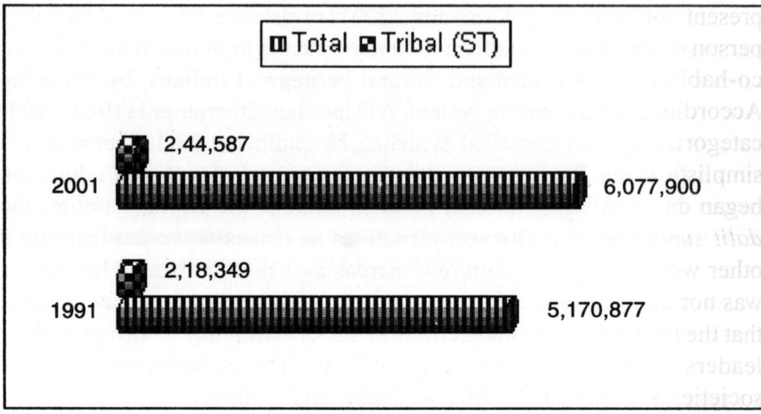

Fig. 2.1: The Tribal and the Total Population of Himachal Pradesh

For me it was a startling experience, how the word '*jan*' evokes people emotionally. Once I was traveling back to Shimla with an officer in the Indian Administrative Services, from a transhumant family. We had been to his village to understand the high altitude socio-religious and physical adaptations of pastoral people near the Indo-Tibetan border. On the way, my sleepy eyes carried to brain a flash of a big hoarding on the National Highway 22 that now we were entering into *jan-jati* area (the Kanaor). At the same moment, my host exclaimed with a deep sigh—now we were entering from *jan-jateeya* (belonging to Scheduled Tribe-Scheduled Caste) to *jateeya* (belonging to caste) area. I (being from the *jateeya* area) sunk deep into the back seat of his car, and there was silence for a long time. At times even aggressive encounters occur between the members belonging to these two categories, '*jan*' and '*jati*,' which are mainly related to their identities. Some leaders of the *dalit samudaya* (oppressed communities) even consider the use of word 'Harijan' (son of the God; used by Mahatma Gandhi for the Scheduled Castes) as derogatory. Their argument is, such names hardly matter unless the upper castes change their oppressive attitudes and behaviours.

According to Singh (1993) the concept of *jan* was "*proposed by Professor Niharranjan Ray to describe the present day tribes of India.*" For Ray there were two fundamental forms of social organizations in India, the hierarchical one represented by *jati*, and the other relatively egalitarian one represented by *jan*. True, as it may be, that the concept of tribe is a creation of colonial mind, but we must understand the processes perpetuating the stratification in the society on caste basis and its relationship with religious institutions. From the point of view of the present study, it would be interesting to look into this statement by a person of the stature of Singh, who had seen the tribals life closely—as a co-habitant in the terrain of tribal people and as an administrator. According to him, the present day tribals have been frozen as social categories by the colonial and post-colonial processes. It would be too simplistic to think that the process of marginalisation of these populations began during colonial period. Is it correct that the overt expression of *dalit sumudaya* towards so-called 'Manuvadi' has no sound basis? In other words, is it correct to believe that the distribution of *jan* and *jati* was not there, before British stepped in India? Although Singh believes that the level of investment in tribal areas has sharply increased, the tribal leaders complain that it has brought distortions in these egalitarian societies. But Singh admits that it is difficult to deny the commercial exploitation of the resources of tribal land.

One can look at the scenario from an entirely different perspective—the development of social identities. Yet, the discrimination already embedded in the society was conducive to throw another large section of society into a downtrodden dustbin, whatsoever developmental concern was there. During post-independence period, the incentives provided to these sections worked perhaps more to maintain their pseudo-identity as *jan*, they are largely misperceived by others similarly as they perceive the scheduled caste people (the lowest class in the *jati* hierarchy). There also appears to be an identity crisis due to these incentives. They are neither accepted to move up socially (though many of them have done it materially), nor are they able to leave the entitlements associated with the *jan* (ST) status (Figure 2.2). Though Singh did not include incentives and entitlements as a factor in social mobility, he has mentioned only two aspects of social mobility. One is the upward movement in *jati*, the *sanskritization*; and the other is the movement of returning towards the tribal roots. The latter one is seen as a quest for identity in a pluralistic society. It is possible that incentives and entitlements are important factors in this mobility.

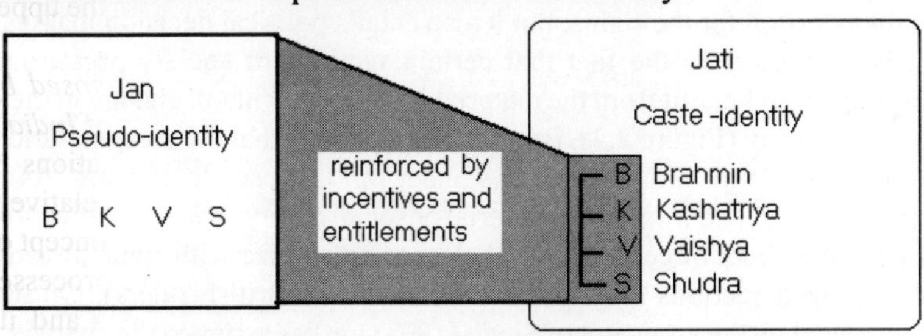

Fig. 2.2: The Relationship between *jan* and *jati*

People of India (POI) project data suggest widespread awareness of *varna system* among people. Nearly 68.5 percent of the communities were aware of it. Though most tribals stood outside the *varna* system, castes were more involved in it. Singh has summarized that, "*More than half of the Indian communities (2804) see themselves as part of the varna order and recognize there place in it. About 8 percent of the communities perceive themselves as Brahmin, 15.9 percent as Kshatriya, 9.36 percent as Vaishya, and 29.1 percent as Shudra.*" (Page 85) Though the leading occupation pursued by 2503 communities was settled cultivation, a considerable number of communities preferred animal husbandry (999).

According to Dharampal (1993), "*Varna include large groups, based on occupations, skills and social responsibilities, into which human society gets divided at a certain stage of the unfolding of the universe. At the stage of highest complexity human society is divided into four Varnas. These are: Brahmin, Kashatriya, Vaisya and Shudra.*" This is where our intellectuals and social workers engage in defence of the prejudices of our past. Despite the laudable efforts of the Gandhians, people from some sections of society, or some communities, are still denied access to temples even in the tribal areas. Another problem with this definition is, these four groupings are not associated with specific tasks and skills as indicated by the POI data. Moreover, until the society denies such opportunities to other communities, there is no evidence that Shudra cannot recite the mantras of Brahmin, and the Brahmin cannot learn to play the music of the courtyard of temple. Even if there is division of labour, which is justified, there is no logical explanation for endogamy, hierarchy and pollution. Individual preferences, without any prejudice of *Varna* or community are valuable psychological qualities, but at the same time one must take care not to hurt the feelings of others.

Legally the conceptualization of Scheduled Tribes or Scheduled Castes is an instrument of policy (Miri, 1993). Therefore, we must realise that the pseudo-concept of *jan* is a recent phenomenon, a consequence of dalit assertion for the rights, but it also entails political decision making. It is supported by the fact that certain sections of society pressurize politicians to benefit from the material incentives, without change in their social identity (Figure 2.3). But my assumption is that the categorisation of certain groups and populations under *jan* is a pseudo-concept. As it does not originate from some material or social reality, it is a classification by the members of certain 'other' class to empathize with some already categorized sections (for which we may blame British rulers). On the other hand, in the argument of Singh (1993) *jan* has assumed the character

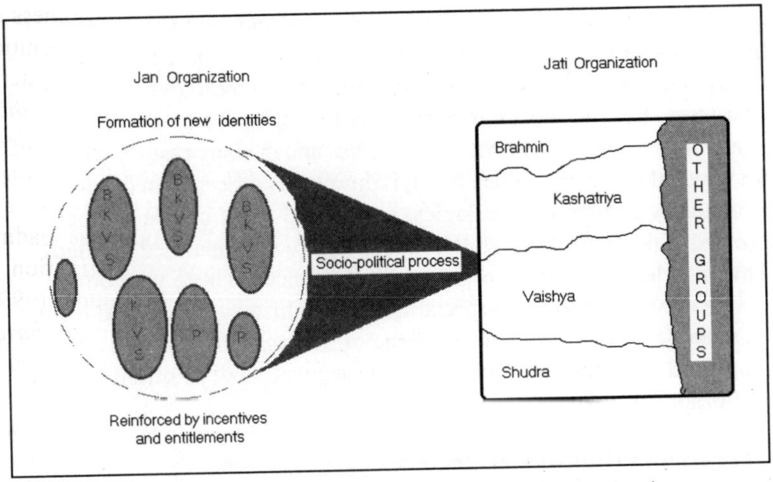

Fig. 2.3: Formation of Identities (B. Brahmin; K. Kashatriya; V. Vaishya; S. Shudra; P. Primitive)

of a realistic category for branding certain communities. As a consequence of which the non-material and material transactions with such sections of society change. But the pseudo nature of *jan* becomes ambiguous when some new groups adopt this new identity (the *jan*) to take certain entitlements but refuse to accept discriminatory material and non-material transactions that has become associated with it. These identities are emerging in various forms, a fact hard to deny—*dalit* literature, *dalit andolan*, *dalit samaj* or *adivasi samaj*.

On the basis of long administrative and research experience, Singh has suggested that tribal ethnicity was closely related to the environment which encompassed the tribal's rights to their resources, the very basis of their survival. However, more fundamental for Miri (1993) was the cognitive self-empowerment. Where the tribesman became aware about his dilemma; articulated his cognitive competence and coherence; and, finally developed an intellectual, moral and spiritual self-confidence. Above all, he would be facing the powerful, coercive, arrogant, and intellectual forces of dominant social sections during this social change.

In a community the particular mode of production is historically conditioned to the specific ways of life for its survival. It may also be referred to as mode of subsistence and has material, social and psychological aspects. At material level it would involve the selection of particular animal and plant species as food and for domestication in case of pastoralists. Social and political institutions then mediate in survival, and also in meeting the needs of production and exchange. Lastly, the psychological factors may involve individual's need satisfaction, behavioural interactions, cognitive processes, ideologies and learning processes. But the most contentious part of this process is the tendency of a group to interact with the other groups, and in many cases it is essential for survival in the day-to-day life. It is during this process that the dominant community thrusts its ideologies, norms and ways of life on the other groups. If the latter fail to fall in line, they are marginalized or alienated. This may lead to various negative consequences. Those who do not fall in line may resort to reinterpretation of their history, myths and legends. Noticeable effects occur in the areas of demography through choice of mates and, in the political arena through acquisition of positions in various institutions of democracy.

Appraisal of Human Competence

An element of humility is needed among 'experts' studying the weaker sections of society including the pastoral communities. In many cases it appears that to achieve the objectives of their study, these investigators become empathizers of the communities. And the entire course of their work becomes an enterprise of an 'expert advice' rather than objective understanding of the subject and his physical, social and psychological contexts. For example, a person embarking upon the study of monkey behaviour, becomes an empathizer of these animals. Though it is not bad to become an empathizer, perhaps it may serve an even greater cause for monkeys and men, if he first of all comes back with some curious observations on the life of monkeys. Our empathy must enliven the scenario with knowledge. We find that Sankrityayan did not show any interest in the animals, which the Kanaoras love, the *arung zet* and *kim zet*, around whom the whole social system revolved. Without concern for the pastoralist and his sheep and goats, it is difficult to improve their condition. This love must extend to plants as well, on which these animals survive. Mira Behn was an embodiment of such love, she not only cared for the pastoralists and their animals, but worked incessantly for the preservation of the oak forests in the Himalayas (see Box 1.4). This preceded with efforts to develop necessary structure, based on knowledge, for the improvement of animals, pastoralists and the Himalayan mountainsides.

It was only due to the sheep and goats, that the trade was possible at a time when roads were absent and there was no vehicular traffic between the Indian plains and the Tibetan plateau. It is important to remember that behaviour and management of sheep and goats is an area of science, where the Kanaoras and Gaddis would like excel. Instead the common trend is to test their cognition in areas that are remotely represented in their cognition. In the language of memory and learning, the art of pastoralism, rearing sheep and goats is part of their non-declarative memory system. These are habits, which have become deep rooted, in the specific areas of brain, through conditioning principles (discovered by the Russian physiologist Pavlov). They facilitate new learning in these areas. It does not mean that the Gaddi and Kanaora children cannot excel in the other novel areas, and enlarge their non-declarative memory system. The acquisition of new experiences would, however, need greater time and effort.

In addition, the contemporary studies in the area of pro-social behaviour suggest that the humility shown towards animals may be transferred to human relationships, which is also evident from the observations on pastoralists. However, investigators studying these populations of the Gaddis and Kanaoras with their sheep and goats, rarely exhibit such concern towards them. Moreover, such lack of concern is overtly exhibited in identities attached to these communities, little bothering about its consequences. Had the problem been considered from humanistic point of view, the backlash of Mandal Commission (Singh, 1996) could have been averted. But a section becomes an expert, as well as develops a self identity that is distinct and in many cases superior to the "tribal" identity of the pastoral communities. It does not stop here, a complexity builds up in the class of 'non-tribals,' as if they are the donors to the 'tribals,' little do they realise that they thrive upon subsidies, seldom available to the 'tribals.'

Long ago, the Russian Physiologist had emphasized that learning in case of humans had taken a new turn in evolution, instead of primary signals, now the secondary signals governed the life of human beings. With the dominance of language and other means of secondary signals, the importance of primary signals 'physical' or 'material' have become less than the 'mental' or 'psychological' signals. The planners tend to forget this difference, their emphasis on 'physical' incentives to the deprived sections of society has utter disregard for the 'social' and 'psychological' aspects. The latter have greater significance in bridging the gulf of social stratification based on caste or tribe.

We shall discuss this issue from various standpoints. An important one, from developmental perspective, is the conceptualisation of disadvantaged groups. Several pastoral communities in Himachal Pradesh have been included under this category, the prominent being those engaged in transhumance or *arung zet* system of sheep and goat rearing. The famous economist Amartya Sen (1997) has cautioned that the economic growth was important to eradicate deprivation but the human capabilities were more instrumental in the generation of even greater economic and social progress. The quality of human life has its intrinsic value. This is not reflected in development reports. The evaluation of human creativity was not possible by the market. Therefore, according to Sen, the market oriented focus of our planners needed drastic modification towards the capability perspective.

A scientist A.P.J. Abdul Kalam, who became the President of India, used to distribute the morning newspaper *Dinamani* to households in Rameswaram, to help his brother. There are large number of people in India who do not have even such opportunities of part time jobs or who do not have enough to eat two times. There may be about sixty percent such people who cannot afford to provide the basic education and health facilities to their children. The lack of education and the poor quality of life perpetuate the poverty of these people. Non-availability of preventive health care further weakens their bodies and therefore their capabilities. This is the message of *INDIA 2020: A vision for the new Millennium* (Abdul Kalam & Rajan, 1998). Such theorization has a built in dilemma that needs exploration.

Ambiguity about the concept of "disadvantage" is related to its measurement, and the target population. Most of the researches have used social *disadvantage* to study its consequences that is as an independent variable. They have not tried to study the various causes of social *disadvantage*. Those causes may be external to the individual or environmental: social or asocial causes. They may lie within the individual or psychological causes. Many times social and psychological factors may just act as mediators or intervening variables. For example, feeling of inferiority or feeling of helplessness, due to having birth in a social group, where a person is deprived of several physical amenities.

Some methodological and social issues that is pertinent to the study of the disadvantaged sections of the society in India. Those issues include: deprivation and learning, testing and screening procedures, appropriate control group, reinforcing or compensatory education, and attitudes towards disadvantaged groups.

Deprivation and Learning: The researchers use two categories or groups to study the consequences of *disadvantage*, i.e., rural or urban; deprived or non-deprived; tribal or non-tribal. They do not specify the magnitude of social and non-social factors involved in the process of deprivation. Deprivation may be a function of temporal experience under a disadvantaged position (Tripathi & Misra, 1975). The effort required for the physical, social, psychological and economical gratification of needs may be another important dimension (Anandalakshmy, 1982).

Investigators generally assume that the children from an upper-class urban families excel intellectually over the lower class rural children. However, the crucial evidence is lacking. Unable to use the preferred subject, many psychologists have turned to animals in search for generalizations that might be applicable to human learning (Harlow & Mears, 1979). It occurred to Singh (1966, 1969) that one might learn from the city dwelling monkeys to provide information about this issue. He asked, has this urban way of life affected the behaviour of monkeys particularly their ability to solve problems? It was found that forest monkeys performed as well in those complex learning tasks as the urban monkeys. The forest monkeys, however, took more time for adaptation to the test situation. By this time Harlow in his laboratory studies on social isolation (extreme deprivation) in monkeys had already shown that monkey infants reared in isolation did not differ from the normal in the intellectual capabilities. However, they found significant differences in social, emotional and exploratory behaviour. Harlow and Mears (1979) emphasized that Singh's data had every indication that partial isolation cages were just as stimulating to intellectual development as were the temples and forests. However, they concluded that when they gave highly complicated learning tasks the performance of deprived monkeys decreased from the monkeys living under socially enriched environment. The superiority may have come from personality factors and not because the deprived monkeys were lacking in some basic cognitive ability.

Testing and Screening Procedures: An eminent psychologist, Das (1998) has said that the intelligence tests discriminate against disadvantaged children. These tests contain items that were familiar to the children who came from middle-class and urban-families. Therefore it was more likely that the children from better socio-economic status groups living in the urban areas performed better than the children who belonged to Scheduled Caste and Scheduled Tribe groups living in the rural areas. For example, take a child who grows up in the remote village of Kanaor district of Himachal Pradesh. The main livelihood of his family is rearing of sheep and goats. He may know a lot of things about the profession of pastoralism. However, it may be very difficult for him to answer those questions that are framed up by a person who has never seen the tribal areas. Sinha, Tripathi and Misra (1982) have also criticized the intelligence tests on the ground that they were biased in favour of middle-class urban culture. Thus the intelligence tests were closely associated with the higher performance of the urban groups in comparison to the rural ones.

Appropriate Control Group: To make precise assessments of the capabilities of the disadvantaged groups the basic requirement is to take an appropriate control group. The studies on the disadvantaged groups are quasi-experimental in nature. In other words the investigators do not have control over the treatments. It is important that under such conditions the researcher takes all other necessary steps so that the results of the study can be used in making reliable assessment of the behaviour of disadvantaged group. Even researchers from the basic sciences are some times ignorant of the fallacy of the appropriate control group that has extremely important consequences on the applied aspects of the results of the study.

For example, a number of FAO experts that visited the animal breeding farms in India after independence have reported that the breeding experiments were being conducted without taking appropriate control groups. This has significance for development of pastoralism in India. An FAO expert (Naerland, 1958) suggested that for making comparative assessments groups of exotic (Polwarth) and indigenous (Rampur Bushair) sheep should be kept under similar conditions. He strongly emphasized the recruitment of hill people, who traditionally reared sheep and goats, as shepherds, trainers, etc. in veterinaries and research centers. Another FAO expert (Warwick, 1959) wrote that it was surprising that the researchers in India were unaware of the desirability of a control group in experiments. Most of his report submitted to FAO in Rome contained the guidelines for taking an appropriate control group. The control group is essential not only to make precise assessments of the capabilities of the disadvantaged groups but also to make measurement of the improvement after a certain learning strategy is applied on the group. Contemporary studies in behavioural sciences even today lack the appropriate control group.

Reinforcing Education or Compensatory Education: Knowledge of the abilities and skills possessed by the disadvantaged population may help in choosing the intervention strategies that match their psychological characteristics. This is essential for policy-makers to take decisions about the nature of education for these groups. A 'reinforcing education' strategy involves an attempt to build upon the skills the groups already possess. A 'compensatory education' strategy will however involve the development of those skills that are less or completely absent in them. The principles of learning tell us that it is economical for a subject to acquire a task about which he has some experience. For example the pastoral Gaddis or Kanaoras are likely to acquire advanced sheep and goat rearing more proficiently than a task like elementary computer programming.

A pioneer study of some tribal groups in Bihar conducted by psychologists under an international collaboration (Mishra, Sinha & Berry, 1996) provides interesting evidence on the distribution of perceptual-cognitive abilities among the tribal people in relation to their eco-cultural characteristics. The three tribes, Birhors, Asurs and Oraons, are the adivasis of Bihar. Primarily, the Birhors are nomadic, the Asurs are hunter-gatherers and agriculturists, and the Oraons are agriculturists. The investigators concluded that the processes of psychological differentiation, pictorial perception, memory and classification are basic to learning and education. The study reported that the nomadic Birhors and Asurs were psychologically more differentiated than the agricultural Oraons. High differentiation ability is an important prerequisite for success in arts, music and many aesthetic activities. In pictorial perception and object classification the Oraons were better than the Birhors and the Asurs. In Birhors and Asurs, tactual modality seemed to be more developed than visual modality.

Attitudes Towards Disadvantaged Groups: It is also important to understand the attitudes of researchers, teachers, politicians and planners toward the disadvantaged groups. Our exploration of the social reality of the dalits, adivasis and slum dwellers in big cities is partial. The social class of investigators, the tests used and the method of survey handicap it. For example a social scientist (Punalekar, 1994) noted that the researchers who belonged to certain nomadic groups of Maharashtra have opened up for us a wide range of human existence, hitherto unexplored by social scientists. Similarly Vidya Sagar Negi (Chapter 6) writing his own migratory life with herds of sheep and goats seems to be distinct from the others who have researched the Scheduled Tribe areas of Kanaor. The use of categories to describe the social life of people such as animists, fatalists, nomadic, tribal, mythical, and polyandrous do not serve any purpose in the educational planning processes.

The politicians and psychologists in India are alike in their national concern. Every politician in his speech takes a vow to lower the number of people below the poverty line. Similarly the psychologists in India consider disadvantage and poverty as the highest priority area of their research (Adair, Pandey, Begum, Puhan & Vohra, 1995). However in practice much remains to be achieved. In a lecture delivered at the Harvard University, the ex-Prime Minister of India V.P. Singh (1996) narrated an incident when the Mandal Commission Report was announced. During the stormy days a group of boys belonging to the lowest of the low castes, the dalits, came to him and said, "*Sir, all those who are abusing you today are the one's who have abused us for thousands of years. If you stand by us you will also get your share of the abuse.*" The important question for us is, are we ready to stand with the disadvantaged groups?

Psychologists rarely study the attitudes of teachers belonging to higher classes toward the disadvantaged groups. Unless there is a basic change in these attitudes it is difficult to impart education in an unbiased manner. A group of social psychologists of Allahabad University (Das, 1998) conducted an experiment that showed the interaction of traditional Indian prejudices and attribution theory. The teachers from the upper caste were prejudiced about low-caste students' potential for achievement. They expected these students to do poorly in their examinations. When investigators (Sharma & Tripathi, 1988) arranged their experiment that low-caste students performed unexpectedly well, their teachers attributed this success to chance. Teachers attributed the success of upper caste students to the student's ability. Therefore it is likely that the low-caste students lost confidence in their internal abilities and showed less effort as they progressed through their schooling (Pandey & Tripathi, 1982).

Paradigms of Study

We come across various versions of challenging the native wisdom, instead the attempts to enrich the disadvantaged, without denigrating them, are rare. Even some current studies are creating 'myths' about these communities. For example, some environmentalists blame tribal and local communities of the Himalayan region for propagating a 'myth'—the relationship of forest and water. In other words, they say that the local people of the Himalayas hold a belief that the protection of forest is necessary for the conservation of water in the springs, lakes and rivers. More than anybody else, the 'myth' can be attributed to 'Chipko,' the pioneer environmental movement from the Himalayas initiated by the natives or tribals, whatever the more enlightened would prefer to call them. But this relationship had a basis in the naturalistic observations of the local people of the Himalayas. Whether the others (among whom there are 'experts' also), who had similar beliefs, learned it themselves, from the local people or from the western world is not a big issue.

Saberwal (1999) in his book on the pastoralists of Himachal Pradesh has spent considerable space and energy to refute the relationship between forest and water, which he considers as 'myth.' Some investigators were even more vociferous to attribute the 'myth' to the people of Himalayas, particularly the officials engaged in executing the conservation programmes in the Changar area financed by the World Bank (for a discussion on this issue see Pirta, 2007). But for natives who learned the relationship that forests conserve the water, through their experience, strongly argue that it is was not a myth. Though they were aware that the relationship would depend on certain factors and work within certain limits. There are 'experts' who frequently take dual stands. For instance, they, on one hand, favour more and more area under sanctuaries and national parks, but on the other hand empathize with the woes of villagers (Singh, Kothari & Pande, 1990). They value the native wisdom professionally (Sarin, 1996), but hesitate to identify with it in practice.

Instead of resolving conflicts, they ignite them. While prompting forestry for harsher rules to control native interference in the forests (for example the timber distribution rights), raise the issue of tribal rights. For example, Kothari (2006) advocated the cause of tribal people through a catchy visual—*Forests and water are inextricably linked, and the Tribal Bill needs to ensure that the link is protected.* This was about the Great Himalayan national Park in Himachal Pradesh where the rights of the pastoralists were being curtailed, taking away a large area of their summer pasture exclusively for the wildlife. But more important for us at present is, an 'expert' (Kothari), propagating the 'myth' about the positive relationship between forest and water.

Yet, irrespective of the origin of such contradictory statements of 'experts', local people show patience and wisdom in accepting or refuting them. For example, the much-publicised inorganic fertilisers, tested for several years by the farmers in apple orchards were being rejected in favour of organic *desi khad*, the cattle dung. Farmers of Himachal Pradesh, on their own, were transporting truck loads of *gobar* (cattle waste) from Punjab and Haryana. Even the droppings of sheep and goats, during migration towards summer and winter pastures were collected from the forest to manure the orchards.

There is another 'myth,' the intention is to prove that the 'forest people' (tribal) were nice persons but circumstances have made them *jangli* or 'savage.' It is another matter that Rabindernath Thakur considered that the culture of Bharatvarsh (Bhartiya Sabhyata) has its origin in the *aranya* (forests). Whereas the Western Culture (Pashchatya

Sabhyata) has its origin in the development of the urban centers. But anyway, Guha (1999) began his thesis to debunk the 'myth' about the forest people (tribal communities), considered 'savages' by the civilized world. Among the various historians and social scientists to whom he attributes this 'myth,' the last one is Gadgil, though as far as my reading of the works of Gadgil is concerned I do not believe so. At the very outset, Guha fleetingly declared that Gadgil's model has fallen in the face of his arguments. As he proceeds to 'prove' his hypothesis (belief would be more appropriate word since hypotheses are accepted or rejected, not proved or disapproved), it seems that, more than anybody else; Guha has enlivened the 'myth' that the forest people were extremely savage in behaviour. He goes on to 'prove' that these people who earlier shifted between pastoralism and sedentary modes of life, depending upon environmental and socio-political conditions (perhaps assuming that there were no caste differences or differences based on resource use as Gadgil assumed), later assumed a lower status. Whenever through opportunistic looting and plundering one assumed a dominant status in an area, the next endeavour of such 'forest people' (who now have occupied a territory) was to embrace Brahmanical order. He compiles enormous evidence on the aspirations of these low status people. Apparently, instead of debunking the 'myth' of 'forest people' or 'savages' Guha has strengthened it.

Amartya Sen (2006) has discussed the root of such cultural prejudices in an essay on "culture and captivity." His thesis is cultural generalizations leading to social observations regarding certain groups (for example in this case 'forest people' or 'savages') are quite defined to phenomenal world. Interestingly, Guha chose to expose a cultural generalization of medieval or colonial rulers about some groups living in various forest tracts of India, but got entangled, and instead seems to support the social observations, the myth of the 'savage.' These groups include pastoral communities as well.

In this scenario of contradictions among the academicians, the voice of pastoralists goes unheard. The pastoral people are largely far away from the places where decisions are being made about their lives, yet there is hope. It lies in our approach to view the whole scenario with a new perspective, using alternative paradigms of study. Where the disadvantaged groups, or communities of interest become the 'figure' and our expertise goes in the 'background,' called in front only to strengthen the figure. These alternative paradigms would enrich our knowledge in two broad areas: (a) about the art, culture, religious and spiritual aspects of a community, and (b) regarding social, psychological and ecological representations. The first group is considered here as common Himalayan heritage whereas the second group of paradigms forms the individual cognitive dimensions.

Common Himalayan Heritage: The message of some of our more experienced historians, spiritualists, philosophers and anthropologists is synthesized here under the common Himalayan heritage. For example, Anand (1990) has questioned the 'classical' as a measure to evaluate works of art. A Pahari painting from the workshop of Kangra or Chamba may however be judged from the point of view of the *sringar rasa*, the mood to which the creative work is trying to approximate the flirtations of Krishna. Yet, the folk drawings on various walls in Kangra valley depicted the fish eyes of the Jain Kalpasutra. And the visit of Raja of Basholi to Jehangir or when Nainsukh of Guler went to Lahore the *Pahari kalam* was refined by the Mughals. In this context, Anand has made an important suggestion to historians, to withdraw from the western chronological and purely formal approaches in appreciating the paintings. These Pahari paintings have an aura of the native earth.

An Amdo Painter (Figure 2.4) of Tibet, living in exile in Dharamsala, Himachal Pradesh, narrated that the art of painting has gradually spread

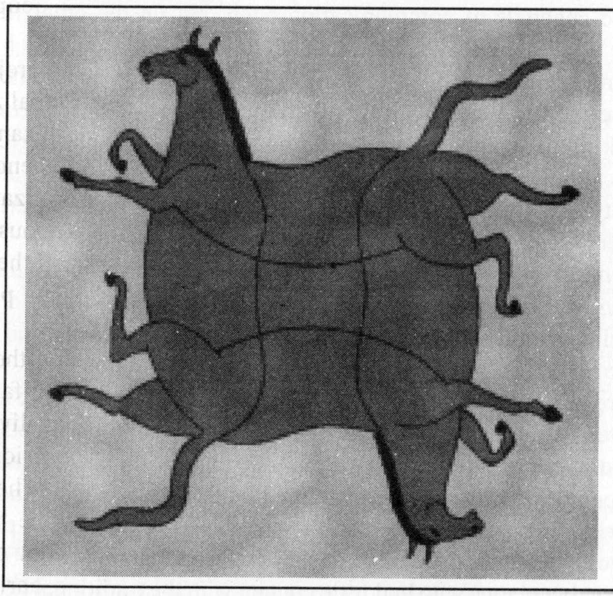

Fig. 2.4: An Illusory Painting (Redrawn from Losal, 1982)

from India to Nepal, China and Tibet. He has described the uniqueness of this art tradition in the form of a dialogue between the painter and a person charmed by a painting. The artist had painted a beautiful flower. A man on seeing the flower mistook it for the real one. So much so that he asked for its seed. The painter said that if he liked the flower, he could take it home. But as the man began to pick up the flower, only then he realised that it was not real (Losal, 1982).

In the same way, Shakspo (1990) has reported that the cultural complexity was so rich in various aspects of life in Ladakh, that sometimes the native was also wonder struck. For example, the music played in worship of the gods (*lha-rna*) had around 360 tunes. Every social and cultural event in Ladakh began and ended with a song of distinctive tune (*dbyangs*). The same was the case with dramas and stories. He strongly disapproved the shallow understanding expressed in a Kashmiri proverb "Ladakhis eat *sattu* (roasted barley flour), wear *pattu* (woolen clothing) and ride *tattu* (ponies)."

Given this background, we introduce here some paradigms as reference points, to build alternative viewpoints to understand and interpret the world-view of the pastoral communities. They may indeed be numerous, however, in this there is a fear of getting lost. On one hand we have to keep the channels of communication open, but on the other hand not become anosmic to the smell of the soil to which a community belongs. In a commentary on tribal art, Malik (1999) has drawn our attention to a character of art that was beyond tribal and non-tribal distinctions, humankind's search for its common identity—psychological and biological—where art transcends its regional identity. It was an act of creativity. However, when seen at regional level, a piece of art would take very specific psychological-metaphysical symbolism. Where, according to Malik, different colours have "*psychic effects, and even religious and spiritual vibrations*." From these local histories, it should be possible to move towards understanding the psychology and history of humankind.

There is, however, an alternative approach to understand the man and nature relationship in the Buddhist Himalayas (Aris, 1990). In particular, he has drawn our attention to the Himalayan crisis, experienced by the native people, but astonishingly refuted by the experts. Even those who felt a crisis, the diagnosis as well as its cure was prescribed as physical. The investigators who refuted the crisis of man and nature in the Himalayas were largely persons who had little contact with the traditional life within the region, whereas the phenomenon required an awareness of the internal history and the spiritual values and attitudes of the Himalayan peoples and their relationships to the natural environment. In the opinion of Aris, the native people whose feelings and aspirations were associated with the Himalayas should have precedence over everyone else's in deciding about the crisis, but at the same time those who had been closely associated with the local people may help in saving this common heritage.

Individual Cognitive Dimensions: In this second group are included the models of investigators involved in cross cultural research where the multidimensional approaches are considered important in understanding the individual. In the eco-cultural model (Segall, Dasen, Berry & Poortinga, 1999), the conceptual framework involves behavioural interactions taking place at individual level and at the population level. Accordingly, the psychological variables (observable behaviours and inferred characteristics) operate at individual level whereas the influence of the background and process variables occurs at the population level. Ecological and socio-political contexts form the background variables. The cultural and biological adaptations taking place in the ecological and socio-political contexts measured through ecological, genetic, cultural and acculturative influences constitute the process variables.

Some cross-cultural psychologists use the concept of the developmental niche, which they think is more appropriate for integrating findings of psychologists and anthropologists, rather than biological or ecological. The developmental niche includes the developmental approach of psychologists and the contextual understanding of anthropologists. At the center of the developmental niche is the individual child, with his or her particular set of inherited dispositions. The child is surrounded by three components or subsystems (Figure 2.5): the settings, or physical and social contexts in which the child lives; the customs, or culturally determined rearing and educational practices; the psychological characteristics of the caretakers, including the parental ethno-theories of child development. Super and Harkness (1997) have explained that the organism and the developmental niche adapt to one another. As the individual adapted to its surroundings, the niche got modified to suit the individual.

In the ecological systems theory (Bronfenbrenner, 1977), the developing individual cannot be isolated from the context, and that interactions are reciprocal, so that the proper unit of analysis is neither the individual out of context, nor the contexts themselves, but the individual in context. Individual child is in the middle, interacts actively through bi-directional, reciprocal, influences with the environment,

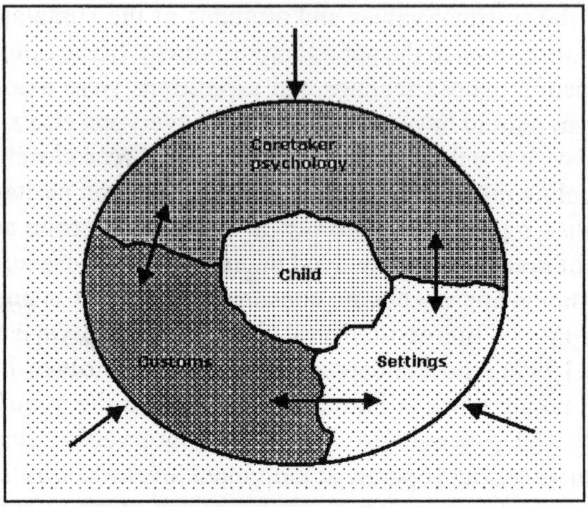

Fig. 2.5: The Developmental Niche

structured in terms of the nested levels of the microsystem, the mesosystem, exosystem, and macrosystem (Figure 2.6). A microsystem is the complex of relationships between the developing person and the environment in an immediate setting, such as home, school, workplace, etc. A mesosystem encompasses interactions among families, school, peer group, religious group and so on. An exosystem encompasses the larger social structures, both formal and informal. Macrosystem consists of general aspects of society, its values, belief systems, and other aspects that are part of culture.

In these ecological perspectives where the psychological processes are assumed to function in transactional terms. Ecology provides important framework for understanding the psychological processes responsible for successful adaptation. In the bio-social psychology approach (Figure 2.7; Dawson, 1969; 1977), adaptation to different biological environments results in the development of particular habits of perceptual inference, cognitive processes, and psychological skills, which are thought to be adaptive for these environments. The term biological environment includes physical and living elements, geography, geology, topography, climate, food resources, altitude and relationships of organisms to that environment. Whereas the bio-social variables include those adaptive socialisation and educational processes that tend in subsistence societies to be the key link between type of ecology and behaviour that reinforce the dominant attitudes and values for that society, whether hunting, fishing, pastoral or agricultural

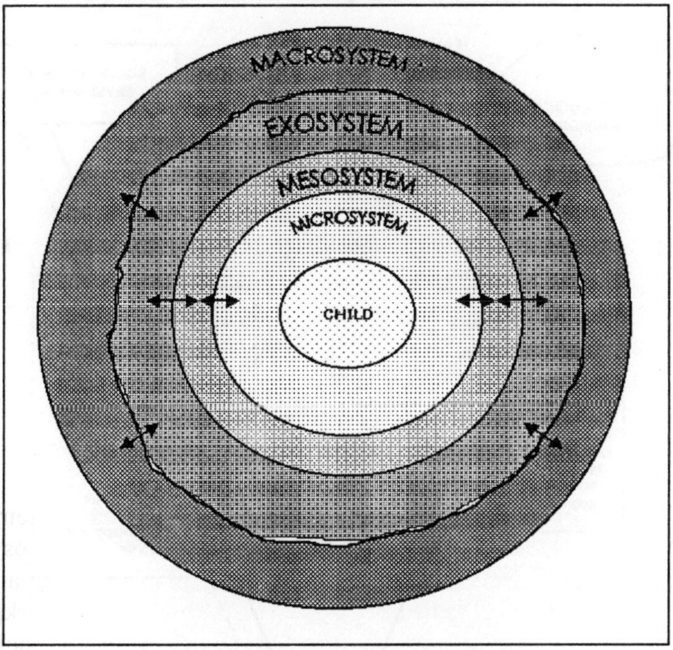

Fig. 2.6: The Ecological System Model

practices. Lastly, biosocial psychology is concerned with the effects of the biological and sociocultural stimuli on the physiological and psychological processes.

Our whole emphasis in this volume is to obtain an understanding of the individual's cognitive aspects keeping in view his contextual factors. Some other paradigms, useful in the pastoral context have been discussed in detail by Pirta (2007), of special significance is the work of Crook and Osmaston (1994) in Ladakh.

Conclusion

In his book on "Kinner Desh", Sankrityayan appears equally uncomfortable with the *Raja* and his *Praja*, the head of the State and its people. It must be seen against the background of India's struggle for its freedom in the middle of the twentieth century. He avoided those involved in the freedom struggle of India at the regional level, and in some cases made a caricature of their efforts. In his writing there is a tendency to undermine the cognitive competency of these people. In fact they, on the one hand, articulated the British policies along with their counterpart in

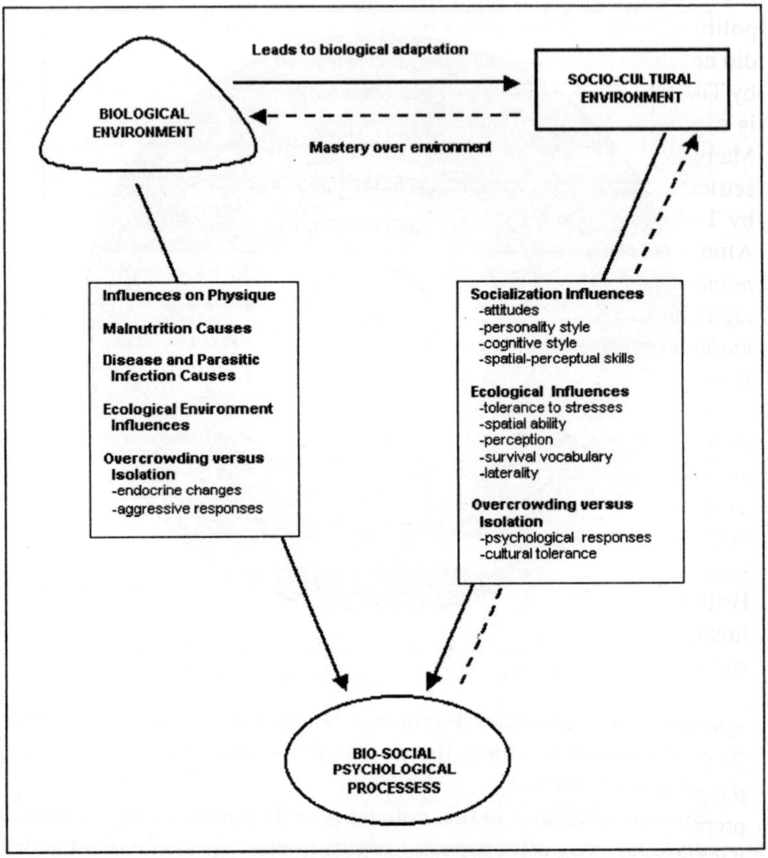

Fig. 2.7: The Bio-social Psychology Model

local rulers, at the same time they were in communication with their leaders far away in Delhi. With a remarkable cognitive quality of assimilation, they succeeded in making a perceptible impact on the folk mind. Undoubtedly, to inspire them against the British and the Raja, was not to cast a spell of trance where the local deity helped them. It needed considerable planning, and above all, the sacrifices of these small invisible people.

There was enhancement in the stature of Sankrityayan and the others of his kind after the independence, otherwise how could have Rajmata of Bushair felt need for his kindness. His curt reference to the young prince only indicated narrowness about a child's cognitive achievements (this young prince Virbhadra Singh became the most important and successful political leader of Himachal Pradesh). The arrogance of Sankrityayan did not stop at this, he even criticised an effort of land revenue settlement by Tikka Raghunath Singh carried out in 1890 and 1891 in Kanaor. Here is a glimpse. In the Himachal Pradesh district gazetteer of Kanaor, Mamgain (1971) has provided a brief comparative account of Barnes settlement with that of a local person. He has written that the settlement by Tikka Raghunath Singh was on the whole beneficial for the people. After this settlement, "*the athwara (forced labour) was reduced from six months to one month. All the burdensome cesses, commonly called as eighteen karahads, were abolished. The landowners were granted adna malkiat (inferior proprietary rights) while previously even their rights of mortgage and transfer of land were restricted.*" (Page 242)

Now I will give some historical evidence to correct the misconception of Sankrityayan about the cognitive backwardness of the people of an adjacent area, the Jubbal State, for the period shortly before independence. This small valley has participated in the freedom struggle of India that culminated in 1947. A well-known leader from the area was Bhagmal Sauta, who had developed a net-work of people right in the Summer Capital of British Raj, at Shimla. Not only they disseminated information having linkages with Lahore as well as Delhi, they raised the issues of local people, such as abolition of *begar* and the grant of civil liberties, through mass protests. One such event, '*Dhami Goli Kand*' took place in 1939 when the ruler of Dhami state apprehended the procession under the leadership of Bhagmal Sauta near Shimla and "*volleys of stones, lathis and golies from the guns were showered*" on the people. There is an important document prepared by the local people and the Gandhians who suffered in this conflict, it is entitled: "*Report of the Non-Official Enquiry into the tragic happenings in Dhami State (Simla Hills) on 16th July, 1939.*" The report of Enquiry Committee was prepared under the chairmanship of Lala Duni Chand advocate, a member of the All India Congress Committee but the local leaders personally met Mahatama Gandhi at Delhi, and Jawahar Lal Nehru at Allahabad. This event was a turning point in stimulating people in the other hill states against the social injustice and the British Rule. A significant point of the Enquiry Committee was that it had a secretary Shri Dev Suman from the Tehri Garhwal, a State farther in the eastern side. He was arrested later, and died in Tehri Jail. But he inspired several young persons—Virendra Dutt Saklani, Sunderlal Bahuguna and Vidya Sagar Nautiyal were prominent among them. They later became crusaders of environment struggles—the Chipko and the Save Himalaya Movement—that modern India can claim for raising environmental consciousness.

Perhaps this should suffice to suggest that these remote valleys were vibrant with life and various social and cultural activities. A very significant part of the regions that characterize its people, for which they have been branded as animists, involve the socio-religious activity that affected every bit of human action taking place in Kanaor, and all over Himachal Pradesh. It has not vanished even when people of Himachal Pradesh have achieved literacy equal to Kerala, leaving behind the Brhamanically dominant states of Bihar and Uttar Pradesh. More important is the scenario of social harmony in this small state when its surrounding area is engaged in conflicts. Perhaps the socio-religious institutions of the local deities are important in it. This questions the general conception spreading all over the world where religion was now seen as a disruptive force to social harmony.

It appears that much of what Sankrityayan (the *Mahapandit* symbolizes other elites as well) other stated was based on hearsay, and there was even personal bias in reporting. Now when we evaluate the ideologies represented by Barnes (representing England) and by Sankrityayan (representing the think tank of Soviet Russia), both the economies have failed. Rather we now have the Nordac social democracies (Denmark, Finland, Norway and Sweden), where the high taxation is used on society's desire for prosperity and social security (Sachs, 2006). These countries have the lowest poverty, much greater investment for social purposes, and highest investment on research and development, in comparison to the English-speaking ones (Australia, Canada, Ireland, New Zeeland, the U.K. and the U.S.) having a historical lineage with the 19th-century Britain.

3

Harmony and Conflict Over Resource Use

Once water covered the whole surface of the Earth. A landmass, Pangaea, appeared that broke into Laurasia and Gondwana (Deitz & Holden, 1970). From the former, Laurasia, originated North America and Eurasia (the Russia, China and European countries). The Gondwana gave birth to five landmasses: Antarctica, South America, Africa, Australia and India about 340 to 285 million years ago (MYA). The triangular landmass, India, started its journey from South Africa and took about 200 million years to join Eurasia through Assam Neck. The separation between India and Eurasia formed the Siwalik Gulf starting from Assam Neck to Arabian Sea towards the western side. Slowly the gulf became a Siwalik River or Indo-Brahm River flowing towards the western side. About 0.25 MYA the Siwalik River, probably due to continuous rise of Himalayas and Peninsular tilt, divided into the westward flowing Indus and eastward flowing Tsangpo or Brahmputra. Ganga, a tributary of Siwalik River also started flowing eastwards. However, an alternative view holds that the majority of the Himalayan rivers were older than the Himalayas. The Sindhu, Satluj, Ganga, Karnali, Kosi, Arun and Brahmputra, these antecedent rivers cut their courses deeper and deeper with the rise of Himalayan range of mountains (Valdiya, 1996). According to geologists, the Indian plate is still moving northwards about 5 to 6 cm per year. The orogenesis or high mountain building, due to collision of Indian plate with the Eurasian plate, is the process of the formation of Himalayas and its fragility.

Changing Biosphere and Noosphere of Himalayas

The Himalayas rises from the Indian plains and stretches up to the Tibetan plateau. It forms a 3,500 km long arc from Hindu Kush to Hengduan (Denniston, 1993). The faults in the plates and other geological changes divide the Himalayas into three major subdivisions. The Outer Himalayas (Sivalik Hills) separates from the Lesser

Himalayas by Main Boundary Thrust. The Lesser Himalayas separates from the Great Himalayas by Main Central Thrust, and the Himadri or Great Himalayas, separates from Tibetan landmass by the Indo-Tsangpo Suture Zone (Valdiya, 1993).

The evolutionary changes and ecological changes occur side by side. About 65 MYA a dramatic event caused the extinction of dinosaurs who dominated the landscape along with more than half of plant and animal species. During this period the landmass that formed India was over a volcanic hot spot, the remnants of which are the Deccan Traps of our country (Courtillot, 1990). The fossils of dinosaurs and other animals of this era lie buried in the Sivalik Hills. During MIOCENE epoch Africa also collided with Eurasia (16 to 17 mya) and the migrations of animals started between the two continents. It was after this period that ape like species migrated from Africa to Europe, Saudi Arabia, India and China. It is clear from the fossils of *Pliopithecus, Dryopithecus, Procunsul, Ramapithecus* and/or *Sivapithecus, Krishnapithecus,* and *Gigantopithecus* (Groves, 1989). The erect walking ancestors of human beings evolved during PLEISTOCENE (5 MYA). The youngest among them is *Homo erectus* (1.4 MYA) that migrated to Asia and Europe from Africa. The Shivalik region of western Himalayas, particularly the area that lies in Himachal Pradesh, is rich in tools of this period.

The ongoing collision of Indian and Eurasian crustal plates caused the fragility of environment in the Himalayas. It is evident from the uplift of land, slope erosion, and unpredictable nature of glaciers (Shroder, 1989). These glaciers might have descended from peaks, and blocked the Indus river forming large lakes which later on caused floods. This was probably the cause of the extinction of *Ramapithecus* and/or *Krishnapithecus*, *Gigantopithecus* and *Homo erectus* in the Sivalik region of western Himalayas. The mighty river Saraswati of Vedic time also might have disappeared due to tectonic movements in Shivalik range in western Himalayas (Possehl, 1982; Valdiya, 1996).

A significant point in the theory of biosphere is the realization that living things also contribute in the atmosphere, which is not merely due to the physical and chemical forces (Goldsmith, 1993). An Austrian geologist, Eduard Suess conceived biosphere in 1875 but did not receive much attention. It is the thin layer of plant and animal life covering the face of the Earth (Grinewald, 1996). In Paris, two geologists, Vernadsky and Teilhard, and a philosopher, Eduard Le Roy, together conceptualized the transition from biosphere to noosphere (Krumbein & Lapo, 1996). Writers often use the ideas of biosphere and noosphere interchangeably.

Vernadsky emphasized the materialistic conception of the biosphere—the biogeochemistry. For Teilhard the noosphere was an anthropocentric idea where human consciousness played the major role. The noosphere (noos=mind) implies that the evolution of human beings added a radical dimension to the evolution of earth. It was a transition from intuitive, mythological unconscious life processes to attributes of human conscious activities. Human beings can change the biogeochemical processes in the biosphere for their survival, and this sphere of interaction is the noosphere. It is an ideal shell of thought or consciousness, the unique human attribute, by which we envelop the globe or its parts, such as the peaks of the Himalayas.

The Himalayas is 'mighty' in our psyche. It is *Nagadhiraja* or the ruler of mountains. This creation of human mind is the noosphere, an envelope of numerous myths around the Himalayas; it evokes unusual imageries from the people of India. A large segment of Indian population looks at these snow clad lofty mountains with deep reverence (Bahuguna, 1987-88). The myths knit together the people living in this region, the rivers originating from its glaciers and lakes, the lofty mountains and the forest that cover it. The same is true for its fauna. For example, monkeys have been depicted in the epic Ramayana as the *vanar sena* (or monkey army) of the Hanuman (Roonwal, 1989). The myth has inspired number of literary works on the life of the people in India (Kipling, 1894, 1895; Das, 1932; Paz, see Davidar, 1990).

Mythological evidence suggests that the Govardhana hill and its surrounding wooded areas which served as pastoral land, *vraja*, for the herds of Krishna, the Chief of Yadavas, was under the sway of fearsome goddess *kali*. The mountain Govardhana is said to have come from the Himalayas. It was carried from the North by Hanuman at the time of the building of bridge across the ocean by Rama and dropped where it now stands (Vaudeville, 1986). It is possible, however, that the territories of transhumants from the Himalayas and Mathura plains overlapped.

There is voluminous evidence from the Buddhist Himalayan villages of Ladakh in the west to the Arunachal Pradesh in the east about the rich cultural heritage in the form of mural paintings—the Vajrayana Buddhist tradition paintings. These highest mountains of the world are home of pastoralists and their tamed animals. They have also developed unique noosphere around each mountain in this region. This activity might have been going on in this region for long. Without them, it would have not been possible for Rin-chen Zang-po to construct the 108 monasteries spread all over the Himalayan range. These monasteries, built in the eleventh century by craftsmen and artists from Kashmir, were not only the institutions of Buddhism, but also became active centers of trans-Himalayan trade. The paintings in these monasteries have created a vision that shaped the culture of the continent (Behl, 2003). He further observed that the monastery of Nako, in Kinnaur district of Himachal Pradesh comprised of four temples within an enclosure of mud walls. The wall paintings at Nako display a considerable delicacy of execution and an inner grace. The villagers of Nako have maintained them. A new trend, however, is that the State administration is now taking possession of these institutions from local bodies. The State preaches through advertisements, and even has websites, in favour of certain deities.

These instances show, to some extent, how people's institutions of faith were taken over by the State. One cannot deny improvement in the administration of the temple affairs due to such takeovers by the State, yet these are places where people voluntarily learn and develop a feeling of attachment and pride in their culture. Due to alienation, people were becoming dependent on the State and even have sought donations from international agencies. In this way, the experts start intervening and undermine the wisdom of local people, who have been taking care of these institutions for centuries. Though people might be hiring a painter from some distant place to do some painting work in the monastery, this normally is a decision taken by the community (see Chapter 8).

The point we want to emphasise is, that the pastoralists have to make such community decisions every time while moving with the herds of sheep and goats. Moreover, collective decision-making is extremely important for the management of pastures. Besides this, development is first of all a holistic effort of the local population according to local needs. Instead we find that experts of different hues enter in the developmental process that are not only alien to local community, they are also alien to each other's goals and ways of work. They have little or no knowledge of the intricate processes taking place in the milieu. Moreover, there is lack of patience as well as time to see the effects of these developmental interventions. Some of them came with potato seeds; other planted poplar trees, the sebuckthorn was advocated with great fanfare; and, a few searched for a poor family that agrees to take loan. The concept of holistic planning keeping in view animals, pastures, lake, monastery, history, social relations and aspirations of the people was entirely lacking. We provide an example of this approach from Kanaor.

Case Study 1: Nako Village, a Cultural Heritage

Verma (2002), in a 300-page volume on Kanaoras of Kinnaur, has reported a case study of the socio-economic development of the village of Nako, at 3,230 m near the border with Tibet. The case report is based on the 'developmental' schemes to help the poorest families of this 'tribal' village of more than 400 people. Though the help provided to these poor families is important, we have to understand how this village survives in the hostile environment. All the villagers in these areas receive some subsidy on fuel wood, solar cookers, smokeless chullahs and solar lights. Besides that a considerable amount came in 1982-83 under the Desert Development Programme to improve the Nako lake. About 50 lakhs were spent on improving the lake for fishing and irrigation purposes. Three main sources of livelihood of the people are agriculture, horticulture and livestock. As far as incentive in the form of daily wage is concerned the author felt that it has benefited the outside labour. But Verma's logic conveys the general attitude where on one hand the villagers were self-sufficient, but at the same time the men folk were shy to do manual work and preferred to waste their time in playing cards and other similar games. The report further says that according to 1991 census, there were 875 sheep and 667 goats in the village. This was more likely *klm zet*, not the *arung zet*, the mobile herds. It does not mention anything about the grazing needs, veterinary and other issues related to pastoralism.

A brief analysis of the preceding report is here. The social life of the people residing in Nako had been entirely neglected, as is the case with the other studies about the people of Kanaor. Even the economic data pertain mainly to some poor families that were visited by the administrative staff to distribute funds. They hardly cared about how the funds were used. This report does not say anything about the livestock and its role in the economy of the village. For the support of animal husbandry, though there was a dispensary, it was not equipped with proper facilities. The same was the case with school, which was in highly impoverished condition. Lastly, it is perhaps most important, the report does not even refer to the significant heritage of the Nako village—its monasteries—that inspired the life of people. Nako is as old as Tabo, the latter attracted greater attention from the scholars and the State. Besides the monastery, there are several important temples owned by the village commonly and individual households. It is these traditions, the works of art in the temples and the monasteries that introduces us to the collective and individual cognitive accomplishments of people. These works of art have received patronage from the pastoralists, who devote a share of their earnings to such creative work. Conscientious historians and archaeologists have been exploring these creative works, however, a task of even greater significance remains to understand the mental processes of common men and women instrumental in its creation and preservation. As the need is to continue these traditions, and not to fossilize them or look for donors from far away places.

In these high altitude Himalayan ranges, transhumance along with trade definitely played a significant role due to lesser scope for agriculture. Movement with herds of sheep and goats required cordial interactions of the herder with diverse ways of life. The people moving with the *arung zet* assimilated various aspects of culture from other groups coming in their contact. They learned skills that suited to the arid environment. Instead of huge temples, that needed masonry work and huge amount of wood, they preferred simple mud walls, but very intricate mural paintings and stuccos. It was not difficult to carry paints, however they lured beautiful painters, and even invited imaginative and learned people like the great translator, Rin-chen Zang-po.

Besides that, for the survival, one needs nutritious diet as well. The meat from sheep and goats, with little supplement from small pieces of farm land was perhaps best combination in such a climate. Meat was dried and processed, and it is easily stored in the dry weather for an year or so. This processing is done in such a way that one does not need to cook the dried meat. Thus they saved fuel as well, which was an important limiting factor. Similarly, the diet was supplemented by *sattu* of roasted barley, which does not need cooking. They mixed the *sattu* with little water and ate it. Moreover, *sattu* was easy to carry on long journeys in the mountains. Even more significant adaptation was the system of turning human night soil to organic manure, which along with the small irrigation system, resulted in high yields from the scarce pieces of land fashioned for agriculture.

Earlier, when vehicular communication was absent, the *transhumantes*, migratory sheep and goats, were the means of transportation from as far as the Shivalik hills touching the Indian plains to the deep valleys of the roof of the world, Tibet. The *arung zet*, the mobile sheep and goats, would thus earn money for the *shalang sa*, their proud owner, not only from the flesh and fibers, but also for the rare commodities that they carried on their back. These sheep and goats needed good pastures managed by the efficient social system where the *shalang sa* had a respectable place. Presently the whole scenario has changed. It appears that the problems of *shalang sa* are not going to end in near future, as will be clear in the following part of this section.

Roy Burmon (1993) has argued that the drive for greater common good is many times in direct conflict with the survival of tribals, particularly those engaged in migratory life of herding. These activities include the extraction of forest resources, submergence of large parts of grazing land, and reservation of forest areas for sanctuaries and national parks. Though they are related to larger interests these developmental activities have restricted the movement of *arung zet* and have drowned the sheep walks and the winter pastures.

The colonial rulers and the post-colonial policy makers have been modifying environment in such a way that it negatively affected the productive activities, social composition and cultural composition of tribal communities. Similar assertions have been made by Singh (1987) in his report that worst affected were the pastoral nomads of Rajasthan as most of them were Scheduled Castes who did not have other resources to fall upon. They were forced to increase the number of goats as the grazing lands degenerated. Moreover, in order to feed their livestock they travelled over long distances, and many have ultimately turned into labourers.

The number of developmental refugees is increasing. Sharma (1987-89) has reported that forced migration of tribals from their traditional habitats was assuming a character of great human tragedy. He was in fact worried about the way the 19th century colonial law like the Land Acquisition Act was being used indiscriminately in the name of development. There seems no regard for the rights of a person, his freedom to live in an area where he and his family have been living for centuries. Mahapatra (1993) has also reiterated that in this process the tribals suffered the most. The customary rights of tribal populations on land and forest were being overlooked, and this according to him was the "predatory role" of the state. In the context of the Himalayan region, Ramakrishnan (1993) has recommended decentralised planning and execution involving local communities, because of the high degree of ecological heterogeneity.

The following case study of Kanaor is an example of the reductionist approach, where the pastoral rights of passage, grazing and even peaceful living in their areas are undermined.

Case Study 2: Dark Night in the Sutlej Valley

On a field visit, in the second week of August 2000, it appeared that nothing wrong had happened only few days ago in this region. The cool breeze slowly gave way to hot humid air rising from the valley floor. Unequally wide narrow strip of muddy water joined the northern and southern steep slopes of the green landscape. It was the Vedic river Shutudri that had rejuvenated as Sutlej in modern times. Originating as Langchen Khabab from the southern slopes of Mount Kailash it travels through the mystic region where once Bonpo flourished, and then enters the Indian territory at Khab. For about three hundred kilometers the river meanders and then abruptly merges with itself, a phenomenon made possible by great human engineering feat, a temple of modern India, the Bhakra Dam. A huge artificial water body came up drowning the town of Bilaspur and its fertile valleys. Over the years, the big reservoir known as Gobind Sagar has become a lake of sorrow for the Himachalis. On the early morning of August 1, 2000 when it was still dark, Sutlej engulfed more than 200 people with their material possessions in its deep waters.

The NH 22 took right turn from Sainj on the left bank of river Sutlej. Human memory abruptly played its magic. Recall processes flashed cognitive maps with limbic arousal. One after another the bridges over Sutlej were conspicuously missing. Nogli, that was yet to recover from the flash flood of 1997, bore the brunt of the Sutlej. Signboard and flags of Ratan Guest House on the edge of road stood witness that there existed a building few days ago. This small township, that catered the need of remote hill villages, was saved by a patch of trees and by an embankment on the sides of the Nogli Khad where it met the Sutlej. On both sides of Nogli town the NH 22 was sinking and may slide down into Sutlej in near future. The gaping crevices were being filled with soil by bulldozers.

After 5 km abruptly the frontal view of Rampur appeared that was once the capital of the princely state of Bushair, perhaps the largest in area among the Shimla Hill States. Presently the right bank of Rampur comprised of Broh (Bron) and Jagatkhana and on the left bank was the main bazaar. Rampur's Lavi Fair reminded of socio-cultural and trade relations with Tibet.

The gushing waters of the Sutlej on August 1 had washed away many concrete structures of Broh and Jagatkhana and filled many of them with silt. Timely warning from the people up in the Sutlej valley saved hundreds of lives. However, the river carried with it a number of people, who could not be woken up at midnight, to Gobind Sagar. All the bridges linking the two sides of Rampur town were washed except one, and was the only route of communication. The old town of Rampur remained untouched by the river as it stands on the solid rock base.

Rampur to Wangtu—A Death Trap: From Rampur to Wangtu the narrow valley has become very fragile. In most of the year this stretch of land turns brown, only in July and August it has greenery. Extensive felling of trees started as early as 1850 in the Sutlej valley by the British contractors who took benefit of the poor condition of the hill chiefs. The deforestation and consequent erosion had never stopped since then. It was noted that wherever there were small patches of trees the erosion was minimum on the banks of river as well as up in the hills.

Over the past several years a number of small hydroelectric projects have come up the stretch between Rampur and Wangtu. They include Ghanvi, Bhaba and Nathpa Jhakri hydroelectric projects. Thus nearly 80-km stretch of the Sutlej valley was exposed to large-scale interventions causing enormous change in the ecosystem. The work was in progress on three more hydroelectric projects, Baspa Stage-I, Baspa Stage-II, and Karchham-Wangtu, up in the Sutlej valley.

This has been going on in utter disregard of high probability of seismic changes in this region. It was essential to consider these human interventions, considering the damage caused by natural disasters, that had recurred every three-year in this small region between Rampur and Wangtu.

Nathpa: 1993: During July-August 1993, a landslide from the right bank of Sutlej obstructed it near Nathpa, 185 km from Shimla, creating an artificial lake. Water of the lake entered through the outlet of 120 MW Bhaba Power House causing it heavy losses. After great efforts the rocks blocking Sutlej were blown into pieces by dynamites making passage for dammed up water. During this period people in the low-lying areas of the Sutlej below that spot spent sleepless nights. A central government team from New Delhi assessed the loss at Bhaba Power House around Rs. 25-lakh daily due to stoppage of power generation.

Nathpa Jhakri Power Corporation had already started work at the site of the 1993 landslide. It included massive tampering, externally as well as internally, with the rock structure. Presently the base of the 60-meter high dam was being laid at this place to divert the Sutlej into a tunnel.

Panvi, Andhra and Nogli: 1997: On the evening of August 11, 1997, the Panvi Khud, a small nullah originating up in the Shatul Ghati brought tons of debris with it and blocked the Sutlej for several days. Six major bridges left no trace cutting the Kanaor from the rest of the country and eroding about 6 km of the NH 22. Big boulders and gravel buried the small habitation and 11 persons at Wangtu. A big lake was formed at Wangtu due to blockage of the Sutlej. For several days people made their way to Kanaor by crossing the artificial lake by boat. On the same night at 8 p.m. the Andhra Khud, flowing on the backside of the same mountain range, washed away a roadside township of Chirgaon with more than 300 inhabitants. A considerable loss did occur on the same night by the Nogli Khud originating from the same ridge. Andhra and Nogli powerhouses suffered heavy losses and did not generate electricity for about one year.

The flash flood was probably caused by a cloudburst on the Shatul Ghati (4640 m), which divides the Sutlej and Pabbar water catchment areas. Here it is important to note that on both sides of Shatul Ghati the elevation of the mountains goes up to 5,260 m. It is the Hansbeshan (5,240 m) mountain that feeds to all the three rivers that caused major damage on August 11, Panvi, Andhra and Nogli. Thus the rapid melting of snow on Hansbeshan range due to environmental factors cannot be ruled out as the cause of the devastating flood.

Mt. Kailash: 2000: The third incident that brought a high column of water on August 1, 2000 occurred far away at the origin of Sutlej in Mt. Kailash, in Tibet. However, the major losses took place in the region between Rampur and Wangtu. The damage ran into several hundred crores as direct loss to the Nathpa Jhakri Hydroelectric Project. The other major loss was the delay in the completion of the project that was estimated to be about one year. Total cost of the project went up to Rs. 10,000 crore. The telecommunication system, however, did a commendable service which needs to be lauded. Hundreds of lives were saved in low lying villages of Kanaor that got warnings of rising Sutlej over telephone from their relatives living farther up in the valley.

The above case study highlights several issues including the displacement of people from their native areas. Thus a new category of disadvantaged people was emerging. The big dams have displaced millions of people by submerging their native areas in water forever. Social conflicts have also displaced people from their place of birth to live their life partially or completely in an unknown land under the mercy of local inhabitants. The Tibetan population of the Himalayas is one such example. Displacement was also occurring due to depletion of natural resources. The migratory pastoralists were encountering scarcity of grazing area for their herds, and many were on the verge of leaving their profession. The rehabilitation of Bhakra and Pong dam oustees is yet to complete even after about forty years. These large scale interventions have severely restricted the winter pastures of sheep and goats and the projects were being constructed on the migratory routes along the rivers.

Whatever may be the factors of displacement, these large populations of people are likely to suffer from identity crisis, which later cause violence

(Kakar, 1995). The separation anxiety afflicts them and increases their vulnerability to emotional problems. Moreover, the reluctant hosts show discrimination against displaced populations, which results in low self-esteem. There is also a feeling of rage due to apathetic attitude of the State. The important point is that the displaced populations in many cases are the disadvantaged groups. For example, the adivasis being uprooted from the Narmada Valley due to construction of Sardar Sarovar Dam. In this way, the displacement of people against their wishes is a precursor to their destitution and eventual destruction, physically and psychologically (WHO, 2001).

Harvest of Sheep and Goats

An advantageous trait for adaptation to uncertain environment is the diversification of subsistence activities. If one looks at the livestock diversity and associated cultural practices of pastoralists in India, it is unparallelled in the world. Some domestic animals are now cosmopolitan whereas the others are restricted to certain geographical areas. The yak and reindeer remain restricted to certain regions but the cow, sheep, goat, pig, and horse occur all over the world. They provide various kinds of services to human beings. The *Homo sapiens* in turn are instrumental in increasing the survival of these domestic animals.

It is the social milieu in the Indian subcontinent that serves as the catalyst for the diversity of domestic animals for various reasons. First, the agriculture and animal husbandry are complementary to each other. It could develop largely due to the drought power and fertilizer derived from animals. Along with it there was the involvement of religious factors. For example, Hindus revere the cow like mother. Social behaviour and institutions also developed that supported man-animal relationship. After a period when relatives meet each other they never forget to ask about the well being of the 'wealth animals' after enquiring about the well-being of house, family and children (Negi, 1996). The Gujars have an elaborate system of greeting each other. While welcoming each other in the name of almighty god, they ask about the well-being of dera (living hut), family members, different age-class buffaloes and the fodder trees, the pasture as well as grass, all the time embracing each other. Traditionally people say 'dhon-pashu' (wealth animals) however for others it is 'pashu-dhan' (animal wealth). The word 'pashu' or animal is confusing here. In most of the Himachal the word 'dhon' means sheep, goat, and cows. The owner of 'dhon' is known as 'dhoni'. When there was barter system the real wealth of a family was its 'dhon' not the money. On the basis of social system that prevails among 'dhoni' and the traditions they follow, Thakur (1994) has suggested that these people are the descendents of 'pani,' the cow herders described in the *vedas*.

Over time, the symbiosis between man and animals moved in a new direction. The exchange of sheep, goat, cow and buffalo for grain and cloth turned domesticated animals into a prized commodity. In addition, the products of these animals became commodities for exchange. The livestock fair, *pashu mela*, probably came into existence to purchase and sell this commodity and to procure necessary items for livelihood. The *pashu mela* of Pushkar in Rajasthan and Sonepur in Bihar not only display the diversity and number of domestic animals but the sea of people from distant places (Kumar, 1993). At a smaller scale the livestock fairs are common all over India. The fairs are the measures of the importance of livestock and change in attitude towards them depending upon their use for human beings (Nain, 1992). In recent times we see two opposite streams. One based upon extreme utilitarian attitude and the other conservative in nature. The utilitarian value of animals has dwindled, as they could not compete with machine as drought power. The chemical fertilizer also reduced the need of livestock manure. The construction of vehicular roads in the interior areas has thrown the pack animals out of job. The good breeds for reproductive purposes are presently available through veterinary hospitals, but in future they are likely to be replaced with gene banks.

The *nalwadi mela* of Bilaspur and *lavi mela* of Rampur in Himachal Pradesh are famous for agropastoralists and pastoralists, respectively. The *lavi mela* has facilitated the Indo-Tibetan trade in pashmina wool and other goods. It is celebrated in second week of December every year since 1681 after the Namagya Treaty between the Tibet and Bushair. The princely state of Bushair, the British rulers, and later the Indian State has promoted the *lavi mela*. The pastoralists from Tibet, Kanaor and Lahaul-Spiti not only brought their produce of sheep and goats, their raw produce and the finished products but they also came with the Chamurthi horses, handicrafts, the various edible products (Sharma, 1990). The pastoralilsts exchange their products with the household commodities that traders bring from plains. Since 1962, when the trade with Tibet was stopped due to war with China, international importance of the *Lavi Mela* also reduced. The road from Tibet border to Shimla that facilitated the trade on mules, sheep and goats due to British Interest in the trade, was closed after 1962 for security considerations. In recent decades it is an important transportation route for the people and their horticulture produce.

It is a great tragedy that a poor peasantry and pastoralists met the ever-increasing demand of urban centers for livestock products in India and other countries. Though the old aphorism "*unn ta sunna*" or the wool is like gold may have lost its charm, the demand for meat was on constant increase. It is reflected in the words of a young pastoralist, the modern version of the old saying, 'the flock of a goat is a mobile bank. Whenever and wherever you need money sell the goat.' The increase in rearing of goats in the Shivalik region, as indicated by the census 2003, may be due to their demand for meat. At the same time, this young pastoralist admits the erosion of the professional values, but then it is also an adaptation to a society that is apathetic to the needs of its important segment. In this way the pastoralist production can impinge on urban economies (Ratnagar, 1991).

In the 1930s tonnes of wool from Lahasa crossed Gelep La to reach Kalimpong on yaks, sheep and goats. The Marwari traders from Rajasthan, after baling the wool shipped it to American merchants in Liverpool (Chaudhuri, 1993). This has been recorded in the British period or even earlier. Zorawar Singh, the famous soldier of Maharaja Ranjeet Singh, made all out effort to channelise the *pashmina* flow from Tibet to Lahore through Kashmir looms (Charak, 1980). The British did not allow him to succeed and wanted all channels from Tibet to India open to the West. They were most successful till 1947, and indirectly after that too. But since 1962 all the flow of *pashmina* from Tibet has been directed to China. Negotiations have taken place between India and China for trickling of this flow to India. In 1992 the Lipu Lekh Pass was reopened from Pithoragarh in Uttar Pradesh to Taklakot in Tibet. In 1993 the Dharma Pass via Mansarovar was also reopened. The pilgrimage to Mansarovar was resumed under the strict provisions of Indian and Chinese army. The businessmen crossed borders to explore their trade opportunities.

It is important to understand the relationship of *arung zet* system and the trade that flourished on it. There are two important questions. What are the gains of a pastoralist from this trade around the world? And, what are the consequences of this trade in general? The answer to these questions exposes the notorious connection between the fragmenting ecosystems, the greedy traders, the suffering society and the capricious state. One generalisation is that greater the pastoralist moves away from its symbiotic relationship with his sheep and goats along with the pastures, the more he is allured to miseries both on himself and his flock and the entire ecosystem. The typical structure of Tibetan society in the beginning of the twentieth century as described by Bell (1928), is shown in Figure 3.1.

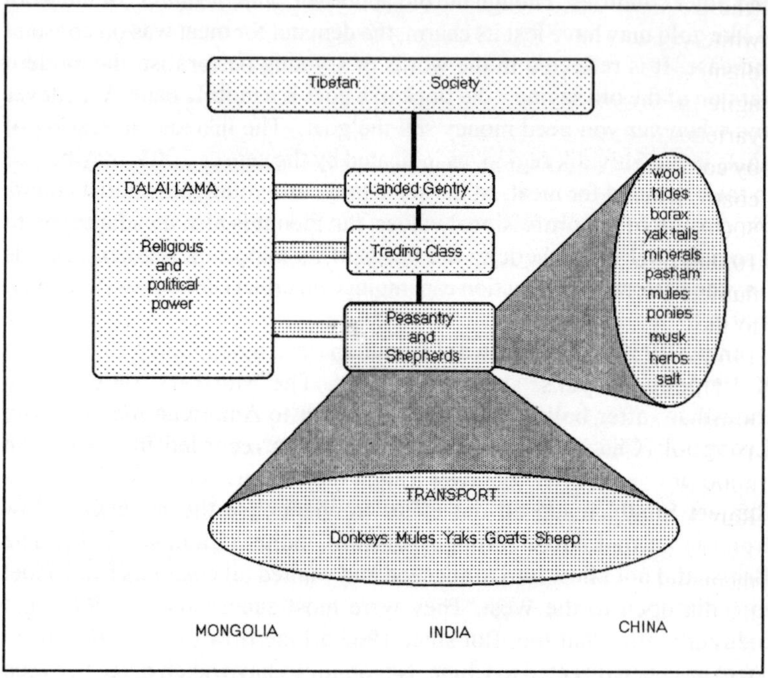

Fig. 3.1: The Typical Structure of the Tibetan Society

A report from the last decade of the twentieth century is illuminating (Joseph, 1991). In Changthang, Ladakh some 40 families of Changpa the nomadic pastoralists reared about 1.40 lakh pashmina goats in 21,000 square kilometers. It should have fetched them about Rs. 5 crore but the revenue that actually came was less than Rs. two lakh. The traders reaped benefit of about 12 times the cost. Most of the Changpa were engaged to barter pashmina for tea, liquor, sugar and food items. They were driven to live a life of extreme poverty by the clever traders. Though earlier Changpas trimmed their flocks of sheep and goats by killing a certain number every year, these traditional checks were being overlooked (Bhattacharji, 1993) due to drastic change in social institutions (Sharma, 1994).

The pashmina wool trade tells how market, society, territory and ecology interact to meet the requirements of the people that are far away from location of the resource. The pashmina goat differs from the ordinary goat in its body built. It shows many physiological adaptations to the cold climate and at 3,500 to 5,500 meter altitude in the western Himalayas, Afghanistan, Tibet and China. The long coarse hair and shorter soft hair (the pasham) cover the whole body. The pasham fibres are mostly in white, brown and blackish shade. The fibres are 10 to 18 milli micron in diameter and 2 to 6 centimeter in length. This medium-sized goat is very agile in running on steep terrain. *Chigu* and *changthangi*, are the two varieties that habitate in India. The pasham is taken with the coarse hairs by combing the body of pashmina goats. In an average goat the weight of coarse hair is twice than the pasham fibres, a male goat may give 300-500 grams of pasham in one year. A pashmina shawl costs above Rs. 10,000 or more. Due to increase in the demand for pashmina shawl the number of goats in Ladakh have increased alarmingly. It is partially due to the migration of pastoralists from Tibet after Indo-China conflict in 1962.

Traditionally the people of Tukpa, Shua and Sialkhar parganas of Kanaor had direct trade with Tibet. The Gazetteer of the Simla Hill States, 1910, mentions that these traders brought wool, pasham, salt, borax, numdahs, carpets, and charas from Tibet and disposed them of at the Rampur *Lavi Fair*.

The pastoralists sold their products to middle men and depended on them for any gain from their hard labour. Except lending money on interest the middleman hardly served any positive role in the lives of pastoralists. It is not a recent phenomenon. A report from the Gazetteer of the Simla Hill States 1910 says that the agriculturists were ruined by such debts. The misery inflicted upon the pastoralists by the moneylenders is depicted even in the folk songs of Kanaor. Although the position has changed, these days in Kanaor, due to increased employment opportunities and the horticulture development, the situation was grim for other pastoral and agro-pastoral communities in Himachal Pradesh and other parts of the country. Khatana (1992) has reported that the bakarwals of Jammu and Kashmir badly suffered due to the grip of moneylenders.

There is scope to establish cooperatives to safeguard the interests of the producers. Such experiments have been done from time to time at the panchayat level and at other regional level. Mostly they are failures for various reasons like other cooperatives of the producers. One success story is the Operation Flood at the national level that took of in the seventies. The Chairman of the National Dairy Development Board claimed that due to Operation Flood project India was self-sufficient in milk and became the world's fastest growing dairy (Padmanabhan, 1992). Though it is difficult to deny the role of financial aid from World Bank and gifts from European Community, the Chairman was confident that the cooperative revolution was not a dream. His argument was that the producer's interests were important to motivate them and improve their living conditions. Increasing the price of their produce for which the government often disagreed can do this. The cooperatives directly helped the villagers by providing inputs to enhance milk production. He advocated the policy of fairly democratic control of cooperatives looked after by the elected representatives of producers without any political interference.

Like the allied sector of forestry, large private industries were making their entry in the fray after assessing the growing needs of milk and milk products. These industries mainly wanted to get more profit from the sail of milk products but the price of milk was kept same. There was though danger that the farmers would become dependent on the private dairy owners. The controversy was going on (Padmanabhan, 1992). The private industry has also entered in the area of rearing livestock. This would harm the interests of they pastoralists by increasing pressure on grazing land. Moreover, they have greater capacity to invest on the livestock. Therefore the liberalisation further aggravates the controversy. A new material relationship is emerging, the traditional dairy system that was primarily complementary to agriculture and embedded in the social structure which has become purely an industry dependent upon the market forces.

An alternative may be to adopt certain agricultural and horticultural practices adaptive to pastoralists' area. In Lahaul where local population keeps only *kim zet* and have sedentary life, people have shown much improvement in their living conditions. A study reported that they grew the cash crops of potatoes, hops and peas. The profitability per bigha was: 600-7,000 for potatoes, 7,000-10,000 for peas and 10,000 to 15,000 for hops. Potatoes have played a significant role in the economy of these people. Particularly they specialised in seed potato and the yield was about 30 tonnes/hectare, more than twice from other parts of India (Srinivas, Kokate & Nand, 1996). The Lahaul Potato Grower's Cooperative Marketing-cum-Processing Society Ltd. has played a crucial role in saving the farmers from exploitation by traders. However it is difficult to say that a similar change will alter the lives of Changpas who live in the adjacent areas of Ladakh. While the Changpas are nomadic pastoralists, people of Lahaul were on the trade route to Lahasa, Samarkand and Bukhara, thus engaged in trade and agropastoral activity. These are, but important distinctions that make Lahaulis better adaptable to agriculture, and also act as astute traders.

The Gaddis keep flocks of sheep and goats, which range over the pastures of Lahaul during summer and go to Shivalik foothills during winter, provide a slightly different picture. They seem to have isolated themselves from the majority of Hindu community by their migratory herds of sheep and goats. Almost half of the Gaddi population keep migratory flocks, however all of them have their sedentary homes in the villages. The total income of a sedentary villager was lower than the one who in addition to agriculture keeps flocks of sheep and goats. About 40 per cent of goats were sold every year (Verma, 1996). This was in response to increase in the prices of meat. The Gaddis have raised the issue of increasing the number of animals in their flocks that was banned in 1972. They have a union to look after their interest and even have elected representatives in the State legislative assembly. Some of the Gaddis are in the Indian Administrative Services. Noble (1983) has observed "*Gaddis may consider shepherding their dharma given to them by Lord Shiva. But it is not just that that makes them follow their ancestors' migratory life. Nor is it a love of it (to me a romantic life). It is the prosperity that the sheep and goats bring—the former largely from wool, the latter from meat.*"

To some extent, this also seems true for the pastoralists of Kanaor, Rohru, Jubbal and Chaupal. However the Gujars are the nomadic pastoralists and there is strong pressure on them to adopt sedentary mode of life despite help from the government. They are spread all over the Western Himalayas. The Bakarwals belong to the same stock as Gujars, but are confined to Jammu and Kashmir and keep sheep and goats. Both Gujars and Bakarwals live with the mainstream population at least in the winter season. It is important to understand why these people have not adopted sedentary life. The Bhotiyas of Uttarakhand were involved in trade with the Tibet till 1962. After the Indo-Chinese conflict the Bhotiyas lost their trade with Tibet. Though they adopted agriculture, sheep and goats were still important part of their life (Hoon, 1996).

There is some provision for support price on wool along with the increase in rates of wool procurement. The mobile weaving units for shawl and carpet are also available. Government also provides compensation on animals killed by epidemic. There is a provision to give compensation on damage to livestock due to natural disasters. Although H.P. Assembly adopted a resolution to recommend tribal status to all Gaddis and Gujars in 1994, there is need to declare other pastoralists also as Scheduled Tribe. The veterinary help is extremely important, but it needs more activity and funding; hundreds of sheep die in Himachal Pradesh due to lack of medical facilities. Medical aid is not available in the pastures. Other important issues are: development of pastures, issuance of permits of winter grazing, and to resolve the issue of increase in number of sheep and goats. There are some social institutions for the welfare of pastoralists, for example, Gujar Kalyan Board and Gaddi Kalyan Board, they are merely engaged in social advocacy, the real efforts need to be taken at the research level—location specific as well as global.

An important decision in favour of pastoralists was due to the efforts of Himachal Pradesh Grazing Advisory Committee—the removal of the restriction on the number of sheep and goats in1996, much to the resentment of some conservationists (see Saberwal, 1999). The constitution of Wool Development Board (H.P.) is also an important achievement. Similarly the Himachal Pradesh State Handicrafts and Handloom Corporation Ltd. is doing good work to promote the handicrafts industry and to accord recognition to the glorious tradition of excellent craftsmen in the pastoral belt. For example, the Kanaori and Kulluvi caps are now familiar all over India. The organization gives State Awards to craftsmen and weavers; helps in freeing artisans and weavers from exploitation of their masters; imparts training to them whereby they can improve their financial welfare; provides assistance in the procurement of raw material; and, undertakes the marketing of crafts items. There are Himachal Emporiums in all District headquarters of the State and in the cities like Bombay, Bangalore and Delhi. The creative consciousness is reflected in artefacts: woollens like shawls, pattus, dohru, mufflers, socks, woolen shoes; the pullans (zomba), gloves, cap, coats, jackets, blankets, carpets, gudmas. The metal ware includes idols of local deities, gods, goddesses; metallic faces; metallic plates; metallic door handles; decorative items and bells for temples. The wood craft can be seen in fruit bowls, toys, decorative carvings, walking sticks, wooden bowls, wooden cutlery, wooden utensils; bamboo baskets, trays, walking sticks. Besides them, the Chamba painting, Kangra painting, Basholi painting, and Gonpa painting have their own place. There are also some other significant items prepared from leather and grass craft: chappal, shoes, grass pullas of Kullu, Paiche footwear from Kanaor; Kapul footwear from Lahaul & Spiti. The embroidery work in the form of Chamba *rumal* has its own place.

These cooperatives of handicrafts, largely based on pastoral produce and their craftsmanship face stiff competition from imitative work and machines. The shawls from the mechanized industries are cheaper and are flooding the market. Same is true for carpets and wooden carvings. The necessary changes in this area include: (a) Provision of small scale mechanization facilities to people: machines for carding, traditionally they do it with hands, carding brushes or carding bow; machines for spinning, traditionally it is done with '*takali*', the various Gandhian institutes have developed different kinds of spinning wheels but they are not easily available; and, mechanized looms, traditionally from yarn the warp is prepared on peg warp and the weaver then weaves. (b) The provision of subsidy on the items needed for handloom production to reduce the prices of their produce and attract people.

A significant step in this direction is the formation of H.P. State Cooperative Wool Procurement and Marketing Federation (Woolfed). It was registered in 1988 but started functioning in 1996-97. The federation was headed by Thakur Singh, a pastoralist and M.L.A. from Bharmour (Box 3.1). The objective is to improve pastoral profession. Himachal, due to its temperate climate and large pasture area, is appropriate for rearing good quality sheep. Breeding of sheep is a traditional profession for the highlanders of Lahaul-Spiti, Kanaor, Pangi, Bharmour, Kangra, Shimla, Mandi and Kullu. The main objectives of the organization are as under:

1. To promote the growth and development of wool industry in Himachal Pradesh.
2. To free wool breeders from exploitation by middlemen/traders.
3. To promote production, shearing, procurement and processing of the wool.
4. To impart training and technical know-how to the breeders.
5. To establish wool procurement and grading centers.
6. To establish wool research and quality control laboratories.
7. To undertake marketing of wool within and outside the state.
8. To initiate welfare measures for sheep breeders.

The Woolfed was actively involved in the procurement and sale of sheep wool, though this was yet at an early stage. Some idea of this activity can be gained from the details of last four years of wool procurement and sale shown in Figure 3.2.

Another major programme taken up by the Woolfed is the implementation of the centrally sponsored scheme of Integrated Wool Improvement Programme for the benefit of the sheep breeders of Chamba, Kangra and Kullu of the state. The major components of this scheme were: health care, breed improvement, product development, marketing assistance, training camps and multi-purpose extension centers. The total

Box 3.1: Views of a Pastoral Leader

There was a spark of excitement in the eyes of Shri Thakur Singh Bharmouri, when I met him in Himachal Pradesh Secretariat to find out his views about pastoralism in the State. He was a proud herder when young. The herd was now with his kin as the transhumance has to survive. Bharmouri confessed that pastoralism was not a profession of choice for younger generation, but it was a hereditary occupation, and has money, too. Moreover, the employment problem was already acute. To some extent Bharmouri is correct, when we see the trend in the countries, which have fallen apart after the demise of the USSR, the unemployed youth there, was looking for pastoralism for livelihood in association with their relatives. For Bharmouri, illiteracy was not the only cause for the shepherds to stick to their profession, it was there since birth, one has not to search for it. Bharmouri underlined that an all out effort should be made to declare pastoralism as an industry. In this endeavour, the government should provide all facilities for its development, because the output of this industry—meat, milk and wool—fulfilled everybody's need. In addition, the pastoral industry provided employment to large number of people, there were at least ten lakh Gaddis alone, stressed Bharmouri, who were directly dependent on the moving herds of sheep and goats.

Bharmouri chided the conservationists for their shallowness. The sheep and goats are efficient pruners of herbs and shrubs and they were part of the ecosystem like the other ungulates. He asked, why were the pastoralists being made scapegoats, when water and air was being polluted by the industries, forests had been denuded for timber extraction, and mining was going on rampantly. If they were enthusiastic about wildlife, the pastoralists also needed alternatives. A better conservation strategy, according to Bharmouri, would be to elicit the cooperation of pastoralists who had experience of living with the animals. The herders, the animals, and the wildlife, all have lived together for centuries.

Although the perseverance of Bharmouri and other Gaddi leaders for the cause of pastoralists is bearing fruits, there is need for a large coalition of pastoral leaders. The efforts of Shri Thakur Sen Negi for the Kanaoras in particular, and pastoralists in general would go a long way, yet there is need for an umbrella organization covering smaller groups.

Shri Bharmouri himself a folksinger of repute, was not sure if something was being done about the folk literature of pastoral population. But he was sure about the man-animal relationship that it was rich and unique, as the pastoralist was associated with it from birth to death. They have rich repository of art and craft as well as other forms of cultural artifacts, which need preservation and enrichment. The cognitive revolution was the hope to revolutionize traditional pastoral systems into a modern industry, and to increase the self-esteem of the pastoralist. A feeling of social identity though is a necessary part of regional politics, it has even significance to enter the global market with products of Gaddi Sheep and Gaddi Goat, like the Merinos of Spain. It is not an unachievable task, but needs thrust in the area of research and development with the involvement of pastoral communities. But the emphasis should be on the quality of products where human hands play major role.

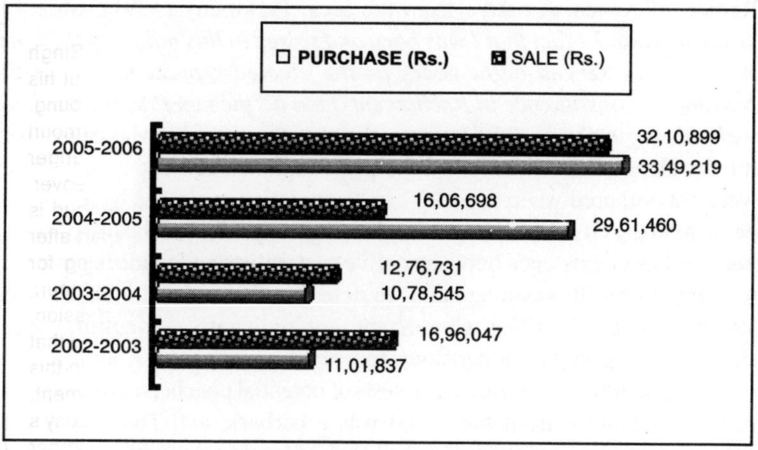

Fig. 3.2: The Purchase and Sale of Wool by Woolfed

outlay of the project, beginning from 2003-04 was about 261.53 lacks for the first two years. The Government of India sanctioned a similar scheme for the sheep breeders of Shimla and Kanaor during 2006-07. Under this new project approximately 3,470 families were likely to receive the benefits.

Although the federation was undertaking the training of herders in various skills, there was need for creating awareness on larger issues like the ecological conservation, global market issues, improvement of quality of products, and the enrichment of their traditional culture and institutions. The dynamic leader of the Woolfed, Vijay Thakur, in an interview raised two important issues: the first was the problem of inbreeding, and the second problem was to attract the younger generation into the pastoral profession. These issues were related with the development of pastoral industry in Himachal Pradesh. It was essential to explore solutions to these problems through multidisciplinary research projects.

Pastures: Harmony and Conflict

The pastoralists are a marginalized profession in Himachal Pradesh. Here, the area for potatoes and apples has grown much faster than that for the sheep and goats. Though the conservation of biological resources is important, the needs of the native people cannot be overlooked. The debate on pastoralism, conservation and development is becoming ever more futile as each party sticks to its argument. It is same in other parts of the world where the pastoral populations thrive, for instance, take the Greater Serengeti

Region of Africa. A native from the area, Parkipuny (1991), observes "*Considering the fact that I was born and raised in this milieu of the land. And, having served eight years as the elected representative of the Norongoro constituency in Parliament, I am all the more deeply involved with this region's issues.*" However the conservationists, who came from the developed countries looked the problem in a fragmentary way. They were not bothered when the wild-beast population increased by about 400 per cent in the Greater Serengiti Region, it greatly affected the life of native people. The coexistence between native pastoralists and wildlife gave way to competition. It was interesting to note that the pastoral areas showed low population densities whereas the predominantly agricultural areas showed high population densities and rapid growth rate. Above all, the local communities were viewed as nests of potential poachers. For the native people, alienation from their land was a barbaric act. The new age in environment management was in the hands of local communities; the sooner we realized it the better it would be (Drijver, 1990).

Colonisation was not always the factor in the denudation of resources, the internal exploitation of the rural areas was even more disastrous. For example, about 50,000 sq km of the area in Aravali Hills inhabited mainly by Bhils had 70 percent forest at the time of Independence of India (Saint, 1991). The forests and pastures were in the control of the local community. After the forests were taken over by the State, a large-scale denudation of green cover set in. In the eighties the whole area turned into brown land with less than 5 percent forest cover. A number of investigators have reiterated that the restoration of the green cover was difficult without the participation of the local communities.

The major issues underlined by investigators were pastoral development policies, organizational structure for development, pastoral land tenure systems, financial institution, food security, improving productivity and designing services (Swift, 1988). He further observed that all the pastoral societies of the dry belt in the past had powerful institutions which regulated economic and social life. But these institutions were weakened, initially by the colonial administration and new institutions of independent states, and later by the incorporation of previously isolated and partly autonomous pastoral economies in wider markets.

The pastoralists use natural resources that include mainly pastures, trees, shrubs and crop residues. They are termed as common property resources and have either 'open access' or socially 'controlled access.' The theory of common property resource management, especially in relation to pastureland, is well publicized in the social science literature, and this has had an unusual influence on practical proposals. The debate started with theories of the "Tragedy of the Commons", and was later developed in game theory as the "Prisoners' Dilemma", both of which emphasize individual decisions within an historical, utility framework (Bennet *et al.*, 1986). Its originator, Hardin (1968) argued that common ownership obliges rural people to pursue strategies that degrade their natural resources. Referring specifically to herders, he claimed that those pastures would inevitably be degraded where animals are privately owned and pasture is open to general use. However, later theorists dispute the inevitable move towards the destruction of the environment by the results of empirical research, which showed the controlled-access, common property regimes were widespread in traditional rural communities (Runge, 1986; Swift, 1988).

The 'tragedy of commons'—private animals using communal pastures, leading inevitably to pasture degradation—has been a powerful force in the minds of government and aid agency officials, and the policy it suggests of privatizing range land ownership has been widely followed. Many pastoralists, especially poorer and less powerful ones, have been dispossessed of traditional access to range land in the process, and made more vulnerable to drought and famine. A more sophisticated analysis and case studies show that members of pastoral groups can negotiate to make rules for the use of resources, and create institutions to enforce them. They are thus able to maintain efficient and sustainable uses of common resources (Lane & Swift, 1989).

One assumption in the minds of managers, coming from developed countries or from the elite class within the country, is that the rural people do not know much about the problems and their solutions. Thus a party may volunteer to help. It suggests that the Maasai of Africa or the Kanaoras of the Himalayas cannot manage their pastures and are likely to over use it. However, there is no such evidence for it. That the pastoralists were ignorant was an outdated myth (Warren & Agnew, 1988). A feeling to help the poor and/or wildlife is shown universally. An alternative hypothesis is that the external intervention has some vested interest. It may be broadening the employment base, to create market for the technology, to achieve some political goal and for some other social motive. Under both conditions it can be argued that the help received by a community also depends upon whether the recipient seeks help. Apparently it is cooperation, but the parties engaging in this cooperative episode have conflicting (different) goals, and the relationship does not continue for long. For the donors it is not the survival of pastoralism but something else (Table 3.1).

Table 3.1: Relationship between Donors and Recipients

GIVER → *RECEIVER ↓*	*NO MOTIVE*	*MOTIVE*
NO HELP SOUGHT	ALTRUISM (MINIMUM AID)	SELFISHNESS (MEDIUM AID)
HELP SOUGHT	BEGGING (MEDIUM AID)	COOPERATION (MAXIMUM AID)

The conflict between the donor and the recipient countries must be resolved by mutual understanding of socio-political and socio-economic phenomena. A learning process approach, in contrast to the blue print approach, is probably more useful in the developmental process. For example, the western experts or the natives trained abroad, have blue prints for irrigation, mechanized farming and ranching. In India the first two models are considered to alleviate the poverty of the country. Ranching has still to take its roots (Table 3.2). And the pastoralism has been relegated to evenmore inferior profession. In his extensive report on the environmental and developmental issues related to pastoralists in the tropical drylands of Africa and Asia, Adams (1988) has asked if traditional pastoralism could be improved by American-style ranching systems. His study indicated that the numerous ranching projects introduced to traditional pastoral areas of semi-arid Africa with the assistance of the World Bank and other donors have failed to take roots.

Table 3.2: Differences between the Two Livestock Systems (Adams, 1988)

Item	*Ranches*	*Traditional System*
Labour	Labour-extensive	Labour-intensive
Animals	Beef cattle	Milk cattle, sheep and goats
Land	Privately owned	Privately owned and shared among kin
Grazing system	Privately owned subdivided and fenced animals rotated round paddocks	Communally owned unenclosed range closely herded on the open range
Foreign exchange	High cost	Negligible cost

The anxiety over desertification due to the grazing herds of sheep and goats needs a correct diagnosis (Warren & Agnew, 1988). The pasture degradation and the creation of more desert-like conditions are different processes. At times the desertification is used to serve the ulterior motives of the institutions and the governments to siphon the funds. Here the desertification is used as the 'institutional fact'. For example, desertification in the Himalayas and its relationship with the soil-erosion. And then traditional livelihood activities like pastoralism are linked with the soil-erosion and policies framed to curtail the livestock population. On the other hand, the relationship between desertification and the climatic changes and the geology of the Himalayas is overlooked.

The case of pastoral development in Mangolia is interesting and it has importance for pastoralism in the Himalayas. In Mongolia the main developmental priority has been the extensive pastoral livestock husbandry (FAO, 1990). Two lessons are important for us. One is the Mongolian model of traditional cooperative livestock production and the more recent pastoral collectives, the *negdel*. The other is the integration of modern science and technology with local knowledge and techniques. These include in the area of development of Mongolian breeds, diversity of milk processing techniques and fodder production by new methods. In Mongolia more than forty percent national population tended around 25 million livestock that comprised mainly five kinds of animals (horses, camels, cattle—including yak, sheep and goats) in semidesert, steppes and high altitudes. Of this total population about 60 per cent were sheep and 20 per cent goats (Tumurjav, 1990). Besides excellent biological characteristics of Mongolian breeds to local environment they possessed some unique behavioural characteristics: intelligence, obedience and high mothering instinct. They located places to save from cold and wind, avoided dirty water, sought fresh pasture, showed strong herd instinct, and they grazed amicably.

Before collectivisation in Mangolia, a political-administrative division was known as *khoshun* (Mearns, 1993). Each *khoshun* had a *noyon* or hereditary overlord through whom the Manchu dynasty ruled. Land allocation within the *khoshun* was at the discretion of *noyon*. Some areas were set aside for grazing by the *noyon's* own herds, which others were forbidden to enter. The highest-ranking lamas (*khutukht*) enjoyed equal rights with *khoshun* noyon and also 'owned' the land within the jurisdiction of their temple territories. Like other pastoral societies, there were customary land tenure arrangements at the local level to regulate herder's access to pasture land. These institutional arrangements were secured through neighbourhood-level groups known as *neg nutgiinhan* ('people of one place'). Group members were often relatives. Like the *khot ail* (the basic herding camp of several cooperating households), neighbourhood-level customary institutions had apparently shown re-emergence in contemporary Mongolia in response to the break-up of the pastoral collectives and other economic reforms. Table 3.3 shows the main pastoral institutions during three periods.

Table 3.3: Historical Evolution of Mongolian Pastoral Institutions (Mearns, 1993)

Scale Level	*Order of Magnitude (Households)*	*Pre-collectivisation (-1930s)*	*Collectivisation (1930s-1980)*	*Decollectivisation and Transition (1990s)*
Encampment	1	herding family	herding family	herding family
	1-2	sakhaltiin ail	suur	sakhaltiin ail
	2	jarsiin ail	sakhaltiin ail	—
	2-12	khot ail	—	khot ail
Neighbourhood	20-50	neg nutgiinhan	team (kheseg)	neg nutgiinhan
	50-100	bag	brigade	cooperative (horshoo)
	100-250	—	—	bag
Administrative unit	500-1000	—	—	company
	1000-1500	khoshun	collective (negdel)	district (sum)
	10000	aimag	& district (sum)	province (aimag)
			province (aimag)	

Another important pastoral group, now of historical significance, was Afghan *powinda*. Over a long period Afghan *powinda* (from *powal*: to graze), from their summer pastures located in South-East Afghanistan (the Khorasan) migrated hundreds of kilometers to low winter grazing areas of India along the left bank of Indus river. The increase in grazing tax (tirni), disarmament and restriction on free movement curtailed the Afghan nomadism in India by the British rulers. A major blow came after the political division of India in 1947 and finally in 1961 by the closure of Pakistan-Afghan border (Balland, 1991). Hundreds of families belonging to different tribes with thousands of camels, sheep, goats, buffaloes, horses, donkeys and mules arrived every year on their winter grazing pastures. With the construction of railway network in India the Afghan nomads, known as *Kabuliwala*, began to visit almost all parts of India and monopolised the trade between India and Central Asia. Although their main activity in India was trade and money lending, a large number of them also engaged in manual labour work.

One can imagine the effects of the restriction of Afghan nomadism in India, and later in Pakistan. Such a huge population of animals was restricted to a small area, and a large number of people who had taken up trade and other activities in addition to pastoralism were thrown away with no work.

The partition of India in 1947 also affected the pastoral migration of sheep and goats from Western Rajasthan to Sind in Pakistan. That in turn increased pressure on the desert region of Barmer, Bikaner, Churu, Jaisalmer, Jalore, Jodhpur, Nagour, Pali, Sirohi, and Ajmer (Kavoori, 1991). Second, the decline in area, degradation and removal of social, control of the common property resources in Rajasthan restricted the activities of pastoralists. Third, the market forces for meat and wool, motivated the pastoralists to intensify pastoralism. These factors were catalysts for evolving new strategies: responded to internal competition on grazing by looking out for more pastures in adjacent states, regulated the herd size in a dynamic fashion, and, abandoned returning to their villages of origin.

The rise in number of sheep and goats and increasing trend of transhumance in Rajasthan had its impact on the adjacent states. One consequence was the development of mutually beneficial relationship. The sheep and goats of Rajasthan came to the fields in Haryana to eat the crop stubble and in turn they fertilized the fields. The deleterious consequence of this migration was the rise in inter-state disputes over grazing. For example, the dispute between Madhya Pradesh and Rajasthan has even gone to the Supreme Court of India. These sheep owners have their organization, the Rajasthan Pradesh Ghumakad Bhed Pashupalak Samiti, to voice their interests. On the other hand, the forest officials and the villagers in the Bilaspur and Raipur districts of Madhya Pradesh have been complaining that the sheep owners from Rajasthan often deviated from their prescribed routes and caused damage to forest and agriculture fields. About 20 lakh to 25 lakh sheep entered from Rajasthan's Jaisalmer, Barmer, Sirohi, Jalore and Pali districts. It was also claimed that besides the traditional pastoralists, the majority of sheep coming to Madhaya Pradesh belonged to the wool manufacturing 'companies' of Rajasthan (Mishra, 1996).

In Rajasthan some social workers were advocating for the revival of the 'Oran tradition'. This tradition protected the forests, water, livestock, pastures, grains, milk and environment (Thanavi, 1992). It was alive due to the fear of deities. These forests belonged to yogis and jhunjharon. Approximately 8,46,000 hectare of land was reserved for 'oran' and common grazing land over the eleven districts of Rajasthan. 'Oran' had a deity that protected it and kept the trees alive.

After the independence, to some extent, the re-alignment of political boundaries has also resulted in inter-state conflicts over grazing. The control of small rulers gives way to larger territorial markings and people took time to realign to new States (the new Rajasthan, the new Punjab, etc.). The elderly persons who were carrying the maps in their cognition passed away. The local issues related to livelihood of common folk slowly became unimportant and the Central issues brought the new agenda (environment, wildlife, afforestration). When the new generation internalized own and other State boundaries the next-door village became an outsider. This is explained by an episode of the dispute over a pasture between the villagers of Dodra-Kewar in Himachal Pradesh. Where a Survey of India team pointed out to the author that due to realignment of political boundaries, in the same valley some villages were in Himachal Pradesh and the others came under Uttaranchal. These villagers lived on one stretch of land, they had same culture, worshipped same deities and had kinship relations among themselves. However, now an invisible political boundary separated them. They had now frequent disputes over grazing, reported the survey team.

In 1986, the author witnessed the *arung zet sa* (people engaged in herding mobile sheep and goats) from Kanaor harassed by local villagers in Chamba, Tehri Garhwal. The local people had formed '*uran dasta*' (flying squads) to warn the pastoralists sneaking in the forests around their villages. The pastoralists from Dodra-Kewar, Kanaor, Rohru, Chaupal and Jubbal areas had been taking their sheep and goats for grazing in winter to the districts of Uttarkashi, Tehri Garhwal and Dehra Dun in Uttaranchal (earlier Uttar Pradesh). The Uttar Pradesh government took unilateral decision to abolish the grazing rights of shepherds of Himachal Pradesh (Anonymous, 1986). In retaliation the Himachal Pradesh government also refused the grazing rights of the people of Uttar Pradesh during summer in the Ranikanda area of Himachal Pradesh. As a result of this dispute the pastoralists in Himachal Pradesh have been forced to confine their sheep and goats during winter in the Shivalik foothills of the own State.

Finally, we conclude this section by evaluating the scenario of pastoralism in Tibet that had directly affected the *arung zet* system of Kanaor in the western Himalayas. The Tibetan plateau spread over 1.65 million square kilometers has by far the most expansive areas of grassland in the world (Richard, 2005). This rangeland was home to five million people and supported a livestock population of some ten million yaks and thirty million sheep and goats. These rangelands and livestock, between 1950-1980, were ambiguously collectivised into management units of 'people's communes,' 'production brigades' and 'production teams' (Yan, Wu, Yeshi & Ru, 2005). Chinese academicians assumed that the traditional system of communal tenure ship of rangeland has degraded it, therefore new policies were aimed at large-scale resettlement of nomadic pastoralists and governed their livelihood by the Grassland Law of the People's Republic of China (PRC) passed in 1985 and revived in 2003. Mainly the land is divided among the households and the access to higher reaches of river catchments has been curtailed. Realising the difficulties in achieving the desired goal—'to provide nomads with better lives'—the Chinese academicians were now thinking that these designs were handicapped by lack of local institutions (Yan, Wu, Yeshi & Ru, 2005).

Most of the grasslands, semi-arid and high plateau pastoral lands, earlier part of western Tibet, were thus under rapid change and were likely to affect pastoralists of India of the Himalayan regions. Therefore it is important to look into the results of some interventions. Renolds (2006) has reported the findings of a project from Altai in Xinjiang, N.W. China on the ancient transhumant system where for centuries Kazakh herders have moved with their livestock. Except for the altitudinal variations, the cycle of these Kazakh herders appeared similar to the Kanaoras of Himachal Pradesh. Kazakh herders reared cattle, sheep, goats, horses and camels. For summer grazing they took their livestock on lands at higher altitudes for about three months (late June to late September), migrated down (mid-September to end November), in winter pasture (December to end March), and the return journey was in spring to summer pasture (April to late June).

The success of the interventions, financed by the schemes under the United Nation's programmes, according to Renolds was visible "*in transforming former (Gobi) desert areas into herder/farmers.*" The families provided external input to irrigate land, grow alfalfa and other social facilities, had much higher incomes than the traditional families. If such interventions created sustainable changes in pastoral life and were able to alleviate their poverty, the innovations were to spread to farther regions, including India.

Survival of Migratory Trails

There are number of questions that arise when we have some domestic animals that need grazing habitat for them. The sheep, goats, cows and buffaloes browse upon herbs, shrubs and tree litter. The browse components are more in the open habitats than the closed forests. In India we have patches of open and closed habitat and both are used by the livestock. The idea of anthropogenic conversion of wooded habitat need cautious look (Rodgers, 1991). Furthermore, there is need to understand that different kinds of domestic animals can live in the same habitat. However, we have a large variety of distinct habitats and domestic animals to adapt to these habitats. For example, in Himachal Pradesh the yak can withstand –40°C temperatures in Lahaul and Spiti and a buffalo is comfortable at +40° C temperature near the Punjab plains. With the closure of high altitude pastures and increase in urban activities in the Shivalik hills, the grazing areas of Himachal Pradesh are under intense pressure. The middle belt is also witnessing drastic changes in the agricultural practices. Even the pastoralists are deriving more benefits from the cash crops in Kanaor. Therefore, it is to be seen what course transhumance take in this region in the near future. The four scenarios of pastoralism in Himachal Pradesh are depicted in Figure 3.3. They include: 1. Nomadic pastoralists, the Gujars; 2. Transhumant Gaddis and Kanaoras; 3. Agro-pastoralists with mobile herds; and, 4. Agro-pastoralists with sedentary animals (see Chapter 6).

Besides these habitat related factors it is important to study the behaviour of animals within the habitat. The domestic animals can be sustained in relatively high densities in a particular habitat if the herders use efficient techniques of regulating the grazing of their livestock. In

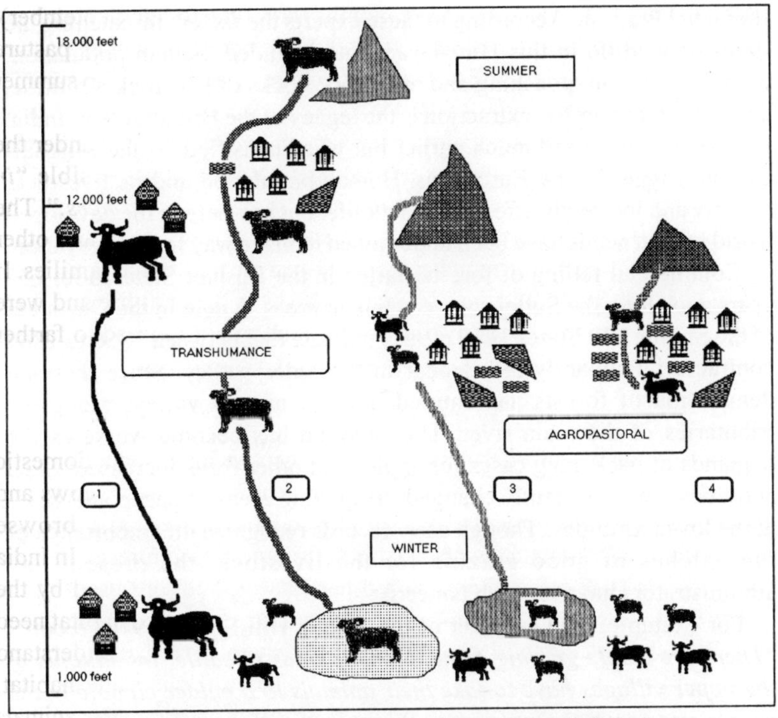

Fig. 3.3: Four Scenarios of Pastoralism in Himachal Pradesh

high altitude pastures the herder does not remain all the time with the flock but at the low altitude pasture the herder is all the time with its herd to monitor the grazing of sheep and goats. Many kinds of herbs and shrubs are present in the forest. Although the animals do show preferences, a good herder always guides the herd through nutritious vegetation.

A naturalist Hingston (1988) who explored the Himalayan valley of Hazara (now in Pakistan), in 1914 and 1916, observed that it was not in the thickest jungles but in the barren valleys of the western Himalayas that there existed the largest number of animals. However, some environmentalists start with a hypothesis that the mammals show homogeneous distribution in space. If they do not find it, the culprit is the native and his livestock. Some wildlife experts have carried surveys on birds and mammals in Himachal Pradesh (Gaston, Hunter & Garson, 1981; Singh, Kothari & Pandey, 1990). They have also provided expertise to the State Government on the conservation of wildlife, particularly on the establishment of Great Himalayan National Park in Kullu District in

Himachal Pradesh. According to these experts the factors threatening the status of wildlife in this Himalayan state included, human population, timber extraction, poaching and migratory flocks of livestock. Of these, they forget, the timber extraction is the legacy of the British rule in India. And poaching started much earlier but was intensified by the Mughals and the trigger happy Europeans. Human population and its livestock, directly and indirectly affected the wildlife, but nowhere in the developed world human needs have been undermined to make way for conservation.

Commercial felling of forests started in the Bushair State about 150 years ago along the Sutlej river catchment areas. A note in the Gazetteer of the Shimla Hill States 1910 clearly indicate that between 1850 to 1864 contractors rampantly fell deodar in the Sutlej valley. Since then the denudation of forests has entered into the narrow valleys along the tributaries of the main river. The situation has become worse as the demands of packaging cases for apples and other fruits increased. Such activities have constantly changed the grazing areas of sheep and goats at the lower altitudes. Though early records recognize the importance of the patches of good grazing for the livestock, the present day administrators have no such concern.

For example, the Gazetteer of the Shimla Hill States (1910) records "*There are ample grazing ground for all kinds of cattle. Inhabitants of the upper villages have to take their animals to a milder climate in the winter and come as far down as Bilaspur and Nahan. Two hills named Chiti Jangram and balthar in pargana Bhaba, Tehsil Chini, are said to have famous grass for cattle.*" (Page 53)

In recent years, the hydroelectric projects have considerably changed the ecosystem of the river valleys. These large-scale interventions have irreversibly destroyed the pastures of sheep, goats and other cattle. The excessive human activity along the migratory routes has made them extremely hazardous. Some negative attitudes against sheep and goats are so deep rooted that it is difficult to change them. For example, consider the observation of Mamgain (1971) that the rearing of goats was dangerous to the soil conservation and consequently to the whole catchment areas of the Bhakra Dam. Though it was the ushering of hydroelectric projects in the Sutlej basin that is reducing the life of Bhakra Dam due to silt, caused by the tunneling operations and road construction. The fear in the minds of wildlife experts and other conservationists is that the main culprit of wildlife were the migratory flocks of sheep, goats and buffaloes. These experts follow the reductionist approach, where few variables are considered significant and other need control or elimination to see results.

If preservation of wildlife is the goal, the extermination of the sheep and goats along with the shepherd is not a wise alternative. It should be possible to evolve ways where human beings co-exist. The grazing cycles of sheep and goats are developed in such a way that herds do not stay in one area for long (Figure 3.4; for more description see Chapter 6).

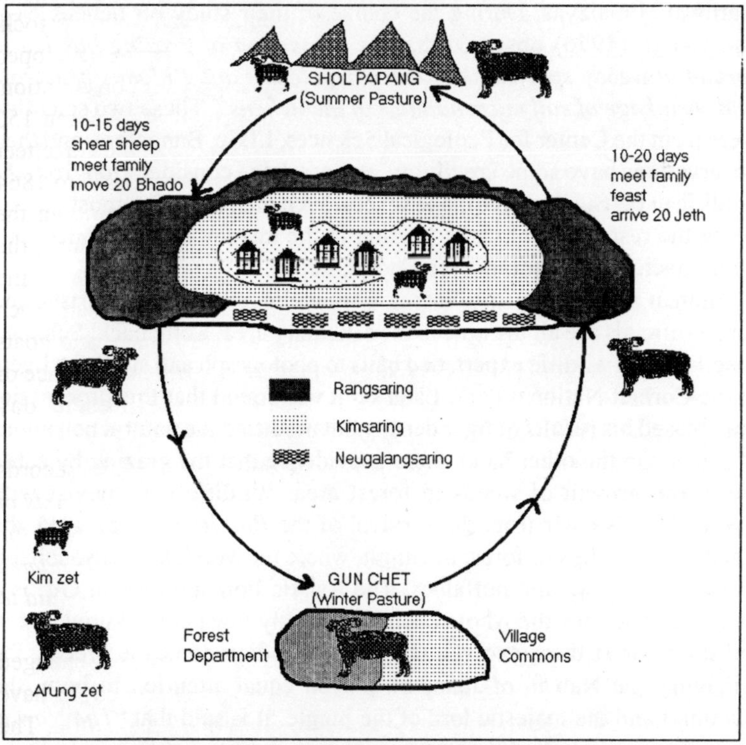

Fig. 3.4: The Grazing Cycle of Sheep and Goats of the Transhumants of Kanaor

It is difficult to understand why should grazing by livestock be harmful to wildlife? Some of the reasons given are grazing competition, disease, plant growth retardation, and human activity. However, one can argue the other way round. The grazing competition may increase if you leave the population of wild animals on its own in a certain area with limited food supply and without predators. Disease may spread in the wild populations from sources other than sheep and goats. Even the plant communities may invade each other. For example, it is common observation that in comparison to the oak forest, fewer species grow under the pine forest. In addition pine trees make the soil acidic and thus prone to erosion. The people's protests against the pine plantation in Himalayas are well documented. More recently, we find that in adjacent Uttaranchal state, the pastoralist Bhotias were prohibited to take their sheep and goats for summer grazing in the Nanda Devi Biosphere Reserve (NDBR) in Garhwal Himalayas. During the course of their study on lichens Negi and Gadgil (1996) observed that the "*cessation of grazing has led to spread of weedy species like Rumex nepalensis and Phlomis bracteata and shrinkage of soil microhabitats of the lichens*." These two scientists were from the Center for Ecological Sciences, I.I.Sc. Bangalore, and their observations have some credibility, and need due consideration from the wildlife experts, who have made several such mistakes. The most glaring being the restriction of cattle grazing in the marshy land of Kaleo Dev Bird Sanctuary, Bharatpur (see Gadgil, 2001).

Human activity may also increase when the researchers, tourists, and forest officials are all the time in the sanctuary area. Long back, Schaller, a well-known wildlife expert, tied baits to photograph and study the tigers in the Corbett National Park. Later on it was found that this process not only biased his results of tiger density but modified the natural behaviour of tigers. On the other hand, there is evidence that the grazing by cattle check the growth of weeds in forest area. Wildlife can coexist with livestock, it is clear from the survival of the *Panthera leo persica*, the Asiatic lion in the Gir forest of Gujrat, where the Maldharies also inhabit it with their cows and buffaloes. The Asiatic lion survived in Gir, is a matter of pride for the whole country, but only few people know that in the same forest there evolved the pride of Indian domestic breeds, the Gir bull. The Nawab of Junagarh played equal attention to both, the Maldhari and the majestic lord of the jungle. It is said that "*The Nawab of Junagarh preserved the last surviving population of lion in India by telling visiting British dignitaries, who wanted their trophies, that there were none left in the royal hunting preserve of Gir*." (Gadgil, 1998) The Gir is famous for its indigenous breeds of cattle largely due to the native pastoralists, the Maldharies, whose *nese* (huts) dot the entire forest. They have survived through a mutually harmonious relationship. However, the wildlife experts (Chavan, 1989) have resolved to oust the Maldharis, to save the lion.

It is extremely important to understand the relationship between grassland production and the needs of livestock. Since lack of such evidence leads to the generalist's accounts damning the pastoralist as a major cause of ecological degradation, but rarely is there an attempt at examining the issue involved (Rodgers, 1991). Therefore to narrow down pastoralism to overgrazing and condemn it, only demonstrates our lack of interest to understand the problem, and find viable solutions to meet society's basic needs. A contemporary manager pens the nomadic herder and the wildlife separately. On surface he wants to improve the lot of both but at deeper levels it helps neither the herder nor wildlife. Moreover, the only solution for the upliftment of pastoral populations so far tried by the various governments all over the world is to sedentarise them. In other words the administrators encapsulate pastoralists by modern social structures (Balland, 1991).

The elite class in India considers domestic animals as burden on the forests and pastures and therefore it recommends a reduction in its number. However, the deterioration and shrinkage of pasture is intimately related to the development 'model' that is being followed (Negi, 1996). The real threats were, timber trade, mining, big dams and industrialisation. There is no concerted effort to develop a national policy for the holistic development of animal husbandry. Rather an idea is being implanted in the minds of villagers that their livestock was inferior and needs replacement by exotic breeds. They perceive this was being done to modify the sacred feelings of people toward animals so that there is no obstruction in the continuous supply of beef.

A myth is widespread that sheep and goats are desert creators. The natural geological processes coupled with the climatic factors and the behaviour of rivers over a period has not only changed the direction of rivers but also caused the death of rivers (Upadhayay, 1994; Valdiya, 1997). It is inaccurate to suggest a cause and effect relationship between grazing and consequent habitat loss by seeing herds of sheep and goats in a habitat already denuded of vegetation, due to other factors. There are instances where wild animal curtailed their population growth through social control mechanisms and the habitat loss was averted. The well-known ecologists, Wynne-Edwards (1991) has concluded on the basis of his research that the animals need food and must consume it prudently.

In the case of domestic animals, the herders who keep watch over the condition of the pasture and increase or decrease the number of sheep and goats exert the social control. In traditional societies "*environmental risks are adjusted by various social groups through a combination of strategies that vary over space, season, sector, and social group. Patterns of diversification are evolved over a long period of time, through trial and error, and not necessarily only with immediate economic ends in view.*" (Gupta, 1991)

The preceding notes may appear eccentric observations considering the national and state level policies of animal husbandry in India. However, the scientists must take responsibility for the miseries inflicted upon the millions of people who are dependent upon their livestock and are affected by technological interventions. Australia has about seven thousand sheep per thousand individual whereas India has only about fifty. It is hardly sufficient for clothing India's large ill-clad population. In India the trend showed that the number of livestock per thousand individual was decreasing over the years (Singh, 1991).

The fact is that, most of the livestock has been kept alive in India by those pastoralists who are traditionally trained in this way of life, and receive little or no support from the Government. They, however, meet the basic needs of the society. For these pastoralists bodily comfort is not the motto, as they do not believe in "*charani bhedan, topne manje*" or the one who takes sheep to graze should not look for a cot. It is true, however, that the fodder is becoming scarce for animals during the migratory period and in the winter pasture. Because for about eight months the migratory herds of sheep, goats and buffaloes compete with the domestic cattle of the agro-pastoralists in the Shivalik hills from Jammu to Nepal in the Terai area. The scarcity of fodder and the developmental activities in this region has broken down the age old mutual relationship of transhumant and agricultural groups. Roughly each agro-pastoral village in the hills got only 65 per cent fodder for its domestic animals from all its resources (Singh, 1991). The situation worsens when the migratory herds visit the lower hills in winter, and share the village commons and forest areas of the local population.

The scientists advocate stall-feeding and improvement in genetic stock. Both these strategies were being followed in India from the early decades of this century. Ever since the experts are divided over this issue. The improvement of the nutritive quality of the pastures is a low priority area. Whether it is an indigenous breed or an exotic breed, both need fodder. The exotic breed in fact consumes large amount of fodder. Though it is true that the exotic breed is more productive than the indigenous, the former requires the technical expertise in terms of artificial insemination, veterinary aid, extra feed in terms of grains, and proximity to urban center to sell the products. The rural agro-pastoral people living in distant parts of the country can not meet these requirements. For the migratory pastoralists it is even more difficult to meet the basic requirements of the exotic breeds.

'Herbal' is a *le dernier cri* (a fad) today. From the traditional healers of villages, the herbal has gone in the hands of muticrore industry, the advanced beauty parlors. In the medical world the new name for the herbal drug is phytomedicine that procures information from ethnotherapeutics practiced in remote cultures (Dev, 1997). A decade ago, the sale of phytomedicine in the countries of European Union was around US $ 600 crore, now the global trade in these medicines may go around $ 2,000 crore. In India alone the herbal product market is to the tune of Rs. 2,500 crore. An important question is what is the source of these herbal drugs? It is extracted by exploiting the natural resources of the marginal people. While for these marginal populations it is essential for their bare survival, the herbal industry primarily caters to the cosmetic desires of the urban people.

In summer the forests and alpine pastures in the Himalayas dot with local villagers and hired labour of contractors to dig up the roots of herbs and shrubs, to collect leaves, flowers and fruits and in some cases the woody portions of trees. There are no surveys to guide how much herb is to be harvested per year, people compete to procure as much raw material as is possible. The deep scars left behind in the soil of the pastures, retardation of vegetative growth due to plucking of all its leaves, and low dispersal due to few seeds left behind constitute the cost born by the pastoralists on which the herbal industry flourishes. In addition extraction of the *guggal dhoop*, mainly used as incense, is causing unimaginable harm to the alpine pastures of the pastoralists. The market forces and ensuing competition has broken down the social control by the local population over the extraction of *guggal dhoop* and other herbs.

In the Shivalik foot hills the khair (*Accacia* species) trees are vanishing to meet the requirements of *pan* (betel leaf) chewing habit of people. A paste, *katha*, is prepared from the wood of khair trees which is an ingredient of herbal medicines, but it is mainly used in *pan.* The *pan* chewing habit is common all over India. The khair provides good forage to goat when the tree is growing. The roots of khair trees goes deep in soil and maintain the moisture level. The pressure on khair trees is so much that the immature trees are also chopped off to prepare the *katha.*

These activities not only accelerate the soil erosion process but also create shortage of fodder. The apprehension of pastoralists is that the urban people were now consuming the nutritious and medicinal natural herbs and shrubs that kept sheep and goats in good health. The shrub of *kashmal* (*Barbaris* species) has been dug all over the State of Himachal Pradesh to meet the demands of drug industry in India and abroad. Besides a preferred browse of sheep and goats, it provided vegetational cover to soil. The birds eat its berries and nest in this shrub. Some exotic ornamental plants have become weeds and are spreading in the grazing lands. One conspicuous example is lantana or *phool lakadi or kesu*. This shrub has covered the forest and open habitat in the Shivaliks. It is difficult for the herders to move with their grazing herds of sheep and goats in the forest infested with lantana. The sheep loose their wool while moving between the lantana shrubs.

During a foot march by Chipko activists in the mid-Himalayan mountains of Himachal Pradesh the impact of commercial felling of trees and agriculture and horticulture expansion was apparent. In their report they noted "*Near Umaradwar, a family of gujjars, migratory buffalo herders who regularly graze their animals up in the mountain, told the Chipko activists that the potato fields had spread right to their front door*." (Levy, 1988) Since then, the apples and potatoes have eaten up more area. The other indirect processes related to this agrarian change are even more dangerous. The apple industry needs more people as labourers, transporters and middlemen. The demand of packaging boxes is so high that besides thinning the local forests, the eucalyptus grown in Punjab and Haryana has also been consumed. In the orchards near the forest, the farmers collect the humus and lop trees of deodar to meet the demands of manure. In the fifties and sixties, potatoes brought improvement in the life of hill people. After seventies it is apples that made the highlanders prosperous. Therefore some people in the hills feel that their miseries are over. All these agrarian activities, besides causing ecological imbalance, due to increase in monoculture plantation, has also led to the shrinkage in grazing area. The government policy to promote the potato and apple cultivation even by distributing *nautor* (breaking forested land) and overlooking the illegal encroachments on forest and common land has reinforced a particular agrarian change, at a heavy cost to the pastoralism. The migratory routes of sheep and goats between summer and winter pastures are severely encroached and forces pastoralists to take motor roads. Consequently the sheep and goats become prone to road accidents.

The ever-increasing number of stray cattle in the townships is the indication of new agrarian change in the hills. The peasants are no more ready to support their cattle, except two to three cows or buffaloes for milk. The change is not only in the external behaviour, but a selfish materialism replacing the mutually beneficial man-animal social ethics. The stray cattle, in order to adapt to the hostile behaviour of human beings, are becoming nocturnal and more agile. They raid the crops during evening and early morning and take flight as soon as a person approaches them. This radical change in their behaviour is creating trouble for the farmers themselves.

Lastly, the forester's plantation policy favours the trees that are fast growing and have timber value, like eucalyptus, poplar and chir pine. Irrespective of the resentment expressed by the villagers, the state policy is geared for the plantation of mono-culture of species. These tree species do not provide fodder for the livestock, rather they increase the problems of pastoralists in various ways.

Conclusion

Though people love to reap the harvest of sheep and goats, they are wary about these animals. Therefore, when we evaluate here few studies on the migratory herds of sheep and goats in the western Himalayas, our focus is on the welfare arung zet sa and his herds, rather than the academic quality of the work. Wildlife enthusiasts, Bagla and Menon (1990) find ancient charm in mythical Kinner country, and suggest its modernisation through the immense potential for microhydel schemes. On the one hand they were worried about the loss of the folklore and culture, but on the other hand considered the sheep and goats as threat to fauna and flora of Kanaor. Same attitude echoes in a study on Changpas of Ladakh. Bhattacharji (1993) reported that the changes in the lifestyle of Changpas had put pressure on the environment. For example, the change from polyandry to monogamy was considered problematic as it increased the growth of population. Earlier the Changpas trimmed their flocks of sheep and goats by killing a certain number every year, but these traditional checks needed strong social institutions. It is difficult to understand the language of these investigators, who were not ready to accept modernization of the traditional life of pastoralists.

There is every indication that these experts, through these popular write-ups create a negative image about the transhumance way of life and their animals. The area between Ladakh and Kanaor, Lahaul has already become seedbed for potatoes, in which scientists like Srinivas, Kokate and Nand (1996) take pride. The external constraints on the lives of shepherds vary. According to Noble (1983), "*If the Gaddis lived solely from the cultivation of those tiny strips of terracing there would not be so many newly built houses on the opposite hill, shops filled with shoes, cloth, Dalda and suchlike, nor women laden with jewellery, nor substantial land owned by them in Kangra.*" Whether the change in pastoral lifestyle is making them happier, or not, remains a fundamental question.

Where external constraints are severe, the end of migratory pastoral life seems imminent. Laffitte (1998) recounted "*The drokpas (nomads) have classically been at the heart of Tibetan civilization and the heart of*

Tibetan identity." But in the Chinese regime, these nomads are under severe stress, and the young and the old stand divided. For the old it is an end of the way of life, not only the obliteration of the wealth of accumulated knowledge of transhumance, but also the end of Guru Rinpoche's teachings that gave them noble place all over the world (Miller, 2008). For the young, it is the attraction towards easy life, though lowly it may be, yet full of western glamour. However, some of them living in exile in India feel proud in their reminiscences. The traditional *drokpa* feels helpless in face of the political change that appears far more formidable than the life freezing storms characteristic of the Tibetan plateau, which they are able to cope up in the company of their animals.

For the Chinese scientists, writes Lafitte (1998), *drokpas* are "*fundamentally stupid, irrational, superstitious, unable to comprehend the consequences of grazing behaviour of their herds*," and not only that, these scientists suggested a new management policy—"*Depopulate the Drokpa areas, both of people and animals.*" It is not limited to Chinese scientists and their government, perhaps international agencies and the World Bank may support projects to change the landscape of Tibet. We also find these changes in the life of Dolpa-pa, the transhumants of highest lands of Nepal, who visited Tibet for salt. The world may have seen it through Eric Valli's celluloid, the last of the salt caravans. The challenge is to avoid such catastrophe for *arung zet sa*.

4

Resilience of Social Bonds

A question raised in the middle of the twentieth century by a brilliant student of animal behaviour Konrad Lorenz in his popular book *King Solomon's Ring*, is becoming evermore imminent as we enter in the twenty-first century. He asked, "*Which is going to be easier for us in future, the production of the weapons or the engendering of the feeling of responsibility that should go along with them, the inhibitions without which our race must perish by virtue of its own creations?*" (Lorenz, 1952/1976; Page 198) The suggestion embedded in it has sound basis in animal behaviour. The 'inhibitions' mentioned by Lorenz, have learned as well as innate aspects, and its exploration needs arduous field works. Otherwise there are chances of error, as one often find in important literary work, which has enormous influence on the minds of people. Rudyard Kipling, for example, has depicted Bagheera (leopard) speaking like human beings (Kipling, 1895/1986).

Yet, Lorenz wants us to learn morals from animals. The error can be reduced if the creativeness of a writer or a scientist knows the limitations of the facts depicted in their work. Since Lorenz's time, the work in animal behaviour has taken fascinating turns, and accordingly the morals derived from this long journey have multiplied and changed in complexity. Dawkins' (2006) recent book, *The God Delusion*, provide glimpses of the generalisations being made from animal behaviour to human behaviour.

My objective in this chapter is twofold, to introduce the reader to some morals, learned through anecdotal and scientific observations on animals, and secondly, to present a few areas of research that a student would like to undertake on sheep, goats or on the *arung zet sa*. The following section introduces a conceptual background about the use of comparative approach in behaviour, essential for making generalisations from animal behaviour to human behaviour.

The method adopted is naturalistic observation. This is the basic scientific method where an investigator, the observer, uses his senses to record the natural phenomena, in our case, for example, the behaviour of sheep and goats. Ethologists, the students of animal and human behaviour take observations under natural and semi natural conditions. They have immensely improved the theory and measurement behind naturalistic observations. The comparative psychology and evolutionary psychology are also engaged in the study of animal behaviour. Accuracy in the observation of behaviour has its own significance, since the information generated is important in day-to-day life. The first requirement is, as Lorenz has pointed out that a good observer must know his animals.

The criterion of a good herder or the *arung zet palas* is—he must be able to identify his *arung zet* (mobile sheep and goats) individually (see Negi in Chapter 6). This is only possible if he is a keen observer. Now consider another observation of shepherds. An *arung zet sa*, generally grazes his sheep and goats separately. Besides other reasons, one reason is the occasional fighting between adult rams and bucks, where severe injury is inflicted to one species member. The reason being two opposite behaviour patterns for fighting. They are in reality aggressive displays of each species. The bucks are taller and stand on hind legs to full length before striking their head against the opponent's head; the latter also assumes a similar posture. And none of them breaks the rule. This is the moral, according to Lorenz. But when the opponent is a ram, in this species during ritual fights the opponents strike heads horizontally against each other. There is no bipedal erect posturing, and additionally, rams are shorter in height. Thus when a ram fights with a buck, each contestant innately exhibits the species-specific behaviour patterns. Though for each contestant it is ritualistic fighting episode (not to damage opponent's vital part), but a ram may directly hit the buck below the belt, though it is not done intentionally. The consequence may be a serious injury to the buck.

Such knowledge, as noted earlier, requires accurate observation of behaviour under natural conditions. But it involves a deeper side of the study of animal behaviour—the explanation and generalisation of behaviour. This is an area where scientists diverge according their theoretical viewpoints.

Explanation and Generalization of Behaviour

For long the western thought propagated the idea that animals differ from human beings as the latter have souls and minds to think. The Indian philosophers, however, believed that all living beings have consciousness or *chetana*. The former rejected his hypothesis as the science of comparative psychology grew whereas the latter integrated nothing new to its traditional wisdom. In early 1930s the comparative psychologists asked where in the animal kingdom mind or consciousness first appeared (Stone, 1964)? Since then, the scientific evidence on this question has been steadily increasing and now there exists a broad area of primate cognition (Zuberbuhler, Cheney & Seyfarth, 1999).

Perhaps the most significant contribution a comparative psychologist can make is to understand the interaction of ultimate and proximate causal factors in behaviour. Without the basic premise that ultimate and proximate factors underlie the evolution and the development of behaviour it is impossible for a psychologist to justify his observations on rats, cats or monkeys and to generalize them to human beings.

Ultimate and Proximate Causation: The investigators often confuse between proximate and ultimate causes of behaviour (Chadwick-Jones, 1987). Where attempt is to explain behaviour with proximate causation, especially in the area of social behaviour, the theoretical vigour is lacking. For example, we have enormous data on aggressive behaviour in different animal species necessary for its evolutionary basis in human beings. But it is not clear how this instinct blends with the proximate factors of aggression. This is essential to understand violent and non-violent behaviour in *Homo sapiens* (Hinde, 1990; Tinbergen, 1968). The search for ultimate causation has rekindled interest in proximate causal factors (Stamps, 1991). The generalizations based on sociobiological and behavioural ecology models need cautious approach, because the experimental evidence shows that, among other factors, the maternal effects provide crucial non-genetic pathways for inheritance of traits. Similarly, the various abilities for information acquisition that are integral part of various evolutionary strategies depend on proximate mechanisms.

There are two areas where information on proximate mechanisms is extremely essential. It helps in knowing what makes behaviour happen at any given moment and how does its machinery work. To make explorations in proximate causation of behaviour the first step is to measure precisely the variations in behaviour. The fluctuations occurring in grazing behaviour during hours of day, in different seasons, and across different habitats give idea of such variations. Once the limits of these variations are known in reliable terms the second step is to measure deviations from it under certain conditions, for example, increase in population density or social control over the pasture management. It is most important from applied animal behaviour viewpoint.

It is easier to invoke an ultimate cause (or survival function) for a behaviour than to understand its proximate mechanism. This is evident from the contradictory explanations about male migration in some animals. For example, in monkeys (Pirta, 2002), during the mating season, from October to January, the peripheral or isolate adult males join the natal or new bisexual groups and mate with the females. Due to which there is competition among the adult males to gain access to oestrous females. However, this is an important mechanism for inbreeding avoidance in rhesus monkey groups. All or most of the males leave their natal group before reaching sexual maturity. The inbreeding-avoidance function of male emigration has its alternate to provide access to mates. A third argument is that the emigration acts to reduce altruism by kin selection. However, an interesting observation is that emigration of males in rhesus monkey is not random. Low ranking males emigrate earlier than the high-ranking lineage males.

Dietary selection provides another interesting example of the interaction between proximate and ultimate factors. It involves the visual, manual, olfactory and oral processing of food. This primary selection through sensory-perceptual mechanisms further involves several proximate factors. A sheep, goat or monkey can discriminate between the edible and non-edible leaf by previous association, innate preference or observational learning (Davey, 1989; Staddon, 1983). However, the preference development for the particular food object also involves physiological and behavioural after effects.

To summarize, the proximate factors explain the variation of behavioural responses to dynamic environmental conditions whereas the ultimate factors explain the variations in behaviour of life forms. The comparison of present day species can give deep insight into the evolutionary history of behaviours (Tinbergen, 1968). Besides precisely measuring the species differences, comparative method explores how natural selection produces differences in allied species, divergent evolution, and similarities in non-allied species, convergent evolution. Pagel and Harvey (1989) give an analysis of reconstructing phylogenetic trees and ancestral character states. They suggest that different models of evolution require different comparative methods based on categorical or continuous nature of a character.

The process of conservation needs a new perspective. It is a kind of interspecies interaction where human beings express pro-social behaviour towards other fellow creatures. However, this pro-social interspecies interaction between a wild animal species and man must have an objective basis. Therefore it is imperative to re-evaluate the subjective protectionism considering adequate demographic and behavioural data from long-term field studies. Apathy towards damage to sheep, goats and crops by animals engenders protests from local people in urban as well as rural areas. A comparative behavioural study revealed that differences in the feeding strategies of rhesus monkeys and Hanuman langurs, which damage crops, were crucial in the formation of positive or negative attitudes of people toward these species (Pirta, Gadgil & Kharshikar, 1997). Rhesus monkeys fed significantly more from human resources than langurs. On the other hand, langurs fed significantly more from natural resources than rhesus monkeys. Although, both species raid the crops, rhesus monkeys engaged in food snatching and stealing. Therefore, people harassed the rhesus monkeys more than the langurs and they also develop negative attitudes towards rhesus monkeys. Such differences in attitudes towards sheep and goats are also common among people. Goats are seen as enemies of plants whereas the image of sheep is that of a docile animal.

India has large variety of animal species that live in natural and semi natural habitats on which there is voluminous mytho-zoological information. Thus, a student of animal behaviour can begin his studies from a sound and unique base. Besides that a student of behaviour may find mobile herds of sheep and goats interesting for observations, which has applied significance as well. Thus, lack of laboratory should not frustrate a student of behaviour in India. He can make significant contributions in the area of explanation and generalization of behaviour by observing the tamed and wild natural populations of animals. The comparative method helps the investigator to collect data on behaviours of his interest across habitats and species. The observed variations in life forms are explored by invoking ultimate causal factors while the variations in responses to environment are explained in terms of proximate factors. The naturalistic observations on the mobile herds of sheep and goats would not only strengthen the theory and method in animal behaviour but also rejuvenate the dying profession of transhumance.

Social movements rooted in the philosophy of non-violence, and traditional ecological prudence of vernacular societies are crucial for the preservation of flora and fauna (Bahuguna, 1997; Goldsmith, 1993). The holistic approach of development that they emphasize, require a core of intrinsic values about the flora, fauna, mountains, valleys, rivers and vernacular societies (Goodwin, 1996a; Naess, 1986). The classical Darwinism has to incorporate cooperative strategies (Goodwin, 1996b; Wynne-Edwards, 1986), and then transcend to Gaian phenomena where human activities, too, come under close scrutiny (Bunyard, 1996).

Formation of Bonds

A pastoralist crosses spatial boundaries over a temporal dimension that is mainly tuned to the annual cycle. We do not know for sure if there had been pastoralists who moved with their herds of cattle and flocks of sheep and goats and returned to their place of origin after several years or did not return at all. Although, there may be cases where the whole tribe from a certain area located a better pasture and migrated to inhabit it. The evidence of this type of acquisition of new areas by segments of a population are plenty in the stories of the place of origin of the inhabitants of a particular village in the agro pastoral population. The nomadic pastoralists occasionally moved from their traditional areas to new locations (e.g. Gujars of Jammu and Kashmir to Garhwal or Gaddis to Pithoragarh or Kanaoras to Pangi). It is probably in association with the warrior groups that the carvans with their cattle population annexed new territories by dominating the populations encountered in their way. Some folk stories provide such kind of evidence. For example, the story of Usha and Anirudh marriage in Kanaor at the regional level and the Yagyas by kings in Mahabharat suggests such territorial excursions.

In this way we can have three scenarios of pastoral adaptation in the utilization of surrounding environment. The most common is the stay in a particular region and have an annual cycle of migration that is affected by climatic, floral and herd structure in an ecosystem. A less common is the continuous but slow migration where some segments of a population selects a new habitat farther from its origin (the members of a royal family, other than the king are given *basa,* suitable land or village) away from the main land of the *thakur* or *raja*. Kavoori (1991) has noted such 'migratory drift' in some pastoralists in Rajasthan. In this case larger or new territories were acquired. The third may be the pastoralists forming warrior groups and conquering new territories. For such large scale social change the social and physical factors both may be responsible, for example, the epic migration of Yadavas from Mathura to Dawarka.

The sedentary agriculturists resort to the last two types of strategies to a great extent even today. Thus, it is important to explore as to why do the pastoralists stick to the annual cycle, though they are more acquainted to shift to new places and have more physical endurance to acclimatize to the harsh environment. Some of the reasons may be: the pastoralist need a larger territory to pasture animals; the livestock adaptation is more important than the human; the pastoralist has to defend himself as well as his herd from external threats; thus, the pastoralist need more elaborate social system in space and time; and, there is already more uncertainty in the daily life of pastoralists therefore the shift involves greater risk for them.

However, for the sedentary agriculturists these issues are not important. It is easier to carry seeds from one place to another, store them in a small place, though growing crops may need adaptation to climatic and soil conditions. In this way the requirements of the pastoralists are quite different from that of sedentary agriculturists. Furthermore, the pastoralists have to adapt to the social life of their herds of sheep, goats, cows, buffaloes and yaks. Therefore, the differences in the habits and social life of the arung zet (mobile herds) bring specialisation in the activities of the *arung zet sa*, the herders.

In social animals, group has its territory or home range. Among them, the migratory activities of several species are tuned to the annual cycle. In some cases the territories of such animals may be some hundred kilometers apart, this is particularly the case in birds. The social animals do not change their territories frequently. Although, individual animals may change territories by migrating from one group to another, it is only under some drastic external threats that the group changes its territory.

On this basis it is possible to hypothesize that the pastoralism is older than the sedentary agriculture. A group of early *Homo sapiens*, besides having its own territory, probably adapted itself to the social life of sheep, goats and pigs as keen observers of their behaviour. They might have killed them more easily than the other mammals and birds. Also these animals did not compete with them for the prey species as they are herbivores. At times the group of *Homo sapiens* may have stumbled on a newborn lamb or goat, left by the ewe or doe while she ran for safety. Some lactating females adopted this newborn, the latter followed the human group. Only few species could show such behavioural adaptations. These explanations are more parsimonious than those based upon the development of artefacts and complex mental traits. Because we have examples of wolf children, the human babies picked up by the wolves and reared by sheer maternal instinct, and then getting protection from other herd members.

Diamond (1989) has raised an important question, why since 4,000 B.C. no new mammal has been added to the list of successful domesticates. He identified some characteristics that were important for domestication. Social animals were easier to domesticate than the solitary animals. In herd life the animals were imprinted at birth and through social learning they followed the leader. This behaviour is generalised during domestication to the herder. The Asian mouflon sheep (the ancestor of domestic sheep) had such submissive behaviour but North American Bighorn sheep did not. Second, some species became nervous and took flight at the signs of danger. For example, out of 40 species of deer that exhibited such behaviour only reindeer showed tolerance to intruders. Third, nonterritorial species were prone to domestication. Fourth, those animals are tamed easily that reproduced in captivity. For example, the finest wool in the world comes from vicunas but it was difficult to domesticate them.

For the management of herds of sheep and goats, ethological studies on the parturition period are important for the improvement of reproductive efficiency. These studies provide detailed knowledge of goats' behavioural patterns around parturition crucial for securing adequate comfort and welfare at this moment in animal management.

Home Range: Grubb and Jewell (in Smith, 1971) have reported the remarkable consistency of the Soay sheep for adhering to particular home-range, usually in small flocks of about thirty, comprising ewes, lambs and young rams. Some ewes were known to have retained the same home range for five years, and for many groups the daily pattern of movement, particularly in the summer, was remarkably regular. Rams also formed groups, which were smaller in numbers, and they remained together until the mating season when members tended to wander and encountered ewes on heat. The group later reformed with the same membership and on the same ground. There is hardly any study on the groups of sheep and goats from India.

Dominance Hierarchy: In Bighorn sheep (*Ovis canadensis*), the chief factor in determining the male dominance hierarchy was the size of the horns (Geist, 1966; Figure 4.1). Where the differences in size were considerable, conflicts were reduced; but fierce, head-on butting contests between rams with horns of comparable size occurred, the challenger being afforded the advantage of charging downhill. By analogy with the 'peck-order' of domestic hens, the more dominant ram kicked those beneath him in the rank order with one of his forefeet and this was accepted without reply. Mounting of the subordinate was also observed. The large, sexually mature males interacted at will with all sheep but associated most with males of comparable horn size and the larger females, whereas younger males and juveniles interacted with sheep of equal or smaller horn and body size.

Fig. 4.1: The Size of Horns Vary with Age in Sheep (Geist, 1966)

In social species (Hayes 1994), threat displays have been found important in limiting the possible serious injury between opponents. For example, the kick with the forefeet on subordinates and 'Flehmen' response (wrinkling of nostrils after sniffing the vulva or immersion in urine) were common displays in many ungulates. The conflicts did occur, but these displays avoided serious damage between contestants. In these displays, during conflicts, the animals engaged in fights with members of their own species, but it involved the non-vital parts of the body. They used their natural weaponary—in the case of mountain sheep, their curly horns—in such a way that the apparent threat was maximized while the real damage was minimized.

Social Organization: For a herder it is important that the flock of sheep or a flock of goats live as a cohesive unit. The animals do not go amiss from each other. Otherwise it is impossible for a pastoralist to herd these sheep and goats during migrations between the summer and winter pastures. It is also essential that the sheep and goats graze in a group, take rest in a group and follow each other. The herder do not teach his animals but he is careful about the behaviour of the individuals of his flock. Some individuals are aggressive and some are docile. Some walk fast and some are slow. During grazing some individuals do not tolerate the others. The stronger may not allow the weaker individuals to graze. Similarly the younger ones require special attention. There are differences in the feeding behaviour of sheep and goats. A good herder knows all these things very minutely and deals with such problems through his experience of grazing with elders and from his own learning.

The attachment between the newborn and its mother or surrogate develops through imprinting (Box 4.1). This early experience with mother or mother figure has long-term effects on the social behaviour of the developing animal. There are numerous studies that show the effects of isolation from mother, which results in abnormal social behaviour in animals and humans. Imprinting is a kind of pre-programmed learning to the blueprint of mother (or parental figure). It serves many important survival functions in the social life of animals.

Box 4.1: Imprinting

The primary social bond for group life is the affectional relationship between mother and her infant. This bond is the basis of all other social bonds that a young one develops in his later life. Ethologists study the behavior of animals and humans under natural and seminatural conditions, and they are poineers in understanding the formation of social bonds in animals. The founder of ethology, Nobel Laureate Konrad Lorenz, discovered the fundamental principles underlying the formation of social bonds in his studies on variety of animals. It is one of the greatest contributions to our understanding of the development of social relationships. His discovery of the phenomenon of imprinting explain how the newborn follows its mother or mother figure and what are the factors that maintains this relationship. Imprinting occurs during a well defined period after birth, the sensitive period of imprinting.

In social animals, such as sheep and goats, shortly after the mother gave birth, the mother goat labeled her offspring by licking them and was sensitive to the smell of her kid (McFarland, 1987). A contact of about five minutes with her kid made a permanent impression on the mother to recognize her own kid later on. A goat that does not have such experience with her kid would not allow him to suckle.

There are few studies on the pre-partum behaviour in the domestic goat. Almost all the wild and domestic ungulates show a tendency to isolate and display an increase in aggressiveness towards herd mates during pre-partum. The goat shows progressive increase in restlessness through such behaviours like grunting, kicking and head moving. It remains stationary for the hour before parturition, either standing up or lying down. The goat selects a shelter to give birth, it may be a place just near a wall.

Mother-infant Behaviour: The work of Smith (1971) on lambing in three domestic breeds of sheep has provided important information which is evident in the traditional practices of lambing among *arung zet sa*. While birth was due, the ewe showed withdrawal for varying distances from the flock. There was sniffing of the grass upon which the amniotic fluid had fallen after the rupture of amnion. If driven away, she frequently returned to it and here, after labour, the lamb was born. The sound of the wet, struggling lamb and in particular its first, feeble bleating usually attracted mother's attention and the licking and nuzzling of the neonate began, accompanied by short, repeated phases of a low pitched bleat. The lamb thus, received tactile, auditory and visual stimulation from a moving object which had definite olfactory characteristics. The ewe in turn also received gustatory and olfactory information which would correspond with the amniotic fluid previously encountered on the grass. Conceivably, the probability of the ewe finding the lamb could be enhanced in this way. According to Smith, this purposiveness in behaviour could be attributed to the mother.

As soon as the lamb has struggled to its feet within twenty minutes of parturition and with its early faltering steps an innate reaction is observed, namely, to place the head under any object or projecting surface at about the height of the lamb's shoulder and under which it can thrust its head (Figure 4.2).

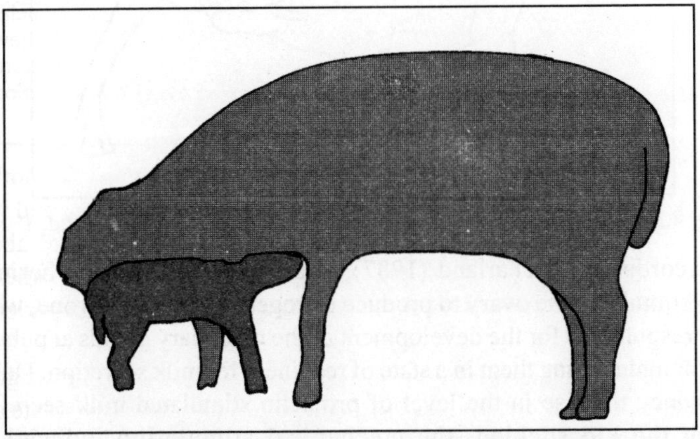

Fig. 4.2: Suckling Response in the Lamb

Further studies on the process of attachment indicated that ewes deprived of the early opportunity for nuzzling would accept any lamb, and not necessarily their own. Moreover, if the doe had already accepted an alien, she would also accept one of her own kids. These studies emphasize the role of the mother in the process of attachment but a study by some investigators of fine wool, merino sheep suggests the operation of some innate tendency in the lamb for the establishment of this bond. The *arung zet sa* not only allows the sheep or goat to suckle the newborn soon after parturition, but makes sure that the infant sucks the nipples of mother for some time. This helps in strengthening the social bond between mother and the offspring. Although, the direct action of hormones on brain is a quick mode of behavioural action, sometimes the effect of hormone is delayed. The peripheral factors, stimulation due to tactual stimulation by the sucking response of kid, comes to mediate this hormone and brain relationship (Figure 4.3).

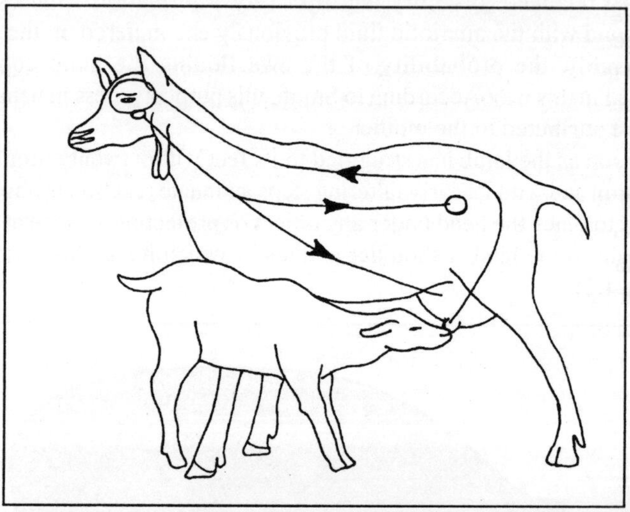

Fig. 4.3: Mediation of Suckling by Brain and Hormones (McFarland, 1987)

According to McFarland (1987), in a goat the luteinizing hormone (LH) stimulated the ovary to produce estrogens and progesterone, which were responsible for the development of the mammary glands at puberty, and for maintaining them in a state of readiness for milk secretion. During pregnancy the rise in the level of prolactin stimulated milk secretion. When the kid suckled, the mechanical stimulation induced the hypothalamus of the brain to release oxytocin from posterior pituitary gland. The rise in blood oxytocin triggered milk letdown. The oxytocin response was very rapid and the kid would normally receive milk within the first 40 seconds of suckling.

Testing Bonds

The pastoralists, through centuries, have selected special varieties of dogs and know to train dogs to look after their flocks of sheep and goats. Some aspects of their training are common, however, some of their traditional ways are unknown to people. The Nobel Laureate Ivan Patrovich Pavlov is remembered for the pioneer experiments on the acquisition of behaviour in dog (Figure 4.4). That the same fundamental laws govern the human and non-human species in learning, was a celebrated discovery of the Russian physiologist Pavlov. Everyone knew that the dog secreted saliva when it was hungry and the food was in vicinity. Although, the secretion of saliva during chewing food served important physiological function, it was not clear why the secretion occurred prior to the reception of food in the mouth cavity. Pavlov, who has learned a lot about the physiology of digestion in dog by his experiments and surgical techniques, was puzzled by the secretion of saliva by dog prior to delivery of food. He dared to call the saliva secreted by dog prior to receiving food as 'psychic secretions.' It roughly suggested, the dog mentally expected the food or has thought about food. It affected his nervous activity controlling the secretion of saliva. Nobody would have agreed to this explanation. Through the classical conditioning experiments, Pavlov demonstrated this in dogs. In fact, this was the fundamental principle in the acquisition of new behaviours in all animals. He showed that the salivary response, can be elicited by such neutral stimulus as sound of a bell, when it is presented few minutes prior to food. After several such paired presentations the dog secretes saliva on hearing the sound of bell alone.

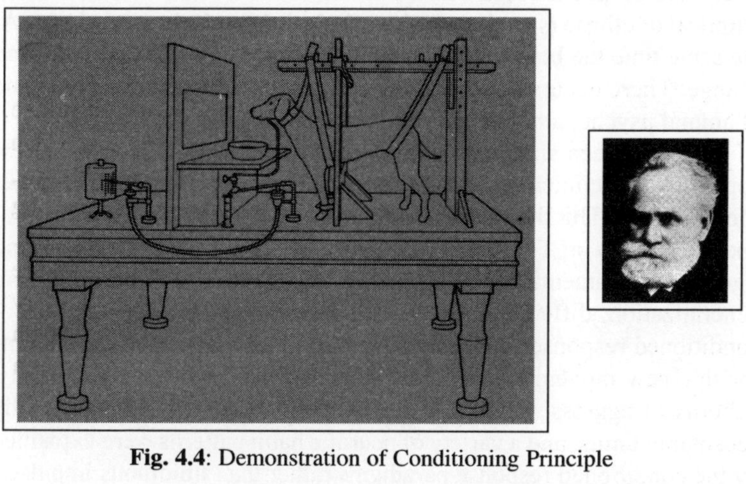

Fig. 4.4: Demonstration of Conditioning Principle

These learning strategies became later important for understanding the acquisition of normal and abnormal behaviours in animals and human beings. In his last works Pavlov was confident that the experiments on dogs in the field of conditioned reflexes, reproduced pathological states of the human nervous system, even he demonstrated return to normal, a recovery (Ivanov-Smolensky, 1954).

Comparative psychologists working with animals had incidentally observed that the behaviour of some animals underwent an abrupt and violent disruption during complex learning experiments. Pavlov was the first scientist to identify, in the beginning of twentieth century, such abnormality as 'experimental-neurosis.' It was a chance discovery. Pavlov admitted that they did not have even the slightest idea of the limits of the endurance of the dog's brains. The demands of the complex experiments caused chronic disturbances in the normal activity of cerebral hemispheres. Some of the dogs recovered from these disturbances after the experiments were discontinued and they had taken rest. The other dogs showed persistent signs of disturbance that required therapeutic measures.

Further support to the theory of experimental neurosis came from experiments on sheep and goats by using different paradigms. A particular strategy that was commonly used in understanding the experimental basis of psychopathological behaviour needs a brief description here.

In this paradigm a dog receives training to salivate to a luminous circle it has association with (delivery of food), as evidence of discrimination between circle and ellipse. Such discrimination occurs quickly when the circle and ellipse are quite different. As the circle is made to look as elliptical or ellipse is made to look as circle the discrimination breaks. At the same time the behaviour of animal undergoes an abrupt and lasting change. There occurs emotional breakdown, and it is a classic example of animal psychopathology.

In the nineteen sixties, these experiments formed the basis of a new applied area in clinical psychology, the Behaviour Therapy (or Behaviour Modification). This therapeutic movement arose in reaction to the psycho-analytic theory of Freudians and neo-Freudians. The systematic and rigorous experimental work in animals and humans on the acquisition, generalization, differentiation, extinction and spontaneous recovery of conditioned responses provided firm and sound theoretical foundations for this new movement. The acquisition of morbid fears and anxiety, patterns of aggressive and submissive behaviours beyond the socially acceptable limits, and a variety of neurotic habit patterns were explained by the conditioned response paradigms rather than libidinous impulses, and can be produced experimentally in the laboratory (Sen, 1968).

Following Pavlov's work on dogs in Russia, Liddell and his co-workers in the United States did a series of experiments on sheep and goats to further explore the principles of experimental neuroses (see Patton, 1964). In Liddell's experiments at the Cornell Behaviour Farm, the animal was first confined to a Pavlovian conditioning frame, mild electric shocks are applied to its foreleg (Figure 4.5). The animal had to learn to anticipate the shock by raising its leg when experimenter presents certain conditioning signals in advance to the shock. However, restraining animals to prevent escape behaviour caused in them different degrees of stress. The animal became alert on the first click and, soon lowered its head and flexed two to three times before shock. It again flexed to the shock, and then returned to its alert behaviour. As the number of trials increase the amount of tension also increases. The animal's rate of respiration increased, it became deeper accompanied by teeth clicking, yawning and immobility of conditioned limb. Animal avoided experimenter and animal room attendant, and resisted vigorously being brought to the laboratory.

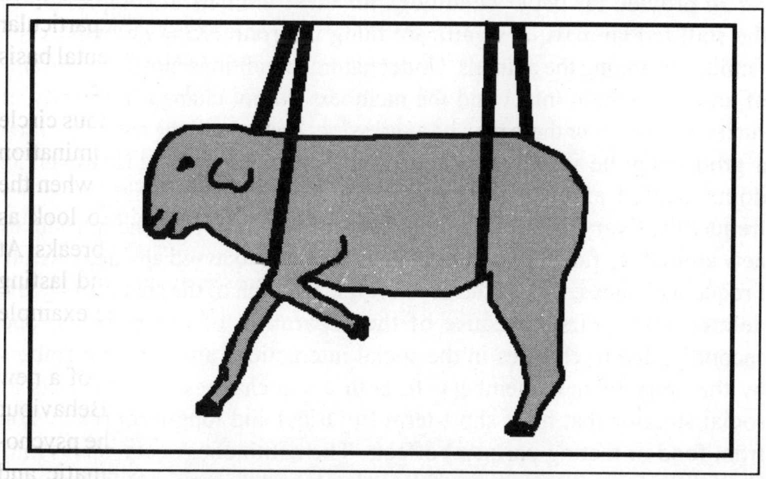

Fig. 4.5: Experimental Neurosis in Sheep

Liddell's study demonstrated the long-range effects of early separation. The kids separated from the doe did not develop normally. Not only were they backward socially in that they shrank from invitations to play or reacted by aggressive butting; but at the age of six months, they were below normal weight. In several cases, their social reactions were so poor that other kids reacted to them as to an inanimate object, such as rock or tree stump. However, a significant finding of Liddell's experiments was the role of mother in reducing the stress of kids under these conditioning procedures. A mother and her kid were kept free in a room with the conditioning equipment tied to kid's back. The other twin was kept alone in the adjacent room with the conditioning equipment on his back. The rooms were lighted. All of a sudden the light went off for ten seconds and as it was turned on the kids received mild shock in the foreleg. The kid with the company of the mother was more tolerant to the stress than the isolated kid. The conditioning in isolation was traumatic. The isolated kid would stop sucking entirely and died during such training. The kid with mother sought the company of the mother during conditioning and moved in the room. On the other hand, the isolated kid assumed a still posture on the corner of the room during conditioning.

These findings have important consequences for the role of a social partner in decreasing the traumatic effects of stressful situations in human beings. For instance, the company of mother and other familiar persons increases stress tolerance. The flocks of sheep and goats kept by *arung zet sa* provide far better conditions for these animals in comparison to the stall fed animals. A significant thing in group living animals is the familiarity among the animals. Under natural conditions mostly the groups of animals remain intact and the members do not change frequently. If such changes occur there may be aggression. Sometimes the animal joining a group may be jointly attacked by the group members. However, in domesticated animals the partners in the group are changed more frequently. Every herder or animal keeper takes care when he introduces new animals to flock, particularly he is cautious to avoid any aggression. Frequent changes, affects the psychological health of the sheep and goats deleteriously. First, because of the separation of companions, and secondly, due to changes in the social interactions among the members by the entry of new members. In both cases changes in group acts as social stressor that have short-term (injuries) and long-term (exclusion from food or mating partners) effects. The continuous social stress may change the immune response of the animals and thus make them prone to diseases.

Affection in Primates

Harlow and his associates (Harlow & Mears, 1979) propounded a theory of affection in primates by conceiving love as a number of affectional systems, and not as a single emotion. They identified five such systems in the rhesus monkey, each of which developed in a series of orderly stages. Anatomical and physiological characteristics underlying each system predisposed the individual to react in particular ways, but the general capacity of the individual to learn with experience was also important. In general, as the sequence of affectional systems developed in the life of an individual, the effects of prior social experience became more and more powerful in shaping affectional responsiveness. The affectional systems observed in the rhesus monkeys were also observed in other species of monkeys, apes and men.

The infants reared in complete social isolation lack in all mannerisms of heterosexual love on reaching sexual maturity. Neither the isolation reared males succeed in making love with normal females nor the isolation reared females solicit properly to normal males. The isolation reared females are not good mothers. These motherless mothers are highly abusive to their infants. The infants reared together form groups in natural habitats however they need extensive care from human investigators. In natural groups the adult members provide this care to infants. Reaching at late juvenile period these infants are able to range freely in the natural habitat (Pirta & Singh, 1978).

The attachment theory of Bowlby (1969, 1973) proposes that the behaviours exhibited during separation are biologically adaptive for the infant and help in coping the loss of attachment object. Although, Bowlby had psychoanalytic background, his theory was largely influenced by ethology. The strong attachment formed early in life when caregivers determine the nature of individual's expectations from himself as well as from relationships.

The predictions of Bowlby's attachment theory have received strong support from numerous studies (Cairns, 1979; Maunder & Hunter, 2001). There is now convincing evidence from various disciplines on affective attachment to place in human beings. These researches indicate that people who show rootedness to their places are negatively affected when forced to leave it. Therefore, it is possible that the usurpation of villagers by the large scale interventions lead to separation syndrome that may have deleterious consequences on their well-being.

These generalisations find support from experiments and observations on the social life of the common Indian monkeys. The negative effects of displacement due to large dams or other interventions have two underlying assumptions. One argument assumes evolutionary continuity of social interchanges, such as the formation of attachment to ones native area and to explain the effects of loss of attachment after forced displacement. This is based on the second assumption. Once the attachment has developed with the mother figure, it is generalized to other living and non-living objects to serve the primary function (evolutionary) of the survival of individual and its group. In this case the attachment is generalized to one's place of birth and development.

Laboratory studies on non-human primates have shown that separation from mother and peers was extremely disastrous for the individual (Harlow

& Mears 1979) and aroused defencive behaviours (Kalin, 1993). Field experiments in India supported these findings (Singh, 1975; Singh, 1977). The home range also had survival value for the members of group (Pirta & Singh, 1978, 1980). Usurpation of a group from its home range had deleterious consequences for the members (Singh & Pirta, 1978). Infants reared in isolation from its mother developed attachment with the place and its cage. When these infant monkeys were separated from their age mates or mother or its place of attachment, they exhibited separation syndrome (Singh & Pirta 1980).

An example of a category of vocal behaviour "coo" would make it clear. To survive an animal must communicate with other members of the group, detect potentially dangerous situations and then start appropriate defensive behaviours. A field observer knows that a rhesus monkey infant separated from its mother gives "coo" calls. The separation studies conducted in laboratory and natural conditions supported this observation. The frequency of "coo" increased immediately after separation from age-mates or mother, but it reached peak in the evening. Infant gave "coo" calls throughout the separation phase, but on reunion (post-separation) the frequency became normal (Singh & Pirta, 1978; Figure 4.6).

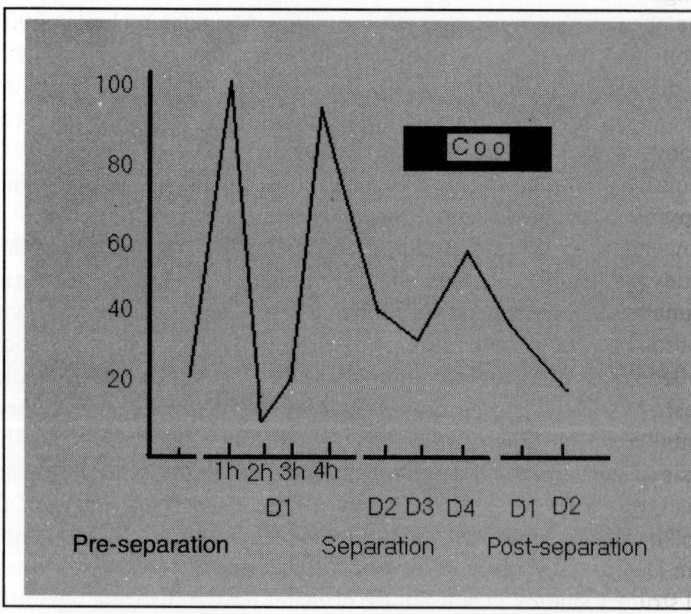

Fig. 4.6: Frequency of "coo' Calls During Three Phases

Two common non-human primates in India have shown some coping behaviours to the ever increasing urbanization stress (Pirta, 1990). Both species adapted to the urban environment by acquiring preference for man made food, resorted to permanent night lodging sites, and considerably decreased their spatial movement. To compete with the human beings, the rhesus monkeys in the urban areas showed increase in communal attack, decrease in agonistic behaviour within the group, and higher social grooming among group members presumably to keep the friendly social ties. Thus, to survive in the urban environment and compete with human beings, the rhesus monkeys increased within group cohesiveness. This was also clear from the proliferation of rhesus monkeys all over the South Asia. Although, the generalization of these findings to human beings has some problems, it is wiser to learn some lessons. One important lesson being to avoid displacement of people. In case it is unavoidable, the oustees must receive social support to enhance within group cohesive relations in the new habitats.

All limits of decency and humanistic values are forgotten when investigators study the social life of pastoral communities. This is especially true with regard to most intimate human relationships. Every investigator goes with his/her yardstick and measures these relationships. On the one hand, these investigators advocate sexual freedom, because it is considered a characteristic of modernism, on the other hand, these same persons look down upon the marital strategies of the pastoral communities. Though the Gazetteer of Chamba State 1904 does not have anything about the mobile herds of Gaddis, it has good description of social life of these "semi-pastoral and semi-agricultural tribe.: (Anonymous, 1904/1996)

However, observations of some investigators are amusing, for example, the study by Shashi (1971) indicated his ignorance about developments in animal social organisations and theory. The knowledge of religious institutions appeared superficial. Verma (1996; 1997; 1999; 2002) has compiled reports on Gaddis, Pangwal, Gujars and Kanaoras in Himachal Pradesh; these reports have referred to almost all aspects of these communities, the accounts are however superficial. In an elaborate analysis of marriage and divorce customs of scheduled tribes in Himachal Pradesh, Kapoor (1993) has raised the legally important issue of "non-Aryan" or "unapproved" forms of marital system in these communities. Bhasin (1996) has however collected minute details of the cooperative social structure in transhumant communities of the Himalayas, including the Gaddis of Himachal Pradesh. These two studies provide link between non-human and human social systems. Finally, there is need for holistic analyses where material and non-material elements harmoniously unite in a social system, and help in its survival.

We find such symbiosis between the herders and their animals. Gujars share their *kotha*, the living space, with buffaloes. The Kanaoras share the open space with their sheep and goats. The social system has developed in such a way that it supports this relationship both physically, and in the cognition. The sheep and goats become part of the mental imagery as we find in the folk songs and folk tales. On festivals animals receive as much attention as the other kin of the *arung zet sa.*

However, with more and more sedentarization this relationship is changing from symbiosis to purely utilitarian one. The studies that consider pastoralism as an adaptation take a highly deterministic view where the co-evolution of man-animal relationship is overlooked and the human evolution is the primary consideration. The social customs are considered as part of the adaptation for bare survival in harsh environment. The selfish point of view has started dominating the present community also. Since they have now alternatives to meet their needs, earlier they were dependent on cattle, sheep and goats.

There was a symbiosis between the sedentary agriculturists and *arung zet sa*, but today the conflict between sedentary agriculturists and the pastoralists is growing in the Shivalik foothills. The agriculturists go for organic manure as it increases agriculture production from their fields. Therefore, they do not wait for the pastoralists to fold (or pen) their sheep and goats in their fields. On the other hand, the grains needed by the pastoralists to feed themselves and occasionally for the sheep and goats are available in the market. Earlier pastoralists enjoyed a secure base to cope up with their problems. They also used the fodder available in the vicinity of sedentary agriculturists.

The Dhangars in Maharashtra, who herd sheep, had symbiotic relationship with the sedentary agricultural populations (Dandekar, 1991). The symbiotic relationship depended on the exchange of grain for sheep manure. In the same area, the buffalo-keeping Gavli had symbiotic relations with the Kunbi agriculturists. The butter and milk has alternated for cereals, lentil and clothes. There has occurred considerable changes in this symbiotic relationship between Gavli and Kunbi. Before 1920, the Gavli were the proud inhabitants of Western Ghat hills. There buffaloes roamed freely in the thick vegetation except for milking by the Gavli during day time. However, the construction of dams and the consequent urbanisation process initiated a change in the life of Kunbi on whom the

Gavli were dependent for grains. After their irrigated rice fields were submerged in the dam water, they moved upward in the area of Gavli and started denuding forest land for agriculture. Besides that, between 1950 to 1970 the entire forest cover of Maharashtra was damaged for various development activities. This was a severe blow on the Gavlis.

Songs of Love and Misery

In his pioneer work on the folk literature of Kanaor, Sharma (1976) has analysed samples of songs, tales, proverbs, festivals, drama, language, deities, social life and culture. Of special importance is an attempt to extract the motifs, the primitive elements essential for understanding the mind of local people. It was found that about 92 percent of the motifs expressed in the folk songs were about the deities worshipped by people. Mainly these motifs were categorized according to Motif Index of Folk Literature by Stith Thompson, but Sharma isolated several new motifs associated with the deities. The folk songs were found particularly rich in depicting various characteristics of the people of Kanaor. Though the author used a broad classification of songs, it is restricted to songs related to deities. The classification of songs include following categories: religious, social, drama, individual, and philosophy. Besides these broad categories, there are a number of sub-categories. The author concluded that the cognition of the folk poet was well developed. Analysis of folk tales show even greater variety and number of motifs. He has also used other indexes to study the motifs. They are indeed very important to explore the complexity of the mind of people living in particular region and compare them with people from other regions.

The following examples of folk songs indicate the fine sensibilities of the people of Kanaor (collected by V.S. Negi and English translation by R.S. Pirta).

While young herders pasture the flocks of sheep and goats there is lot of fun, these lines are from the song *Shalang of Bagto Herders.*

A storm arises in the afternoon
The storm arises and it blew away the cap
The storm arises and it blew away the cap
(He) crouches and starts weeping, after wind blew away the cap
(He) crouches and starts weeping, after wind blew away the cap
"O younger brother Hiradas" says Dharamdas
"O younger brother Hiradas" says Dharamdas
Don't weep for the cap, (I) will search (your) cap
Don't weep for the cap, (I) will search (your) cap

The elder brother Dharamdas gives cap after searching it out
The elder brother Dharamdas gives cap after searching it out
On giving the cap after searching it out, (younger one) laughs
On giving the cap after searching it out, (younger one) laughs

Far away, the young girls, on seeing the plight of their boy-friends, make the situation more amusing in the following lines of the song:

What kind of male, (who) weeps for a cap
What kind of male, (who) weeps for a cap
Weeps for a cap, (the male who) can not bear a single sorrow
Weeps for a cap, (the male who) can not bear a single sorrow

In many communities, including the Kanaoras, the adolescents of the village meet in a room to sing, dance, eat and to share viewpoints, in the evenings. On certain occasions, when they are departing on a long journey, these sessions continue throughout the night. During such special gathering the discussions may focus on things such as moments of joy and sorrow in life, or even about death, as we find in this *Song of Separation.*

In the Ransingh room all (girls and boys) friends gather
All (girls and boys) friends gather
All (girls and boys) friends gather (and) sit on khayarcha (goat hair mattress)
Sit on khayarcha
Sit on khayarcha, take tea in bowl
Take tea in bowl
Take tea in bowl, exchange happiness and misery
Exchange happiness and misery
Exchange happiness and misery, if (someone among them) talk of misery
If (someone among them) talk of misery
If (someone among them) talk of misery, then all friends feel sad
Then all friends feel sad

There is a song of *Dava Vazeer* (minister of Raja). In Kanoar, all rich and poor have flocks of sheep and goats. The Minister is in the pasture with the flock.

Dava vazeer, herder of his sheep and goats
Dava vazeer, herder of his sheep and goats
Herder after sheep and goats, takes away the sheep and goats
Herder after sheep and goats, takes away the sheep and goats

Takes away the sheep and goats to upper pasture
Takes away the sheep and goats to upper pasture
Dava vazeer in upper pasture
Dava vazeer in upper pasture
Dava vazeer sitting on the (top of) hillock
Dava vazeer sitting on the (top of) hillock
Sitting on the (top of) hillock playing flute
Sitting on the (top of) hillock playing flute

At this time his *bethu* (servent) visits him, there is conversation between the two, the proud Vazeer expresses his grief due to social isolation from family members and women friends in the village. He requests his *bethu* to take gifts of flowers to his beloved ladies in the village.

Present bags to girl friends, (there) is a garland of Tinkyong (flowers)
Present bags to girl friends, (there) is a garland of Tinkyong (flowers)
A garland of Tinkyong as well as a bunch of Zabisang (flowers)
A garland of Tinkyong as well as a bunch of Zabisang (flowers)
A bunch of Zabisang (flowers) on the head of girl friend
A bunch of Zabisang (flowers) on the head of girl friend

Even the village deities have flocks of sheep and goats, each family takes them to pasture with their flocks. The herder of this particular flock of the Maheshwar Devata is a beautiful girl, *Banthen Chheringmall*, she has a majestic look. It is also a live portrait of a herder in the words of the folk poet.

In Tholang (village) forest, in Tholang (village) forest
In Tholang (village) forest, in Tholang (village) forest
In upper pasture, in upper pasture
A flock of sheep and goats, a flock of sheep and goats
A flock of sheep and goats, a flock of sheep and goats
Whose sheep and goats are they? Whose sheep and goats are they?
Don't say whose? Don't say whose?
Half of Maheshwar (village deity), Half of Maheshwar
And half of Tholag bhat (family), and half of Tholag bhat
After those sheep and goats, after those sheep and goats
Who is herder? Who is herder?
If (we) say herder, if (we) say herder
Pretty Chheringmall, pretty Chheringmall

With narrow waist, with narrow waist
With narrow waist, with narrow waist
With teeth like white pebbles, with teeth like white pebbles
She (wears) male dress, she (wears) male dress
If (we) look at (her) body, if (we) look at (her) body
Gown of lamb wool, gown of lamb wool
If (we) look at (her) waist, if (we) look at (her) waist
Belt of burra (from insect fibre), belt of burra
(Below) cotton trouser, (below) cotton trouser
If (we) look at (her) feet, if (we) look at (her) feet
Shoes of Suket make, shoes of Suket make
Pretty Chheringmall, pretty Chheringmall
With a sickle (tucked) in waist-belt, with a sickle in waist-belt
Flute in hand, flute in hand
Plays flute, plays flute

There are occasions when the flock of sheep and goats get lost in the pastures. When the herders get tired of searching the flock, they come to their village and seek the help of village deity to locate the flock. The *Song of Pitiram Negi and Patiram Negi* describes such an event:

Now what to do? The sheep and goats are not there
And what to do? Let us go home
In my house, in corner (of house) "O my parents!"
In corner "O my parents!" The sheep and goats are not there
At upper temple, they ask the (village) deity
The village deity says, niece knows
Niece knows, dakhenang (a special worship)
Perform dakhenang, on dakhenang stone
(They) perform worship on dakhenang stone
(They) perform dakhenang, ahead of
Ahead of, a pair of my young dogs
A pair of my young dogs, Khablu and Dhumru
After (them follows) my 900 sheep and goats
Ahead of sheep and goats my Phleoreya ram
My spotted mouth ram comes ringing bell

The departure for winter pasture is a moment of separation from the family and friends, it arouses separation anxiety in the mind of *zet palas* as well as his family members and friends. In this song, *Ramu's Son Ramgopal*, the herder is taking his flocks far away for about seven months.

The depiction of separation is realistic, but more important is to lessen it through ritualistic ways.

Ramu's son Ramgopal
Ramu's son Ramgopal, takes out 900 sheep and goats
Takes out 900 sheep and goats
Takes out 900 sheep and goats, from the door of lower story
From the door of lower story
Outside the door of lower story, (his) mother stands
Mother stands
Mother stands, in her hand holding dhoop (burning incense)
In her hand holding dhoop
In her hand holding dhoop, in other hand korang
(worshipping liquid)
In other hand korang
Outside the door of lower story, his mother advises
His mother advises
His mother advises, O (my) offspring Ramgopal!
O (my) offspring Ramgopal!
O (my) offspring Ramgopal!, go carefully to winter area
Go carefully to winter area
Go carefully to winter area, come back
Come back
Below in shongthong road, (stands) his girl friend
His girl friend
His girl friend, in her hand dhoop
In her hand dhoop
In her hand dhoop, in the other hand a bottle (of liquor)
In the other hand a bottle
In the other hand a bottle, in her gachi (the cloth waist-band)
roasted wheat
In her gachi roasted wheat
In her gachi roasted wheat, tears (of separation) in her eyes
Tears (of separation) in her eyes

The song of *Banthen Krishna Mani* is perhaps the finest description of the balance of human emotions, harsh environment of the Tibetan plateau, its strong attraction for the pashmina wool, and above all the responsibilities of a trader. The whole song is reproduced here to give a feeling of the mind of the folk poet, and to describe the folk mind for its complexity.

Down from there and if (we) go up-up from there;
If (we) go up-up from there
If (we) go up-up from there, in the plain of Pooh (village);
In the plain of Pooh
In the plain of Pooh, at the house of Mathas (family) of Pooh
At the house of Mathas of Pooh
At the house of Mathas of Pooh, is there (any) offspring?
Is there (any) offspring?
Instead of any offspring, (this family) has a pair of offspring
Has a pair of offspring
What are the names of their pair of offspring?; What are the names?
If (we) say names, the name of elder brother; The name of elder brother
The name of elder brother is Gurkum Ram trader; Gurkum Ram trader
The name of younger brother is Kangyur Chhosphel headman
Kangyur Chhosphel headman
From where is the beloved wife of those two brothers?
From where is the beloved wife
(If we) say their beloved wife, a girl from Asrang (village); A girl from Asrang
A girl from Asrang, a daughter of Asrang's lama (family)
A daughter of Asrang's lama
What is the name of the daughter of Asrang's lama (family)?
What is the name?; (If we) say name, (she) is pretty Krishna Mani
Pretty Krishna Mani
Gurukum Ram asks "(O) my house full family!"; "(O) my house full family!"
"(O) my house full family!" Are you happy or not?
Are you happy or not?
Are you happy or not? I go for trade; I go for trade
All others are happy but his beloved wife is not happy
But his beloved wife is not happy
Krishna Mani says "O (my) beloved husband!"; "O (my) beloved husband!"
"O (my) beloved husband!" (If) you go for trade; (If) you go for trade
(If) you go for trade I will also accompany; I will also accompany

Gurukum Ram advises "O (my) beloved wife!";
"O (my) beloved wife!"
"O (my) beloved wife!" Don't come with me;
Don't come with me
Don't come with me (because) you are a lady; You are a lady
You are a lady, it is not in your capacity; It is not
in your capacity
It is not in your capacity (because) Tibet's mountains are bad
Tibet's mountains are bad; Tibet's mountains are bad,
storm will blow (you)
Storm will blow (you); Krishna Mani says "O (my) beloved
husband!"
"O (my) beloved husband!"
"O (my) beloved husband!" (If) you don't want to take me
(If) you don't want to take me
(If) you don't want to take me, I return to my father's house
I return to my father's house
I return to my father's house, to my sweet father's house
To my sweet father's house
Gurkum Ram advises why do you go to father's house
Why do you go to father's house
Why do you go to father's house, there is my brother
There is my brother
Krishan Mani replies, why say my brother, my brother
Why say my brother, my brother
Why say my brother, my brother, (I) have no word with (your)
brother
(I) have no word with brother
(I) have no word with brother, my word is with you
My word is with you
My word is with you, pretty Krishna Mani; Pretty Krishna
Mani
Pretty Krishna Mani, in the last quarter of night
In the last quarter of night
In the last quarter of night, puts tea (pot) on fireplace
Puts tea (pot) on fireplace
Puts tea (pot) on fireplace, (and) goes down to courtyard
Goes down to courtyard
Goes down to courtyard, (she) loads goods carrying sheep
and goats

Loads goods carrying sheep and goats
Gurkum Ram trader takes tea in a bowl; Takes tea in a bowl
Takes tea in a bowl (and) smiles; Smiles
Smiles and thinks in mind; And thinks in mind
And thinks in mind, wife (of people) like me; Wife (of people) like me
Wife (of people) like me, (she is) matchless with others
Matchless with others
Matchless with others, brave as a male; Brave as a male
Now (it is time) to lead (flock of sheep and goats); To lead
To lead, pretty Krishan Mani (goes)
Pretty Krishan Mani
Pretty Krishan Mani, calls sheep and goats; Calls sheep and goats
In the rear (of sheep and goats) (Gurkum Ram) follows whistling
Follows whistling
If (we) go higher up from there, on the top of Tibetan mountain
On the top of Tibetan mountain
On the top of Tibetan mountain, storm flows; Storm flows
Storm flows (that) blows the cap (of Gurkum Ram); Blows the cap
Gurkum Ram says (in dejection) leave aside other things
Leave aside other things
Leave aside other things, that (special) cap of mine; That (special) cap of mine
Krishan Mani advises "O (my) beloved husband!"
"O (my) beloved husband!"
"O (my) beloved husband!" let our life be there; Let our life be there
Let our life be there, is there lack of caps?
Is there lack of caps? Is there lack of caps? If one (goes we have) another
If one (goes we have) another
Going up and up from there, in Guge Changthang
In Guge Changthang
In Guge Changthang, what a Changthang? What a Changthang?
What a Changthang? There is no wood to light fire

There is no wood to light fire
There is no wood to light fire, burning dung for fire
Burning dung for fire
Burning dung for fire, no stone to throw; No stone to throw
No stone to throw, no rock shelter (for) rains
No rock shelter (for) rains; In Guge Changthang Gurkum Ram trader
Gurkum Ram trader
Gurkum Ram trader's illness increases
Illness increases; Illness increases, unbearable pain in body
Unbearable pain in body
Gurukum Ram says "O (my) beloved wife!"; "O (my) beloved wife!"
"O (my) beloved wife!" Now (I am) sinking
Now (I am) sinking; Gurukum Ram says "Brother-in-law O Brother-in-law"
"Brother-in-law O Brother-in-law"
"Brother-in-law O Brother-in-law", my 900 sheep and goats in your hands
My 900 sheep and goats in your hands
My 900 sheep and goats in your hands, your sister (also) in your hands
Your sister (also) in your hands; At the time of saying this
Gurkum Ram trader
Gurkum Ram trader
Gurkum Ram trader, leaves his breathe; Leaves his breathe
Pretty Krishan Mani weeps beating her chest
Weeps beating her chest; Weeps beating her chest, weeps twisting her hands
Weeps twisting her hands
"O lord" my that (unique beloved) husband
My that (unique beloved) husband
My that (unique beloved) husband, where do you conceal?
Where do you conceal?
Where do you conceal? Leave aside to think in reality
Leave aside to think in reality
Leave aside to think in reality, (I) never thought in dreams
(I) never thought in dreams; Pretty Krishan Mani, brave as a male
Brave as a male

Brave as a male, in forenoon; In forenoon
In forenoon, torches the pyre of (her) husband
Torches the pyre of (her) husband
In the afternoon, (she) starts trade; (She) starts trade
(She) starts trade, with weighing balance in hand
With weighing balance in hand
With weighing balance in hand, weighs pashmina wool of kids
Weighs pashmina wool of kids
Weighs pashmina wool of kids, (and) weighs wool of one year lambs
Weighs wool of one year lambs
Pretty Krishan Mani, weeps with tearful eyes; Weeps with tearful eyes
She returns weeping with tearful eyes;
She returns
She returns to the plain of Pooh (village);
To the plain of Pooh (village)

The above sample of songs show that Sharma (1976) has missed two important areas in his analysis. It has bearing upon the theoretical viewpoint of affectional systems presented earlier in this chapter. He has concluded that folk songs depicting separation were almost negligible. He explained that this was because in Kanaora society there was freedom for making heterosexual relationships, under such conditions, generally the husband and wife or romantic lovers did not suffer from separation anxiety. This is a general case with all the investigators belonging to upper castes, as they perceive the tribal population permissive in sexual relations. However, we would like to emphasize that there is no dearth of separation anxiety, or its opposite, longing for romantic relationship, among the adolescents and married couples in Kanaor.

In fact, the affectional systems theory, that was presented earlier, predict preponderance of such separation syndromes in healthy heterosexual relationships when one of the partners leave. Sharma's explanation that the absence of separation anxiety and creation of songs related to it, were missing in Kanaor due to polyandry, has no basis for two reasons. First, it can happen even before marriage, in the adolescent age, when members of the opposite sex are attracted toward each other. Many of these young boys and girls make romantic relationships which do not succeed for various reasons, and thus, the separation anxiety is obvious. We found it amply depicted in songs, not only in Kanaor, but also in adjacent regions.

Even if one raises the issue of polyandrous marital relationship, we have to keep in mind that its distribution is not uniform in the families. Different families vary considerably in number of children and according to the sex of the children in a family. If there is only one adult male and he gets married, where does the question of polyandry arise. This is a common mistake by the investigators who find polyandry mysterious, they hardly try to verify the percentage of polyandrous relationships in the society.

Furthermore, the Freudian influence on the psyche of the intellectuals is so deep that it is assumed that all affectional relationships are sexual. One may feel separation anxiety from the age mate, it may be a boy or a girl. The same may happen while departing from mother, father and other elder members of the family. These emotions are also evoked when an *arung zet sa* or *zet palas* move with the flocks of sheep and goats to winter or summer pastures. It is a grave error to undermine the finer emotional sensibilities of the marginalized people or those belonging to the lower section of society.

The second major drawback of the study by Sharma is his failure to notice to explore the motifs related to the livelihood of the people of Kanaor. Although it is amusing that the two elite investigators, Sankrityayan (1948/1957) and Sharma (1976), chose to focus upon the institution of deities prevalent in Kanaor, to study the society, they present diametrically opposite viewpoints. However, both of them entirely miss the fundamental man-animal bond, which has been important for the survival of these populations. The moving herds of the sheep and goats are real *Lakshmi*, the basis of prosperity for the people of Kanaor, and the other pastoralists as well. How did these investigators overlook *Lakshmi*, is difficult to understand. In the songs that we collected, there is deep concern in the mind of herders, from the *zet palas* (hired herder) to the *vazeer* (minister of Raja), for their flocks of sheep and goats, the *shalang*. Even in the most contemporary scenario, Thakur Sen Negi, a political leader of great repute in Himachal Pradesh, and a proud Kanaora at that, was deeply concerned about the opening of pastoral trade between India and Tibet.

Last and most significant point is that the affectional systems theory emphasizes the formation of social relationships not only between the individuals of same species, but even between the individuals of different species. These affectional relationships, *not the sexual bonds*, are considered the fundamental basis of society. It is only among those individuals who are raised in normal social groups, that the attachment relations prosper, and they only show separation anxiety and grief when there is threat to these relationships. Where there is deprivation of the development of attachment relations at an early age, in animals as well as humans, the adult social relationships are severely affected. They are quite ineffective in the expression or perception of normal social relations at the adult stage.

Unsafe Environment for Pastoralists

Resolution of conflicts involve changes at the individual and group level according to a context where socio-cultural factors are important. More than two decades ago the people in the Himalayan region, while resolving social conflicts engaged in a non-violent struggle, the war of *dharma*, to save their forests, rivers and the culture. The movement was known as the Chipko, hug-to-the-tree, which later transformed into a broad based Himalaya Bachao Andolan (the Save Himalaya Movement). There are excellent sources, which have given general information and provide extensive analyses of this pioneer social movement of India. One must, however, be careful about the biases of those analysts regarding the social issues taken up by the movement and the actors involved in it. They are confined to the early phase of the movement. Some of the basic issues taken up by the movement have escaped the scrutiny of psychologists, however Pirta (2003) has articulated them in a cognitive model that has deeper socio-psychological ramifications.

The studies on cooperative interdependence in primate groups along with the co-evolutionary approach have been combined with the vision of sustainable development observed among people of the Himalayas, which has much wider application to understand ecology and behaviour relationship. The main points of the native's cognitive model as articulated by Pirta are presented here in brief; the other aspects have been described elsewhere (Pirta, 2007). The native people of the Himalayas perceive development from a holistic point of view (Bahuguna, 1968). In such a paradigm, the development of both the individual and community are important. For the normal functioning of the individual head (knowledge), heart (compassion) and hands (actions) must function in harmony with one another during the mundane activities and to achieve self-enlightenment, the ultimate goal. At the community level, 'humanitarian' scientists, compassionate poets and writers, and social workers should work towards the attainment of welfare of all and sundry. The native's cognition reminds the modern man that his 'material development' is path towards *vikriti* (destruction). It is not intended to be a form of escapism. The world is believed to be a form of *Prakriti* (Nature) in which we feel happiness and sorrow. The native says 'Yes' to life and 'No' to death while following the way towards culture, *sanskriti*, which is characterized by qualities such as peace, happiness and fulfillment. In such a paradigm one has to engage in the *yagna*, a noble cause, of preserving the nature's order, the *Rita* (Chaitanya, 2000).

Although, many issues formed part of earlier inquiries, the issue of the resilience of the natives of the Himalayas has significance here. The Gandhians working in the Himalayas have believed in the resilience of the local people as a peculiar biological and cultural adaptation to the mountains. They, however, recognized various large-scale interventions increasing the vulnerability of people in the mountain ecosystem (Bahuguna, 1968; Bhatt, 1992; Kunwar, 1982; Mira Behn, 1993; Sarala Devi, 1978; 1980). Psychiatrists and psychologists associate resilience-vulnerability approach to the mental health of people as affected by environmental conditions. These new conceptualizations have been incorporated in the native cognitive model as shown in Figure 4.7. It would help in understanding the wear and tear occurring in the mind and body (allostasis) of a native. These modifications in the native cognitive model as proposed here, in addition, involve the resilience-vulnerability approach of human well-being. The physiological mechanisms that mediate between the measures of resilience and vulnerability, and the psychosocial and physical environment, have been underlined in the studies of medical scientists (McEven, 1998; Porges, 2003; Segerstrom & Miller, 2004). The lower part of the Figure 4.7 integrates these concepts to understand the consequences of threatening environmental interventions on the mental health of people.

This is particularly relevant in the context of Himalayas where pastoral and other populations are facing threatening changes in their environment. The various large scale interventions made in the Himalayas are associated with the vulnerability and resiliency dimension (Charney, 2004; Ray, 2004). This approach, together with the cognitive viewpoint of native people, may help to understand the mental health of these displaced populations. Migration is a global problem. The World Health Report 2001 on mental health mentioned a huge accumulation of the displaced persons from their native areas. These events are generally overlooked and forgotten as far as remote rural and tribal populations are concerned. For example, such displacements have been taking place for over a century in the Sutlej valley in Himachal Pradesh due to construction of hydroelectric projects.

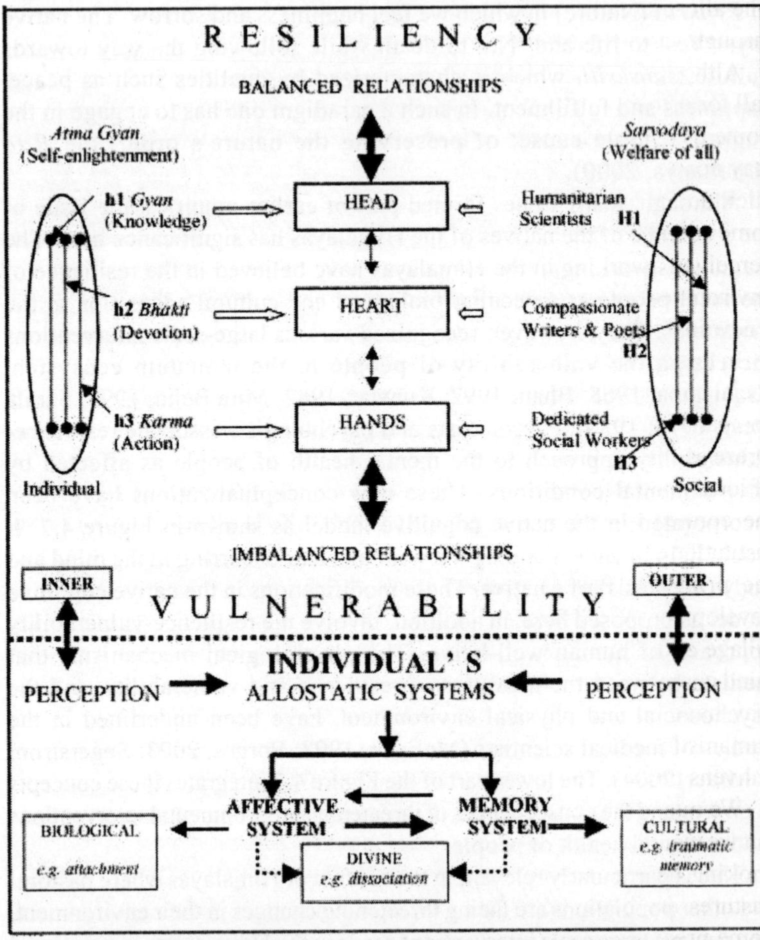

Fig. 4.7: The Holistic Model in the Area of Human Well-Being

Moreover, the problem of displacement has several theoretically important issues in the areas of affect and memory. Thus, it is possible to test predictions based on Bowlby's attachment theory (Ciechanowski, Walker, Katon & Russo, 2002; Stroebe, Gergen & Gergen, 1992) to understand psychological vulnerability of the displaced people. In addition to the attachment theory, there are two significant and related viewpoints developed by psychiatrists. One issue involves the concept of allostatic load and the other is related to the polyvagal theory that emphasizes adaptations to environments perceived as safe, unsafe or life threatening.

The allostatic load refers to the wear and tear of body and it is measured through various physiological measures.

Although, human groups adapt to diverse habitats, different situations call for different behavioural strategies of survival in a particular habitat. Some of these responses involve enormous energy mobilization, which may not be possible at individual level. In such cases individuals would elicit social support. For the elicitation of social support he/she needs some social signals from reliable caregivers. In case such caregivers are perceived as unreliable or unapproachable, a group would perceive such environment as unsafe or life threatening. The polyvagal theory provides a new insight to probe this issue (Porges, 2001; 2003).

In this approach, besides ideas, peoples are major focus of concern and social context has important role in a cooperative action. While explaining comparatively better performance by a north Indian state, Himachal Pradesh, Dreze and Sen (2002) observed that it was possible due to a strong tradition of local cooperative action. An important factor, relatively unexplored in the context of village social structure in the Himalayan region is the institution of deity (Pirta, 2007; see Chapter 8). Through these local deities, the primitive heroes become alive from folklore and mediate the development and maintenance of cohesiveness among the people of the village and the region. It is here that the ecology, culture and the brain-mind complex interact. The other areas where the native's cognitive model may have application are the creation of environmental conciousness, humanistic approach to ecological issues and mental health problems. It enlivens the folk psychology tradition of Wundt.

We may think that the people of Kanaor are living in remote terrain, but we would be entirely wrong. The tentacles of development are steadily choking its lifeline, the Sutlej and its tributaries. Many of its beautiful pastures are being considered for wildlife and biodiversity preserves. Some precious lofty peaks and trade routes of pastoralists have already become the high altitude battlefield. Many of us, the elites, choose to "look away" and refuse to take the responsibility of evaluating the social consequences of these changes and even greater ones that are in the process. The result may be rise in social distress, as we witnessed in a recent conflict over the hydroelectric project in Kanaor. In the snowy December of 2006, many of us were awakened by the visuals in newspapers, the "animistic" Kanaoras with the deity of Chagaon, having a face to face conflict with the armed forces, which is supposed to protect them. Our ability of governance faces a big question. Even greater surprise awaited the intellectuals, the communists and the deity of Chagaon, together protested for the sake of local community's rights and the deleterious consequence of the large scale intervention in the fragile Himalayan environment. The material and non-material coalesced at "Karchham" (literally a bridge for sheep). We hope these are not the last battles of the *arung zet sa* for their survival.

Conclusion

All analyses in the People of India (POI) project uses community as a basic social unit to which an individual belongs or identifies itself and was studied at four levels: general nature about a community's perception of itself, ethnography of a community, interaction and interrelation of communities at the grassroots level and community's attitude and perception of many elements of development (Singh, 2002). As far as social bonding is concerned, there are several indicators of this relationship in the POI data. For example, the POI data on 4,693 communities studied and located, indicate that the primary role of acquiring a mate was through negotiation. The next was by mutual consent followed by exchange, elopement, service, courtship, intrusion, symbolic capture, capture, purchase, and trial. However, more than one mode of acquiring mates prevailed in many communities, particularly among the tribal communities.

There are, however, some unresolved issues, which need further exploration. It was found that polyandry prevailed mostly among Scheduled Tribes, particularly in the hills in Nilgiris and along the Himalayas. Such marriages took place only with the elder brother, whereas the other brothers had a right to cohabit with the wife. That monogamy was a norm in all the Indian communities needed a cautionary approach. Srinivas (2002) has distinguished between perceptions and institutions in the context of behaviours such as the preference for monogamy. If one community followed monogamy, it was perhaps equally important to respect the choice of the other community that practiced polyandry. There was no justification for the negative attitudes prevalent among elite classes towards the pastoral communities who followed different marital systems.

As a system of marriage, polyandry baffles every investigator. But it is one example, there are others too, where a group challenges the primal group of the 'civilised' ones. Without any fierce competition for mate, a social arrangement evolved to meet the needs of the *arung zet* system. However, the investigators hide two important questions in their curiosity about polyandry. Is sex the only binding force for the group? A second, related question is, what is the harm in the sublimation of the sexual urge? Whether polyandry has roots in biological evolution, or not, is an important question, but we find its examples in various animal species.

The institution of deity undoubtedly indicates the development of a complex culture. Though scientists have made considerable success in exploring the principles of biological evolution, the evolution of culture is still a mystery. For people, the local deities of pastoralists are society's mirror images, except the supernatural element. But the uniqueness of this little tradition is, the society can at times override this supernatural element, which is not the case with the greater tradition. "I am because of you; if you are not there my existence is immaterial," said the *mali*, the spokesperson of the deity to a group of villagers during the resolution of a complex social issue.

If one is not enameled by the libidinal urges, it is possible to discern that these institutions of deities that depicts the bonds of love (not sex) that keep the society in far flung mountainside closely knit (see Chapter 8 for more information). Social reforms have hardly come by sexual freedom, rather sublimation of sexual energy has been instrumental in various movements and social upliftment—Buddhism is one of them. The Great Lotsaba, also known as Ratan Bhadra (A.D. 958-1055) was an important personality who not only facilitated the 'Second Advancement' or 'Second Epoch' of Buddhism from Kashmir to Arunachal, but established a basis for social upliftment of people in the Himalayan region. There are different stories about the place of his birth; but he was born in Guge kingdom which included upper part of the Kanaor and extended into Tibet along the river Sutlej. Handa (1998) has written that it was under the patronage of the kings of Guge and the scholarly devotion of Rin-chen-bZang-po and his school of translators the entire population of western Tibet was galvanised into as the Buddhistic creed. Moreover, he has made a very significant remark that for Rin-chen-bZang-po, the monasteries and translation of texts were the means for social uplift, an affirmative action. In the context of pastoral populations of Chamba, the Gaddis, Handa (2005) has hypothesised that the Rigvedic deity Pushan was perhaps a pastoral god.

5

Lessons from Naturalistic Life

Sociopolitical and technological developments in the last century have radically changed the scenario of movement along the Silk Route and Grand Trunk Road in the western Himalayas. Whereas up to the middle of the twentieth century the flow of caravans in these Himalayan regions was governed more by ecological factors and human spiritual needs, the dawn of the twenty-first century saw a display of fearsome global herding mediated by the advanced cognitive competence. For people having an aura of tiny hill states it is yet hard to figure out these contrasting scenarios of peace and war. Now that the dimension has become global is one issue, the more significant challenge is to acquire cognitive ability to grasp it. The spiritual elements that dominated this vast pastoral region from the Roof of the World, and gave humanity unique cognitive elements are retraced by primordial instincts. The study of transhumance, a unique pastoral system illuminates these changes, and challenges the cognitive scientist if he has a way out.

A child born in an *arung zet sa* family at the downstream village of the Sangla Valley of Kanaor, grows up and matures, reaches Great Britain and meets his senior officer Sir Edward Panderel Moon. At the time of this meeting Thakur Sen Negi was a familiar name in Himachal Pradesh, the Hon'ble Speaker of the State Legislative Assembly, the latter was a retired Indian Civil Service officer, who had been the Chief Commissioner of the then Himachal Pradesh in the late 1940s, now living in his 'Manor Farm' away from London. On hearing Negi's views about global parliament, Moon exclaimed, "From Shong to World Government. What a jump." (Chitkara, 1999) Shong is where Mr. Negi was born.

Even an ordinary person can set "A Goal Too Far" to go. In this lies the crux of human cognition, call it a Darwinian achievement or God's gift. Realising the narrow-mindedness of the civilised and modern towards the tribal, Negi's humble plea was that there were a few things to learn from these people close to nature (Negi, 1998). As a proud *arung zet sa*, who loves vast expanse of pasture for his sheep and goats, the vision of Negi was perhaps to demolish the primordial and man-made territories by mutual friendship and make this Globe a common place for living.

Uncertain Knowledge

There is need to define the kind of development we want. A biologist has given an account of the human progress in these words: "*The technoscientific revolution continued, globalized, and unstoppable; computer capacity approaching that of the human brain; robotic auxiliaries proliferating; cells rebuilt from molecules; space colonized; population growth slackening; the world democratized; international trade accelerated; people better fed and healthier than ever before; life span stretched; religion holding firm.*" (Wilson, 2006; Page 129) In future his main worry is perhaps to generate knowledge about what it means to be a human being. The future, thus, lies in the development of humanistic values.

If the use of modern technology is unavoidable then there is no justification that the children of certain section of society should not acquire this knowledge. Yet, equally significant is the propagation of the accumulated wisdom of the human civilisations. If the western way of dissemination of knowledge is through education, the eastern way is through *shiksha*. In the Buddhist tradition, according to Samdhong Rinpoche (an *acharya* and presently the Prime Minister of Tibetan Government in Exile; see Dharampal, 1993) it meant the acquisition of the knowledge of *Prajna*, *Sila* and *Samadhi* (roughly right intellect, right conduct and right meditation). The same is true for the Indian system of *shiksha*. The dichotomy between education and *shiksha* needs conscious resolution, not avoidance from either side. It is difficult to understand why should learning of various arts, crafts, and various physical techniques and sciences not come in the purview of *shiksha*. Similarly, there should be no hesitation for a scientist to learn right intellect, right conduct and right meditation.

There is another dimension to the preceding concern about acquisition and propagation of knowledge. This is a concern for a large segment of society that perhaps remained outside the sphere of *shiksha* in Tibet as well as in India. The pastoralists were among them. Though they provided enough to support the propagation of *shiksha*, its fruits were not easily available to them. Rather they were categorised as tribal, belonging to the lowest section of the society. Social worker and environmentalist, Sunderlal Bahuguna (1968) has emphasized the need to take science, technology and *shiksha* to these people who live in the *bugyals* (alpine pastures above 12,000 feet) and graze the sheep and goats. They live in the open and sleep with their flocks. Bahuguna lamented, though the industrial revolution made the professional intellect sharp and man has succeeded in knowing mysteries of the physical world, there was need to explore the human qualities that transcended space and time. It included love and affection towards others, and was embedded in heart, rather than mind. Pastoralists have survived through this power which they share among themselves, with their animals, with larger social sphere and even among material elements.

In an important study on pastoralists of Himachal Pradesh, though Saberwal (1999) has given some intellectual insights to lessen the miseries of Gaddis and others engaged in this occupation, in disguise he has made a strong case, even stronger than the forester Parmar (1959), against the pastoralists. Saberwal did not spare even the politicians who occasionally resolved the problems of these communities He spat venom on the politicians and painted a beautiful picture of helpless foresters facing dauntless pastoralists. In order to support his thesis, Suberwal has brought out the names of politicians, from the official files, who wrote notes to help the shepherds. They were introduced in this way. "*Vir Bhadra Singh, a kinnauri, has been the Chief Minister of Himachal for over a decade, but for a brief hiatus during 1990-2. Thakur Singh Negi, another Kinnauri, has been an elected member of the Legislative Assembly for over two decades, and was the speaker of the Vidhan Sabha for at least a decade during that period. First Devi Singh, and now Sant Ram, both elected from the Baijnath Constituency of Kangra district, have been Forest Ministers in the state government. The names of these specific individuals occur commonly in the files of the F.D., often, though not exclusively, supporting an application of a herder from their own state or constituency.*" (Saberwal, 1999; Page 81)

Saberwal has thus, succeeded in playing '*Pastoral Politics*' as the title of his book says, however, this is a very shallow politics. Since he has omitted many other players of this game. As a social scientist, following a molar approach, this appears rather consciously chosen strategy. Even greater methodological flaw of the study is the absence of any direct interview with these political leaders who were deeply attached to the well being of their people. In fact, it was their duty too. Saberwal belittles the efforts of persons like Thakur Sen Negi (not 'Thakur Singh Negi') in the upliftment of his fellowmen. Negi fought for their cause. Though he dogmatically pursued the re-opening of Indo-Tibetan trade across the

Himalayas, the national interest was always in his mind. It is incredible to overlook a genius like Thakur Sen Negi, when one talks about shepherds in Himachal. Similarly Saberwal has restricted the role of politicians like Virbhadra Singh, to a few file notings on the applications of shepherds, forgetting his greater role in the development of Himachal Pradesh, and particularly in the conservation of forests. Commenting on Saberwal, the Gaddi leader Thakur Singh Bharmouri (pers. comm.) said that it was the *dharma* of politicians like him to protect the rights of pastoralists and look into their problems in a just manner. He asked, had the forest department ever developed a strip of grazing pasture?

Investigators like Saberwal, and his brand of conservationists even undermine the science of ecology, a science that needs much broader vision if the intention is to resolve conflicting environmental issues. For example, Soule (1986) has called attention to study the "real world." He said conservation biologists must involve in face-to-face interactions with others and with their desires, priorities, and prejudices. In this endeavor we need help from philosophers, anthropologists, sociologists and community development workers, when there are conflicts about values. According to Soule (1986), there was need to consider conflicting interests, for example, the rights of wolves versus those of sheep in Scandinavia. For Bharmouri, a pastoralist himself, the moving herds of sheep and goats were as much parts of nature as were the other wild animals. How could they harm each other?

It is a great coincidence that Theodore Roosevelt a Dakota rancher, who later on became President of the United States, considered environmental conservation an important domestic issue. In the Tibetan plateau where pastoralism is a major occupation of the people, the environment is a sacred thing. The Fourteenth Dalai Lama of Tibet, even from exile in India, has shown deep interest in the global environmental issues, as it was our universal responsibility. The Kanaor had both cultural and economic relationships with Tibet. This relationship flourished with the movement of the caravan of the sheep and goats between the two countries. With the seasonal movement of sheep and goats up and down in the Himalayas, the people of Kanaor enriched their culture by integrating Tibetan (Mahayani) Buddhism. This had long lasting cultural and spiritual impact, but above all it was unique cognitive enrichment.

It may perhaps be an extreme overconfidence on the part of the scientist to state that the *drokpa* is unable to comprehend the consequences of the grazing behaviour of his herd. In the same way, it may also be erroneous to conclude, considering the following scenario, that scientific technology has the alternative approach to reduce overexploitation of resources.

On shore of Lake Victoria, Leslie (2005) saw the fate of the modern ranching system through his eyes and has described it in these words. *"The ranch, called Ned's Corner, was once an iconic part of the vast farm holding of Sir Sidney Kidman, the "Cattle King" .... In the 1930s, his properties extended across four Australian states, and were as big as the British Isles. Ned's Corner itself is the largest privately held landholding fronting the River Murray and one of the largest in Victoria. Yet after 150 years of sheep and cattle grazing, its thoroughly degraded."* (Page 290)

The preceding conflicting scenarios are common, and similar issues were discussed in a recent Global Pastoral Programme Foundation Workshop (UNDP-GEF, 2004). In this conference it was concluded that, first, the notion of "overgrazing" was a scapegoat to undermine the mobile populations. Second, mobile pastoralism was an important production system in the dry areas. Third, there was, however, need to work for sustainable pastoral land management. These issues has significance, as they threaten the resilience of social bonds that pastoralists had developed with the living and non-living, man-animal, and within their social system.

A sense of right and wrong, many biologists believe, can be derived from our Darwinian past (Dawkins, 2006). They suggest that there are four good reasons for individuals to be altruistic, generous or 'moral' towards each other. They are: genetic kinship, reciprocation, reputation for generosity, and advertisement of conspicuous generosity. Our villages have facilitated conditions for these four kinds of moral behaviours to far greater extent than the ancestral primate band. Besides these altruistic urges, the natural selection has also endowed our brains with deep innate urges for sex, hunger, xenophobia and so on. Though the ultimate reason of the evolution of these urges was procreation, Dawkins has argued, there was no check for the 'misfiring' of these urges. For example, an intelligent male, knowing fully that his mate was on the pill, would not show any decrease in his sexual urge. In this way, sexual desire can 'misfire,' or can be channeled through symbols in countless forms, for example, with the help of words one can fashion poetry like *Heer Ranjha*. The same is the case with the misfiring of altruistic urges in the form of religious pursuits.

But the significant point that Dawkins wanted to make was that the 'misfiring' occurred in highly intricate ways, and required higher levels of cognitive awareness, which was still confined to a minority of scientific specialists. Even the most talented mind of our times, Sigmund Freud was entangled by the 'misfiring' of sexual urges, he could not even imagine the finer emotions of mother so important for the survival of an infant, be it sheep, goat, monkey or human infant. This section refers to certain misconceptions about the communities that scientist study, which may have its basis in the 'misfiring' on the part of investigators as well as the subjects, and secondly, there is lack of understanding about the finer emotions that keep sheep and goats in flocks or the human beings in social groups.

While Darwin was fascinated by the competition between sperms and ova (mate selection), on the other hand Freud was worried about the taboos on libidinal urges by the dominant father of the herd. Darwin's insight resulted in exploring various mating patterns in nature, the psychological theory of Freud guides the society even today in explaining aberrations in sexual behaviour. Sankrityayan (a symbolic investigator already reffered in this volume) too expressed his Freudian (libidinal) urges, but in disguise. For example, in the story narrated by a Yogi, in fact Sankrityayan hits at two (or perhaps three) targets with a single arrow. The first target is a Yogi (one who shuns sex for higher up-liftment). Second target was the Jubbal State, and its public, especially of a particular gender—women depicted as low in chastity. Third was the clergy in monastery where the Yogi looses his spiritual rigor in face of seductive woman of Kanaor. For his gender bias in Kanaor one would find an answer in the comments of Yadav (1998), whereas for women and society in Jubbal, it is my *dharma* to respond as a native of the area.

> *"While discussing the people of Kinnaur,"* wrote Yadav (1998), *"it is not just Sankrityayan's book which bemoans the comparative laziness and the drinking habits of the local men, and leaves it at that. The women are praised for being much more hard working and Sankrityayan remembers with a Wordsworthian nostalgia the extraordinarily sweet singing of Kinnauri women working in the fields. In his book, he also makes a spirited appeal for the rights of women, blaming Manu for his justification of 'force' marriages (p. 200). This, however, does not prevent him from declaring that women make greater cooks because God 'created' them for this job (p. 156). ... In fact, on seeing a young 'Khampa' (i.e., one from 'kham') he expresses his desire for a relationship of brotherhood with him sharing with the young man his work, his sorrows and his wife (p. 26)."*

Jubbal was an important State at that time, and became much better known soon after the independence. I do not assume any change in the genes of people; rather it suggests some measurement errors in the assessment of the cognition of people of this area by the *mahapandit* Sankrityayan. Perhaps he could have used some evidence to support his argument rather than the indirect way through an unknown Yogi. In brief, the respect for women existed in the cultural practices; for example, there was no dowry or female infanticide in the Jubbal State, that infested the Brahmanical culture of the plains. People of Jubbal respected women as was evident from an enclosed bathing place at the *Har ki Pauri* in Haridwar constructed by the Raja of Jubbal and its people. As far as other economic achievements were concerned, Jubbal had a small hydroelectric powerhouse before independence, as well as a modern palace, combining western and traditional science and architecture. It had a sound management plan for its forests. The State owned the only sugar mill in Doon Valley as well as a big agriculture farm. After independence of India, the area has given two Chief Ministers to Himachal Pradesh. And Jubbal has become well known for its horticulture development.

Sankrityayan visited temples and monasteries of Kanaor, not to pay obeisance, but to search for historical records and the authenticity of the deities and their spokespersons. It is the humility of the local community that he had access to the premises, search them, test the deity's power and even express or write whatever he liked. But he was not explicit about his atheist agenda. Do we need proof that these deities are *not* the creations of our minds? Yet from time to time, instead of looking at this as an important mental and behavioural phenomenon, as pointed out by the father of modern psychology at the turn of the twentieth century (James, 1902), some intellectuals have a tendency to test the irrefutable hypotheses. The most recent attempt is by Dawkins (2006) in his book *The God Delusion*. Science deals with hypotheses that can be tested, the investigator conducts his inquiry, analyses the data, and accepts or rejects a hypothesis. But for some in Kanaor, there exists a local deity Narainus, for others it is the Buddha, and for the majority both of them exist. It is an irrefutable hypothesis to test the existence of Buddha or Narainus. In the same way, the belief that there is no god is an irrefutable hypothesis. However, if temples and monasteries provide some of its funds for the purchase of books, and then take care of some children who come to learn these books, it may serve some additional purpose. But it is another matter what sort of books we may prefer to keep in the monasteries and temples, and how to use the knowledge gained from the books.

For transhumant Gaddis Manimahesh is the abode of Shiva, while the people of Kanaor visualize Shiva's abode in Raldang Kailash (Negi,

1995). In his book Sankrityayan (1948/1957) has made some very definitive remarks about such beliefs of these local communities, though the more civilised Hindus have the Kashi Vishwanath in Varanasi. He has written that this Raldang Kailash was unreal one (Page 80: *Kinner-Kailash—jhootha Kailash*). This would mean that there was also a real Kailash (he seemed to refer to Kailash which was near lake Mansarovar). This is also irrefutable hypothesis. As if this was not enough, he even refuted the perceptions of local people that Raldang Kailash changed its colour during the day. If the reference is to the snow-clad mountains of unique shape, as is the case with Raldang Kailash, the phenomenon of change in colour seems to be real phenomenon according to modern science. At least, for the benefit of people of Kanaor and for the readers, the great pundit should have mentioned about the discovery of Professor C.V. Raman who had been, by that time, awarded the Nobel Prize in Physics. His research, for a lay person, was about why the water of a lake appears blue in sunlight? But in fact he was curious to know the phenomenon of light. A strange property of light is the perception of the colour of objects, a psychological phenomenon (Raman, 1968), though it is not difficult to find intellectuals for whom colour is a physical property. However, the knowledge that the colour is an experiential phenomenon, not material, has nothing to do with the artist's perfection in painting colourful scenery. The interest in colour has proliferated independently and moreover highly imaginatively. This is visible in the beautiful paintings in the monasteries, such as Tabo (Thakur, 2001), that characterise the Buddhist Himalayas, the abode of *arung zet sa*. The small precincts of *Devi ki Kothi* in the remote Churah, another important pastoral area in Chamba, also have such grand cognitive feast of colour (Fisher, Ohri & Sharma, 2003).

The various schools of painting that flourished in some parts of Himachal Pradesh, introduces one to the complex cognitive faculties of the common people and those who patronised the works of art, besides the artists. They painted gods and goddesses as well as the mundane pleasurable activities of human beings or even animals (Sharma, 1983). Human imagination is transformed in various artifacts that describe our culture. Sankrityayan discovered that people in Kanaor have even enshrined one of their marital systems, the polyandry, in their gods and goddesses. This cognition is the result of curious imagination and might have taken some centuries to evolve. The myths behind them depict dynamic relationships, physical (over territory) and mental (manifested in behaviour). These relationships extend beyond Kanaor to as far as

Mathura, the abode of the pastoral deity Krishna. Paintings of Krishna's *raas leela* are beautifully drawn on the walls of *Devi ki Kothi*.

To conclude, the curiosity about the innate aspects of human behaviour, in terms of the altruistic urges or some other arguments such as the 'misfiring', is as much necessary to explore the folk mind of the *arung zet sa* as they are for reading the mind of an American rancher. For this is the imperative of modern evolutionary biology and psychology. It is in these searches among the mental world of pastoralists, that the investigator is likely to stumble upon the unexplored interactions of innate and acquired. But of greater pragmatic value is the discovery of factors that would act as stimuli to ignite the minds of the *arung zet sa*, from uncertain to certain domain. The next two sections look into the elements of knowledge that transcends from uncertain (empirical) to certain or greater knowledge.

Evolution of Values

The preceding section introduces to pragmatic and theoretical issues in the area of cognition. Here we have made an heuristic attempt to learn few lessons from the animal life to develop an ethics of behaviour for harmonious coexistence on earth.

Origin of Ethics: Human beings have elaborate norms of behaving with each other, which are highly dynamic. There is a belief that it is the unique feature of human species, most probably the outcome of the extra mass of neurons in the brain and its ability to make any kind of association. Although, these generalizations from animal behaviour to human behaviour have been questioned by some critiques, there is however agreement among scientists about some core issues. In a famous and controversial scientific treatise, *Sociobiology: The new Synthesis*, Wilson (1975) started with the following verse of Gita.

Arjuna to Lord Krishna: *Although these are my enemies, whose wits are overthrown by greed, see not the guilt of destroying a family, see not the treason to friends, yet how, O Troubler of the Folk, shall we with clear sight not see the sin of destroying a family.*

Lord Krishna to Arjuna: *He who thinks this Self to be the slayer, and he who thinks this self to be the slain, are both without discernment; the Soul slays not, neither is it slain.*

As a true materialist Wilson has equated the Self with the gene and asked, what was the morality of gene? In exploring the evolutionary history, he speculated that self-knowledge was constrained and shaped by the emotional control centers in the hypothalamus and limbic system of the brain. These centers colour our consciousness with all the emotions—hate, love, guilt, fear, aggression and others—that are consulted by ethical philosophers who give opinions about the standards of good and evil. Though the hypothalamus and the limbic system evolved by natural selection, there is need to pursue it constantly to develop the ethics of behaviour. For example, the need to constrain aggressive behaviour in human species is becoming graver day by day. A central thesis about this problem is related to the counteracting pressures on the units of natural selection. In other words, what is good for the individual can be destructive to the family; what preserves the family can be harsh on both the individual and the tribe to which its family belongs; what promotes the tribe can weaken the family and destroy the individual; and so on upward through the permutations of the levels of organization. This is the essence of sociobiology defined as the systematic study of the biological basis of all forms of social behaviour. Thus the morality of the gene, according to Wilson is to replicate itself. In this endeavor, Dawkins (2006) has dogmatically emphasized that gene was purely selfish in maximising its fitness.

It is argued that scientists and humanists sit together to consider the possibility that the ethics be removed temporarily from the hands of the philosophers and biologists. It may help in evolving an accurate and hence universal code of ethics.

Prudence: The fierce competition and consequent breakdown of social systems make people realize from time to time about the absolute imperative of exploring cooperative strategies. This would be possible through the discovery of social mechanisms that keep disruption under control and promote behaviours where self-interest is sacrificed. Scientists do believe that during the course of evolution animal societies have achieved a balance between two conflicting forces such as, cooperation and competition or egoistic and altruistic drives. The impact of Darwin's theory was largely on exploration of competitive strategies, the cooperation, help and altruism have remained virtually unexplored. Some neo-Darwinians as well as common public have even misused Darwin's concepts, the struggle for existence and survival of the fittest. The slogan of class struggle was propagated. However struggle is irrelevant in the modern understanding of the evolutionary process. The fitness depends upon differential reproduction, wherein peaceful and cooperative intragroup and intergroup association is advantageous.

Most of these conflicts involve individual's interest in getting access to food, space, mate and other things. To a great extent the conflict is resolved by the curtailment of egoistic tendencies by one or both interacting members or parties. This is further associated with prudent use of resources for survival. On the basis of enormous experience gained from animal behaviour studies, Wynne-Edwards (1986) observed that animals used food resources prudently, and cooperators competed with rivals under set rules and accepted the results as binding. Their regime depended on coercing individuals to behave as they do in the interests of posterity. Given that populations were structured in various ways, selection has favoured groups that were efficient in husbanding their food resources. They were ways for securing the future survival of populations as a whole. Group selection was therefore the second level of natural selection. Though it was slower in action than the individual selection.

Mutual Aid: In the foreword to Kropotkin's (1914) classic book, *Mutual Aid: a Factor in Evolution*, Ashley Montagu wrote that the point of view it represents has slowly but steadily made its way, and, indeed, we were not far removed from the time when it would become part of the generally accepted cannon of evolutionary biology. Kropotkin has described that the two aspects of animal life that impressed him most were, the extreme severity of the struggle for existence, and the mutual aid. In the mutual aid, Kropotkin saw a feature of the greatest importance for the maintenance of life forms in each species, and for its further evolution. However, these two forces of life, selfishness and altruism, have bothered philosophers and social scientists for long. It is recently that it has attracted the attention of biologists.

For example, in India researchers have explored the cooperative behaviour in rhesus monkeys and Hanuman langurs (Pirta, 1990; 2007). Furthermore, urbanization in macaques and langurs, and contrasts in their social structure, provide culture free models to test hypotheses derived from the socio-psychological theories. The basic approach was to collect information on cooperation in nonhuman primates by observing their naturalistic life. The question was: has the urban environment affected the quality and quantity of cooperative behaviour in rhesus monkeys and Hanuman langurs? It was found that within the group the rhesus monkeys were friendlier than the Hanuman langurs, as evidenced by grooming behaviour. The rhesus monkeys groomed each other more than the langurs. Another significant observation was that the rhesus monkeys interfered within group fights more often than the Hanuman langurs. In other words there was greater effort among the rhesus monkeys to help each other during social conflicts. Scientists exploring these processes in monkeys and apes have named it reconciliation. These social mechanisms, according to de Waal (1989) were rudiments of forgiveness, assumed unique to human beings. Forgiveness, noted de Waal, did not originate in the minds of people and cannot therefore, be appropriated by an ideology or a religion. The fact that monkeys, apes, and humans all engage in reconciliation behaviour means that it is probably over thirty million years old, preceding the evolutionary divergence of these primates.

These behaviours are not easy to explain even in humanistic terms. Vinoba (1951/1995), the sarvodaya leader and close associate of Gandhi, has described this conflict in the context of violent and non-violent behaviour adopted by individuals. He visualized four scenarios. An individual who adopts non-violent strategy may have to protect itself from the attack of individual following a violent strategy. One way is to leave non-violence and use tit-for-tat strategy. The second way is to continue non-violence but seek help from violent individuals for protection. The third way is to remain non-violent and face the consequences at the individual level that may be complete surrender or slavery. The fourth way is to prepare the masses for non-violent action by convincing them that a joint non-violent action is an efficient way to isolate the violent individuals.

Bonds of Love: The famous psychologist Harlow, who spent most of his life studying the socialization in monkeys, once mentioned that the credit for focusing scientific attention on love goes to Freud. He conceived of a broad life force, the libido, as the basis of interpersonal attachments, and traced its development from cradle to adulthood. This conceptualisation left a permanent imprint on psychologists, psychiatrists, and anthropologists. But according to Harlow, the evolution of potentialities for the formation of strong affectional bonds must have played a role in the success of the Primate Order in the development of adaptable social organisations. In this theorization there is no need to bring in sexual drive as a binding force, the formation of attachment in itself is a positive social factor. With positive ties within and between sexes and within and between age ranges, the group could cohere, permitting animals relatively weak and poorly designed for individual defence to act cooperatively to hold predators in check.

These two theoretical views, though far apart from each other, refer to the finer elements of human cognition and emotion. While the Freudian psychoanalytic theory was based on clinical observations on patients with mental disorders, the affectional systems of Harlow has a sound basis in observations and experiments in animals. Third section in Chapter 4 explored various aspects of affectional bonds, whereas, the last section analysed the songs of love and misery sung by the *arung zet sa* of Kanaor. The affectional systems form the basis of social life in animal and human species.

The Greater Knowledge

The communities that live in the higher reaches of the Himalayas, from Ladakh to Arunachal, are pastoralists and follow the greater knowledge, which has its origin in Indian soil. However, it was further enriched in the Tibetan plateau. It is *Buddha's Noble Eightfold Path*, which shows us the way for right livelihood. For Mahatama Gandhi the Buddhist concept of *nirvana* was not like the black, dead peace of the grave, but the living peace, the living happiness of a soul (Prabhu & Rao, 1967). The founder of *Deep Ecology*, Arne Naess (1989) has noted that the two greatest catastrophes in India have been the elimination of Buddhism and deaf ear turned towards the teachings of Gandhi. They, however, have surfaced from time to time in the debates over environmental issues and in the context of the deprived sections of society. As the uncertain knowledge has failed to deal with the problems related to inequality rampant in the society in general and in the use of resources in particular. For some thinkers the hope lies in the teachings of Buddha and Gandhi (Schumacher, 1973/1993). An enlightening example is the Chipko Movement of the Himalayas (Bahuguna, 1987-88; Baker, 1989). The Buddhism is invoked for creating environmental consciousness through the spiritual ceremonies and speeches by the XIV Dalai Lama of Tibet from exile in India (Anonymous, 1995; Dalai Lama, 1992).

A Buddhist is instructed to develop compassionate and loving attitude towards all sentient beings on Earth. They inculcate these attitudes of compassion in common people through various modes. The Jataka tales, stories about the Buddha's previous lives are important folk medium for it (Batchelor, 1994). The neglect of social and cultural factors by modern science in shaping quality of life may only increase the human misery, if not for all, but definitely for a greater section of society. It would be tragic if the situation is allowed to worsen. Our *dharma* is to do our duty, the acquisition of the knowledge that is for the benefit of all. The classic question is where to search for it. Some thinkers suggested that the wisdom in the traditional societies spread all over the world contain the seeds for our better future. Equally important has been the change in the thinking of some modern philosophers and scientists with regard to development of concepts, such as the *noosphere*. The next section describes the concept of noosphere, which takes into consideration the evolutionary history.

But this approach transcends from material to non-material dimension. It is now entirely embedded in the all-encompassing Gaia. It will be followed by a brief recourse to the Wheel of Life, the greater knowledge of the pastoral communities in the Himalayas.

Cognitive Web: The idea that Earth is a living entity is immanent in human in various traditional cultures. Though it is difficult to establish it through contemporary scientific methods, some concepts have been proposed that contributes positively to this belief. Biosphere and Noosphere, proposed by some thinkers in recent times, have imminence to the view that Earth is a living system. The earliest reference to it has been ascribed to James Hutton. He was first to consider the earth to be a super-organism, in 1785, analogous to physiological systems. About two hundred years later Lovelock (1987; 1996) independently developed the idea of a living Earth by proposing the Gaia Hypothesis. The Gaia theory looks at the life on Earth in a new way. At a certain moment in the evolution of Earth the living matter and its host fused to form a system called Gaia. This super-organism behaves differently then the theories of conventional science of the Earth as a nonliving matter predicts.

The concepts of Noosphere originated in the meetings of geologists Vernadsky and Teilhard, and a philosopher Roy in Paris. They developed the idea of Biosphere into Noosphere (Krumbein & Lapo, 1996). In literature it is not uncommon to find differences in use of these two concepts, in Biosphere the emphasis is on material side, whereas in Noosphere the non-material dominates. Vernadsky emphasized the materialistic conception of the Biosphere—the bio-geo-chemistry, that living and non-living systems interact in unique ways to influence each other. At the same time, for Teilhard the Noosphere was an anthropocentric idea where human consciousness played a major role. The Noosphere (noos=mind) implied that the evolution of human beings added a much more significant dimension to the evolution of Earth. In this way, it was a long transition from intuitive, mythological or unconscious life processes to attributes of human conscious activities. Human beings can change the biogeochemical processes in the biosphere for their own survival; this sphere of interaction is the Noosphere. Human beings envelope the entire globe or its parts by an ideal shell of thought or consciousness. Scientists and philosophers have expressed such opinions in different contexts. Trusov (1983) felt that the formation and development of the Noosphere was the rationally directed interaction of nature and society. Even there was need to define the properties of living states as dynamical systems (Goodwin, 1996a). Such evolutionary course has also been propounded by Sri Aurobindo in the ideas of the development of the *psychic being* (Ranchan, 2001). Though Teilhard and Sri Aurobindo did not meet each other, they were aware of each other's views (Feys, 1973).

The important problem for humankind is to develop the Noosphere. One way is to go ahead with conventional science and technology. The other way is to develop our traditional wisdom to envelope the living Earth. Schumacher (1973/1993) clarified that while the materialist was mainly interested in goods and considered it essential for the development. Whereas the traditional ideologies such as the Buddhism has believed in liberation from material attachment. Though it was not antagonistic to physical well being, the attachment to wealth stands in the way of liberation. The enjoyment of wealth creates more craving for it, and thus the individual's ties with material pleasure gets stronger. If these desires are not fulfilled then life becomes miserable.

The pioneer of *Chipko* Movement, Bahuguna (1987) has underlined that, "*Humankind has always aspired for peace, happiness and fulfilment. Buddha was the first social revolutionary who searched for the root causes of human misery. He found that the main cause of all misery (Dukh) was insatiable desire (Trishna) and the way to peace, happiness and fulfillment, which he defined as the goal of true development, was ending of desires (Trishna Kchhayya). Buddha made basic difference between needs and desires. The needs of all living beings should be satisfied, but the materialistic civilization advocates the continued increase in desires.*" This is how ideas get assimilated in the mind and then they are used to develop a web of consciousness, for example, around the Ganges or the Himalayas. It echoes in the words of Trussell (1990). He has stressed that writers have a vital task the development of the Noosphere or a web of consciousness around the planet Earth. The other vital task of literature was to maintain the health of Noosphere.

It is imperative that we develop culture specific socio-ecological perspectives for spreading an environmental ethos among people (Young, 1983). For a truly socio-ecological perspective, analogies are to be drawn between the socio-biological systems (Eibl-Eibesfeldt, 1975; Harlow & Harlow, 1979; Lorenz, 1981) and the socio-cultural systems (Mann, 1981; Rappaport, 1979). On one side is the realm of science that is ingrained in materialism, whereas on the other side touches the realm of spiritualism, both incomprehensible to a common man. Therefore, we should bring both these realms at the cultural level so that the "cognized models" of human beings assimilate the "operational models" of nature (Rappaport, 1979). In other words, we want to stress that the ecological and social issues are closely related and are most fundamental to our analysis, where the material and non-material interactions are to evolve through the cognitive interaction of human beings (Bueva, 1981; Crook, 1995; Parmar, 1985; Singh, 1998; Southwick, 1972). Therefore, attempt should be to build new Gestalts of the surrounding environment by absorbing the current data into it (Naess, 1989; Rock & Palmer, 1999). As it is easier for a common man to grasp the new ideas related to ecology by associating them with existing perceptions of environment in their culture, particularly entrenched in the mythological and spiritual beliefs of people. Therefore, a holistic approach is needed that takes into account all aspects of human life. One such example is the Gestalt approach that highlights the integration of parts into a whole that creates an impression different from the sum of its parts (Pirta, 2004, 2005). It is more meaningful, more beautiful, more comprehensible and perhaps more natural for us, for example the Wheel of Life in Buddhism.

Interdependence: A look at the figure of the Wheel of Life (Clifford, 1984; Haas & Minke, 1978; Losal, 1982; Read *et al.*, 1959) makes it easier for a commoner to understand the various principles of the Buddhist doctrine. It is common to observe the figure of Wheel of Life in the monasteries and texts in the Buddhist Himalayas. Dummer (1994) has summarised that the wheel graphically depicted the whole of samsara (phenomenal existence) not only in terms of karma and rebirth in the long term but also the states of mental confusion as they occurred in existing life.

The principle of dependent origination (*pratityasamutpada*) (Clifford, 1984; Chhogdup, 1986) can be explained easily to a layman through the figure of the Wheel of Life. This idea is analogous to the biological idea of interdependence among all living beings. It is fundamental for understanding the relationship of various components of an ecosystem, which refers to the dynamic interaction of all parts of the environment. The study of such interactions between plant and animal species in their natural environment had begun at the end of 19th Century and named 'ecology' by Haeckel (Trusov, 1983). Then nobody knew that ecology would concern everybody on this planet by the end of the 20th Century. Ecology simply means looking about our household things. The spiritual leader, Dalai Lama also says that there was nothing special and sacred in taking care of planet earth (Anonymous, 1995). As there was no other planet or house except this one for human beings, it becomes more important to talk of the house where we are living.

Considering the influence of Buddhism among the pastoral

communities of the Himalayas, it is important to understand its basic tenet, the principle of interdependence, or in other words the mystery of phenomenal world, that is its impermanence. The greater knowledge teaches an *arung zet sa* that this world is characterized by impermanence, whereas his experience enriches the vision of the interdependence of object in nature around him. The latter knowledge is uncertain, as it is constantly modified by own experience and through the experiences of the others. Intellectuals need to act as catalysts in the integration and assimilation of uncertain knowledge with certain or greater knowledge to enrich the life of these communities. This is holistic way of bridging the gulf between science and spiritualism or certain and uncertain knowledge. In this journey of new cognitive revolution, for example, the ritualistic turning of the Wheel of Life, has to be replaced with acquiring knowledge behind it. And side by side there must be acquisition of knowledge from the phenomenal understanding of the deeper and deeper meaning of dependent origination, such as the relationship of sheep with the pasture.

Radhakrishnan (1940) has recapitulated the concept of *Pratityasamutpada* (*pratitya* = dependent; *samutpada*=origination) as follows: "*From ignorance spring the samskaras (conformations), from the samskaras springs consciousness, from consciousness spring name and form, from name and form spring the six provinces (of the six senses, eye, ear, nose, tongue, body or touch and mind), from the six provinces springs contact, from contact springs sensation, from sensation springs thirst (or desire), from thirst springs attachment, from attachment springs becoming, from becoming springs birth, from birth springs old age and death, grief, lamentation, suffering, dejection and despair. Such is the origin of this whole mass of suffering. Again, by the destruction of ignorance, which consists in the complete absence of lust, the samaskaras are destroyed; by the destruction of the samaskaras, consciousness is destroyed; by the destruction of consciousness, name and form are destroyed; by the destruction of name and form, six provinces are destroyed; by the destruction of the six provinces, contact is destroyed, by the destruction of contact, sensation is destroyed; by the destruction of sensation, thirst is destroyed, by the destruction of thirst, attachment becoming is destroyed, by the destruction of becoming, birth is destroyed by the destruction of birth, old age and death, grief, lamentation, suffering, dejection and despair are destroyed. Such is the cessation of this whole mass of suffering.*" (pp. 410-411)

Another important aspect of dependent origination is the view of *Karma*. It says that since cause and effect are inseparable there is a natural relationship between the actions and thoughts of the individual and its consequences. Our past *karmic* influences affect our present life and our present *karmic* influences affect our future life (Radhakrishnan, 1940). The rotating wheel is the symbol of the series of lives determined by the principles of karma. The dissolution of the old is the formation of the new.

To summarize, according to Radhakrishnan, the Wheel of Life presents us fresh opportunities where one has freedom to improve his fate. In the context of preservation of our environment, Dalai Lama has given a new interpretation of *Karma*. He has been preaching all over the world that, "*Our belief in reincarnation is one example of our concern for the future. If you think that you will be reborn, you are likely to say to yourself, I have to preserve such and such because my future reincarnation will be able to continue with these things. Even though there is a chance you may be reborn as a different creature, perhaps on a different planet, the idea of reincarnation gives you reason to have direct concern about this planet and future generations.*" (Anonymous, 1995; p. 16). The major problem today is to make people responsive to current environmental issues related to the destructive influences of modern science and technology. It is difficult for common people to understand these dangers. A fear shared by those associated with the study of or living in traditional societies (Zoller, 1990). In a recent study on nomadic pastoralists of Tibet, Miller (2008) noted that belief in *karma* in the landscape of Tibetan Plateau and the Himalayas served to influence one's moral behaviour. The beliefs of pastoralists condition their behaviour.

In view of this impending threat, Dalai Lama (2000) has underlined the need to grasp the subtleties of uncertain and certain knowledge, and cleanse one or the other where ignorance has made its way. This is true way of becoming a Bauddha. This is illustrated in the positive dialogue between modern scientists exploring brain and the Tibetan Buddhism's quest for acquiring higher levels of mind. They are doing experiments on monks meditating in the caves in the upper regions of the Himalayas (Carter, Presti, Callistemon, Ungerer, Liu & Pettigrew, 2005; Goleman & Thurman, 1991). These monks are the aspirants of the greater knowledge in the monasteries of Tibetan Buddhism, entirely supported by the pastorlalists living in these regions. These are therefore, signs of movement towards the integration of two knowledge systems. In the following section, we shall explore more areas where harmonious exchange of knowledge is required between uncertain and certain knowledge to enrich the life and culture of pastoralists.

Lessons from Pastoral World: undoubtedly, few investigators, however, can study the environmental problems rigorously, global and the region specific, to find out their solutions we will have to involve the masses. It is our firm belief that religion and culture can play an important role in the latter process. For example, An Appeal for the Mountains (Mountain Agenda, 1992), circulated on the occasion of the United Nations Conference on Environment and Development held at Rio de Janiero 1992, stated, "*All the major and many minor religions render mountains spiritually significant. And despite the spread of modern skepticism, these emotional, religious or spiritual forces prevail throughout much of the world.*" (p. 10).

Though this viewpoint may annoy some people for whom religion and culture are hindrances in people's thinking, however, the recent experience tells that, at least in the protection of environment, science and religion are compatible. A few examples are: the devotion of Richard St. Barbe Baker popularly known as the Man of the Trees, the nonviolent and compassionate struggle of the Buddhist monk His Holiness the XIV Dalai Lama, the altruistic service by Vedanti Sanyasi Swami Chidananda of Divine Life Society, and the crusade of the Gandhian social worker Sunderlal Bahuguna. The spiritual leaders of India have a crucial role to play in spreading environmental consciousness. They represent the Bhartiya *chit*, *manasa* and *kala* (Dharampal, 1993), the Indian mind and the Indian sense of the flow of time.

The Gaia hypothesis (Lovelock, 1987), besides a scientific basis, has its origin in viewpoints of various religions that the Earth is alive (Goldsmith, 1993). In contrast to the modern viewpoint, Lovelock has suggested that the Earth surrounded by atmosphere was maintained effectively by the living things and together they form a self regulating system, the Mother Earth or Gaia. Lovelock's father, a gardener, living close to mother Earth shaped the thoughts of his child. He remembered the father rescuing wasps from drowning after they have blundered into the water butt. The gardener would explain to the young child that the wasps were there for a purpose, like they controlled aphids on plum trees. As a propounder of Gaia hypothesis the scientist in Lovelock later on reasoned that like country people his father inherited a moral system from his religion by which he felt an innate kinship with all living things. Similarly the pioneer of eco-philosophy, Naess developed the intuitions of his thinking about Nature over a long life spent in the wild (Rothenberg, 1989).

Box 5.1: The Four Harmonious Friends (Dorje, 1993)

The Lord Buddha said: I am talking of those virtues by which many people from this Jambudweepa had gone to trayatrinshata deva loka at some early period.

All the people asked with great curiosity from the Lord Buddha, how was that?

The Buddha said:

O monks listen! At an ancient time four kinds of living beings inhabited a dense forest in the northern part of the Kashi janpad. They were - a bird *kapinjal*, the second was a rabbit, the third was a monkey and fourth was an elephant. All the four lived with close friendship In that part of the forest, they were heartly well wishers of each other. They greeted each other on meeting, they addressed each other without doubt and with great confidence, and they were ranging in the forest with happy mind and without conflict. Their close friendship and immovable love were not able to stop the movement of time. In other words they were also flowing with the movement of time. The memories of sweet life formed in their heart slowly with the passage of time.

Such relationship is the message of many Jataka Tales (Choudhary, 1971; Dorjee, 1987; Jones, 1979; Wray *et al.,* 1979) in which the main theme is an altruistic feeling towards all living beings. For example, in a story (Choudhary, 1971) the lioness after giving birth to cubs felt herself too weak to kill a prey for herself. She decided to kill her own offspring for food. A *bodhisattava* perceived her intentions. He thought, the lioness, a protector of her offspring, was turning into a killer. She would receive the severest punishment in her rebirth for committing this sin. Besides, the innocent offspring will die. Therefore, the *bodhisattava* presented himself to the lioness as food. Another story is depicted in Box 5.1

The dehumanization occurring in the industrial society has found its expression even in works of art that were becoming devoid of meaning, the Gestalt. The paintings (Pal & Fournier, 1982; Snellgrove, 1978; Tucci, 1988; Wray *et al.*, 1979) on wall, roof, cloth or paper provide powerful medium for communicating complex ideas to illiterate and literate people. It is a very popular tradition in Buddhism and can be found even in a remote Mahayani Buddhist village of Lahaul and Spiti in Himachal Pradesh or the famous Ajanta caves (Menon, 1991). *Thankas*, paintings on the cloth, are attractive and colourful visuals, conveying difficult Buddhists concepts in very simple language that is understood by all. For example, in the story of Shavaripa a cruel hunter of Vikrama hills, the great Avlokiteshvara taught him about the ill effects of cruelty to animals. Shavaripa later gave up hunting and made profound penance for his deeds. Though this preaches avoidance of consuming meat, in case it is essential for survival there was no need to invoke religious or environmental pretensions.

From time to time the followers of the Wheel (Dargey, 1978; Joshi, 1967; Narendradeva, 1971; Shantideva, 1979; Snellgrove, 1978; Suzuki, 1981) have enriched human consciousness by the precious knowledge gained over a long period in the pastoral environs of the Himalayas. For example, one may ask what message Tibetan Buddhism, which flourished under the patronage of pastoralists engaged in transhumance (Haas & Minke, 1978; Yonfan, 1981) has for solving our environmental problems? The Tibetan Buddhists do not have technology to cap the ozone holes and stop acid rains, nor have they specific plan to develop some meditations or tantric prescriptions for it. The holy lamas do not have unique potential to evolve new varieties of plants and animals so that pastoralism flourishes. There is certainly a Way of Life open to all for observation and experimentation. In this there are ingredients of wisdom for developing human consciousness in a unique way (Dalai Lama, 2000; Govinda, 1969; Miller, 2008; Sinha, 1958; Rhys Davids, 1900) to envelope this planet for its safe delivery to future generations. These spiritual and moral traditions contain the secret of harmony among humankind and the sacred nature .

The Jataka tales are rich in information about activities of traders. According to historians, the Gupta empire declined after 5th century AD onwards (Dhavalikar, 1997). For about five centuries there was severe drought, lowering of water in rivers and consequently famine all over India. The urban centres started decaying due to fall in trade. These instances make us realise that there is need to improve the water harvesting technologies to avoid the repetition of the similar situation in the 21st century. For this we have to learn lessons from those cultures that have survived in the scarcity of water. It is the deserts of Rajasthan and the cold deserts up in the Himalayas. In Rajasthan people over the centuries have learnt to store each drop of water. There was well established, practical, and widespread organization to collect the rain drops in the desert land. The system was so large in space and time that the whole community seems unified with it (Mishra, 1995).

People in these areas, particularly the Vishnoi, an agro-pastoral group, regard trees essential for their survival. "*The story of Amrita Devi, the leader of first Chipko movement, is well-known. She lived in the desert area of Rajasthan in the domain of Maharaja of Jodhpur, when it was covered with trees. As a child Amrita had been taught to love and protect their trees. Tree care was one of the most important tenets of the Vishnoi faith of her family. When the Maharaja wanted to build a new palace he sent his men to fell timber for lime burning. When they came to Amrita's village they found the villagers hugging the trees, and had to return with only one part of the wood they were sent to fetch, and reported to the Maharaja that to get that amount they had to cut through the bodies of 363 people.*" (Baker, 1989; Page 80). Vishnois, even today, greatly cherish the cordial man-animal relationship.

Bhagsunag, the habitat of Gaddi pastoralists near Dharamsala in Himachal Pradesh, is associated with a folk story related to the scarcity of water in Rajasthan. In *dwapar yuga* a king named Bhagsu of Ajmer in Rajasthan came to the Himalayas for meditation. His aim was to take water for his famine struck kingdom. When the king Bhagsu reached at Dal Lake in Dhauladhars above Dharamsala he thought that it was a right place to carry water. But to his utter surprise, the *nags* (snakes) guarded the Dal Lake. After charming the snakes with magic power he filled the *kamandal* (a holy pot) with water and began climbing down. He felt tired after some downhill walk and slept under a tree. By this time the *nags* recovered from the spell of charm and bit the king. The latter died on the spot, his *kamandal* rolled down releasing the water that became a permanent stream. This place is known as Bhagsunag. This story indicates the association of snakes with water.

This is a mid-Himalayan region, which has plenty of water, but at higher altitudes in the Himalayas, the water is very scarce. A myth corroborates the linkage between snake and water and highlights the innovative way to resolve water scarcity. Rin-chen bZang-po (Ratan Bhadra) was a great scholar of Tibetan and Sanskrit (Negi, 1991). He was a renowned translator and a distinguished tantrik. Once he carried three water snakes in a box of rhinoceros skin, from Hopu in Kanaor to Kyuvang in Guge Province of Western Tibet, for the sake of water. While carrying the box, a disciple of Ratan Bhadra opened the lid of the box at Drati of Sumanam Village. A big and blue water snake came out of the box and disappeared. Afterwards the spot turned into a bubbling brook. Another snake fled, when under some influence of the snake, the disciples again opened the lid of the box, at Tugthang near Spu (Pooh village) by the side of Sutlej river. At this Ratan Bhadra said that had they been able to carry all the three water snakes up to Kyuwang, a township of about a hundred households could have been established, but now that would be a place devoid of livelihood and prone to famine.

In *triskandhadharamaparyaya* (Dorje, 1991a) one form of the Buddha described is *Nag Vyapi*, in blue shade, having twigs of *nagavriksha* and blue snakes in his hands. He possessed knowledge of *the nag*, the lord of the sea. The sea showers sweet water so essential for germination of seeds. It has a variety of precious jewels in it. The sea can destroy enemies with its highly concentrated poisons. It is perhaps due to this belief that people in Mahayani Buddhist areas worship snakes. There is a ritual to bring rains, in which the people pollute the area surrounding a spring, because of which the *nags* living nearby it become annoyed. To clean the pollution the *nags* start showering rains in that area. In a folktale (Dorje, 1991b) of Kanaor one finds a unique conjugal love between a *Nagakanya* and a Kanaori boy, a form of communion between man and animal. Such stories greatly affect the consciousness of young ones and perhaps develop caring attitude towards snakes.

People believe that there is relationship between the water snake and the availability of water. If one kills a water snake near his house or drives it away, the water source will dry up. Not only this, if you pollute the area around a water source, the water snake becomes unhealthy causing scarcity of water. But worship and care of the water source pleases the water snake, the consequence is plenty of water and prosperity. It is common to find the outlets of springs having snakeheads, carved out of wood or chiseled out of stone.

The myths about *nags* among the pastoralists of the Himalayas (Miller, 2008; Vogel, 1972) charm us for another reason also, which is their duality in form. A *Nagkanya* as a female reptile and as a charming young woman is an elusive phenomenon for artists and biologists. Similarly the paintings of a large variety of known and unknown animals in Mahayani Buddhist areas are a rich treasure for a new area, the mythozoology (Roonwal, 1989; Pirta, 1993).

The purity of environment is essential for living beings. The message of Mahayani (Tibetan) Buddhism is that the internal environment is very important and external environment is secondary. It is only by purifying the internal environment that we can improve the external environment. The story of Thunpa Poonshi or Kapinjjal Pakshi explains in very simple terms the harmonious coexistence of different living beings and their mutual dependence for common people (Dorje, 1993; see English translation in Pirta & Negi, 2000; Box 5.1).

The rich cultural heritage of the pastoralists in the Himalayas exhibit their abilities for paintings, weaving, dances, and the other rituals, associated with the grand religious ceremonies. It is a treasure to mobilize rural masses for a social change. Social scientists dare transform the empirical knowledge in the language of common people (Mukhopadhyay, 1997), and use the folk arts for the enrichment of the Noosphere. Some success stories are there from various parts of India. In the Himalayas the pioneers of Chipko Movement spread the message of saving forests by folk songs and *Bhagvat Katha*. A local poet Ghanashayam Sailani would lead the procession singing in Garhwali with *dholak*, a beating drum. At times he used the harmonium while singing his poems and songs in a gathering of villagers. These poems and songs had the message for the conservation of forests, tree plantation, biodiversity and local traditions, but above all it was to boost their self-esteem. Indu Tikekar a philosopher and activist conveyed the message through interpretations of *Srimad Bhagavat* (Tikekar, 1988) which men and women heard with devotion. It brought a spiritual quality in the men and women who joined the movement. The tradition forbids women as exponent of Srimad Bhagavat but Swami Chidananda told her that she must not hesitate and go ahead with this good work and warned that those who associate such pious deeds with physical personality were ignorant.

There are some lessons from pastoralists, the followers of Mahayani Buddhism relevant for resolving current environmental issues. They are: follow the Wheel to mobilize your inner energy to enrich the web of consciousness around the Mother Earth; explore it for awakening the caring side of humankind; seek it to save one's psyche from alluring consumerism; propagate the Way of Life to strengthen the bonds of love between living and nonliving; and, utilize its artistic work to spread the message of environment protection among the people from all walks of life.

Wildlife has unique association with the folklore and beliefs among people in India. In *The Book of Indian Animals*, Prater (1980) wrote that such an interest did not remain confined to India alone, but has spread among men of culture everywhere because of the esteem and admiration in which her sacred books and writings are held. He further said that the third century BC Fifth Pillar Edict of Ashoka was still far the first record of the laws of the preservation of animals in India. The various species of monkeys, the rhesus monkey (*Macaca mulatta*) in north, the bonnet monkey (*Macaca radiata*) in south, and the

Hanuman langur (*Semnopithecus entellus* or *Presbytis entellus*) all over India are surviving in the temples and streets of villages, towns and cities due to religious belief of Hindus in the monkey god Hanuman (Pirta, 1993).

The styles of tail carriage of monkey god Hanuman show interesting variations. For example, in its images carved on the wooden panels in the temples located in the mid-Himalayan agro-pastoral region of Himachal Pradesh, depicts tail carriage of south Indian langur (Fig. 5.1 a & b). Quite incidentally, on the basis of such observations in depiction of tail carriage styles in different parts of India, a well-known zoologist of India undertook a study on various sub-species of Hanuman langurs, the *Semnopithecus* (*Presbytis*) *entellus* (Roonwal, 1989). The findings have suggested a novel way of classifying the sub-species of Hanuman langur in India, the northern and southern hanuman langurs, though similar in various features can be easily distinguished by the tail carriage styles (Figure 5.2; Brandon-Jones, 2004).

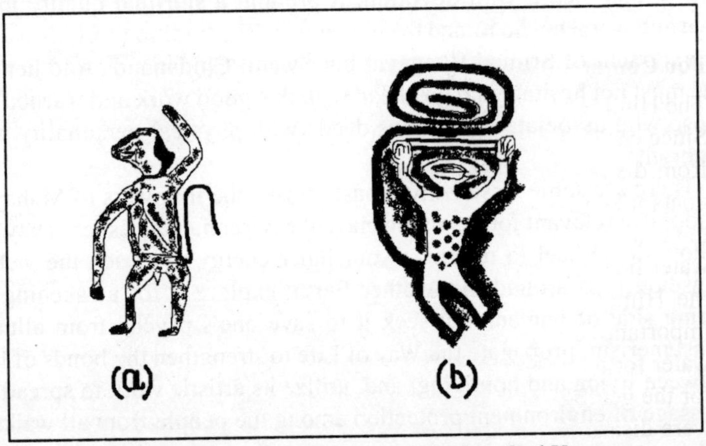

Fig. 5.1: The Tail Carriage Styles of Monkey God Hanuman

A closely related species of monkeys, the Tibetan macaque (*Macaca thibetana*) studied on a slope of Mt. Emei in China, was provisioned by Buddhists in the name of Lord Buddha (Zhao & Deng, 1988). There are several other examples of man-animal worship in India (Gadgil, 2001). These attitudes are a rich and worthy source for conservation practices. In addition, these pastoral communities have powerful mediums of dissemination of information such as paintings, stories and ceremonies.

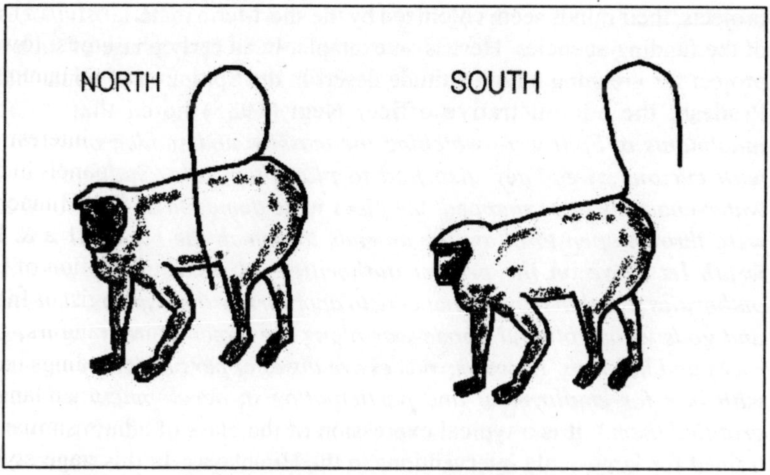

Fig. 5.2: The Tail Carriage Styles of North Indian and South Indian Sub-species of Hanuman Langurs

For Common Good

The Himalayas have acquired a special significance for various reasons. Since earlier times it has association with spiritual aspirations of people from distant places. As a habitat of the special varieties of sheep and goats it became the niche for pastoralists, particularly those engaged in the *arung zet system*. Its snow-clad mountains are permanent source of water for the rivers that irrigate the north Indian plains. In recent times, the Himalayan mountains have become source of debate for three important factors. They include exploitation of its forests for timber, its water for hydroelectricity, and its landmass for minerals, without caring for the geological fragility of the Himalayas. Though these three factors were disastrous for the pastoralists, the turning of the Himalayas into a battlefield was a much severe blow to transhumance. It has shattered the social fabric arduously woven by the *arung zet sa* over a long period. This section briefly explores these changes, however, the focus will be to introduce some issues of theoretical significance, which draw parallel between Hinayana and Mahayana on one hand, and the individual selection and group selection on the other.

A common practice today for the greening of the Himalayas involves the shot-term patchwork from hired technology, it seldom uses local cognition. These activities lack sensitivity to the socio-cultural milieu. Even where local officers are involved in the implementation of the projects, their minds seem colonized by the short-term materialistic ideas of the funding agencies. Here is an example. In an early phase of such a project for greening a high altitude desert in the Spiti area of Himachal Pradesh, the administrative officer Negi (1985) noted that, "*The inhabitants of Spiti were watching the massive and sudden operation with curious awe. They also had to play their role. Suddenly, the water-channels were snapped, the pipes were damaged and enclosures were thrown open to allow the animals to munch the barks. It was a wrath let loose on the project authorities. Mistake on the part of authorities was that they did not care to appropriate their spirits, demons and gods whose blissful abode was along the water-sources, in trees, rocks and hill-tops. However, successive doses of persuasion, tempered with lure for employment and participation in development process gratified them.*" It is a typical expression of the class of administrators trained for large-scale interventions in the Himalayas. In this approach the nature has no value apart from being a commodity. It undermines the feelings and aspirations of local people on the pretext of latter's scientific backwardness.

In a study of the people of Jaunsar-Bawar (adjacent to Kanaor and categorized as backward area), Zoller (1990) has argued that mystical thinking was as rational as the scientific. It was the arrogance of modern human beings that the relationship of man and nature is getting distorted. The developmental problems find amicable solution where assimilation of local knowledge and conventional science approach each other in friendly manner. Scott and Walter (1993) have reported an example of this approach at a village of Shivalik Himalayas, where conventional techniques complemented the local skills to increase the productivity and decrease sedimentation due to soil erosion.

In Ladakh, predominantly inhabited by Mahayani Buddhists, Norberg-Hodge (1994) has narrated similar experiences. She helped in establishing the Ladakh Ecological Group in 1983 to promote use of modern technologies by local pastoral population that promoted their traditional lifestyles and values. The people of Ladakh showed positive attitude to acquire these new technologies. The higher values of Buddhism were their way of life. For example, before ploughing their fields the Ladakhi villagers recited prayers to please the spirits of earth and water. While sowing the seeds, they wished enough grains to worship Buddhas and Boddhisatwas to feed the poor and to support the Sangha.

This thinking has roots in the common Indian ethos. People received motivation to grow more by ploughing the land. However, they freely distributed the surplus to the other sections of the society and to the animals (Bajaj & Srinivas, 1996). The cooperative endeavours, with people's active participation in management of our natural resources, are successful in diverse regions of India (Singh & Ballabh, 1996). The privatisation and nationalisation have miserably failed in maintaining a harmonious link between people and their development. Sarin (1996) has narrated the success story of Sukhomajri and Nada villages in the Shivalik foothills in Haryana in the joint management of forest on common land. The local institutions and the state forest departments developed a partnership for sustainable development of degraded forestlands, by sharing forest management responsibilities and benefits of forest produce. It is a revitalization of destabilized and destroyed system of using daily need items from the area surrounding the village. We have described the success of Chipko Movement in the protection of the forest cover of the Himalayas (see Chapter 4). These are but minute, though important, cognitive inputs in the face of large-scale interventions. Thus, the emphasis on the importance of cultural factors need ever more recognition in the search for alternatives.

It is through the cultural ceremonies that large sections of people become aware of the complexities of nature. Imagine the Herculean task of greening our planet. The modern tool, the biotechnology, may be of limited use in this task, whereas a simple traditional cultural approach has the potential to attain our goal of greening the Mother Earth. For example, on the occasion of the *Kalachakra* initiation at Sarnath, Varanasi on December 29, 1990 His Holiness the XIV Dalai Lama distributed seeds of fruit-bearing trees to the large gathering of the devotees (Anonymous, 1995). They were bought with part of his Nobel Peace Prize money and included seeds of apricot, walnut, papaya, guava, etc., suitable for planting under varying geographical conditions. Dalai Lama advised the devotees to plant them with great care and protect them for the sake of present and future generations.

The devotees on their return from Kalachakra ceremony carried seeds of various species of trees with great reverence to their native places all over India for planting. Vidya Sagar Negi (pers. comm.) witnessed the success story of this idea in the district of Kanaor, Himachal Pradesh. Everyone wanted at least one seed for plantation in his land. Each seedling that came out received utmost care and protection from the owner. Nobody counts the number of trees planted in this way. This is the quickest and efficient method to achieve the desired results, moreover it incurs little or no financial burden on a central agency, and the people ensure aftercare.

Here people plant trees with an intrinsic motivation, to follow the path of the Wheel of Life.

There should be respect for tradition as well as no hesitation to assimilate new areas of knowledge for the benefit of the society. But it is common to observe that technical experts from various spheres refute a healthy relationship between tradition and science. Rather their effort is to disturb it. Twenty-five years ago, in his Presidential Address, at the meeting of American Psychological Association Campbell (1975) clarified that by the "respect for tradition" we mean the propagation of wisdom accumulated through biological and social evolution. The new information was to be assimilated into it from time to time, and required an open dialogue between tradition and science. This he was talking with reference to incorporation of new ideas of altruism and cooperation developed by socio-biologists. Even in the domain of science, the new theories sometimes face strong resistance from the scientists carrying on their traditional views. Theory of biological evolution is one such example.

The Darwinian and neo-Darwinian concepts of biological evolution have significant role in revolutionizing human thought about his own origin and development. It is unconvincing even today for many intellectuals and religious groups. They find it hard to believe that human beings were not the creation of God, but a product of biological evolution. Then there is conflict over the selfish and altruistic nature of gene, which carry the blueprint of life form generation to generation. This has special significance for developing ecological models for resolving conflicts over the use of natural resources. For our long term survival the prudent use of natural resources is a basic requirement. This is the central problem of evolutionary biology that involves selfish and altruistic behaviours. If a group of individuals start behaving prudently by restricting their population, slowly the genes for prudence will propagate. On the other hand, if an individual do not behave prudently and increases his fitness or go on producing more number of individuals, it will have two consequences, the genes for non-prudent behaviour will increase and the individuals carrying genes for prudent behaviour will suffer. Therefore, one group of evolutionary biologists believe that the prudent behaviour will not evolve, and on similar reasoning they believe that behaviours which decrease the fitness of the individual would not evolve, except in those cases where the fitness of a genetically close relative can be increased. However, there is another group of biologists who believe that evolution takes place through group selection (Wynne-Edwards, 1986), which is expressed, in various forms of social behaviourists including the cooperative and altruistic behaviours. In simple words, the evolutionary theory if it has any value for the conservation of natural resources, it is through the understanding of cooperation and mutualism (Goldsmith, 1993; Goodwin, 1996b; Pirta, 2007). These theoretical insights have to become part of common sense. Though it is a fact that these ideas await incorporation in biology textbooks, some concepts of Buddhism common among pastoralists are analogous to it.

There is analogy of individual selection and group selection with two sects of Buddhism, *Hinayana* and *Mahayana*, respectively. In *Hinayana* (the lesser vehicle), the individual prefers solitude and silence and carries his own burden for the attainment of complete salvation from the World. He becomes an *Arhat*. In the other, *Mahayana* (the great vehicle), the individual has compassion for all sentient beings and carries the burden of all including oneself for attainment of Buddha-hood. He practices the way of *Bodhisattvas*. A *Bodhisattva* is an embodiment of compassion, ready to sacrifice himself for others. First he equates himself with others (*paratmasamata*), and then substitutes others for himself (*paratmaparivartana*). 'Self' and 'others' are considered equal, ego becomes non-entity, and finally 'others' are substituted for 'self' (Joshi, 1967). In this state of mind and action the idea of altruism or self-sacrificing behaviour becomes an ineffective term. These ideas are the basis of the teachings of *Bodhisattava* (Tripathi, 1989).

Though the group selection denotes a sociobiological process, and the Mahayana denotes a sociocultural process, both have relation to the phenomenon of altruism towards fellow beings. In the former case an individual has a predisposition to behave in a way that curtails his own fitness but increases the fitness of the group as a whole. But this is true for groups of genetically related individuals. In the latter case the individual learns to follow certain social norms by which he develops self-sacrificing behaviour to reduce others' sufferings, as a duty towards the society. However, in both cases, it is the benefit of all that is the main force for our action. Some new models of group selection are considering evolution of cooperation among non-genetically related individuals (Nowak, 2006). For such cases of cooperation and altruism some social constraints are essential, for example, punishment for non-cooperation (Boyd & Methew, 2007).

After attaining enlightenment, the Buddha took up the task of educating people to alleviate their sufferings, he said to his group of disciples, "Monks roam for the benefit and happiness of all (Mahavagga—1-2.2.5.1). However, he cautioned that believe nothing no matter where you read it, unless it agrees with your reason and your common sense (Tatava-3587). Whether there is social constraint, or not, it inspires to make some cognitive effort. In the present case, for example, the attempt is to draw an analogy between Mahayana and group selection, unification of evolutionary process with a cultural process. Our hypothesis is as follows. A distinguishing feature of human groups, from the other social animals, is to form large congregations where cooperation for the sake of some non-material cause is a dominant factor. This has remained a great puzzle of human sociability. And even a greater mystery is its continuity from earliest periods of human history to the present times. This surprising feature is its universality, a quest for some sublime entity, which unites the humanity.

PART II

In association with

Vidya Sagar Negi
Chhaya Pirta
Sonia Pakhretia
Randhir Singh Ranta

6

Life of Arung Zet Sa
The Pastoralists of Kanaor

*Vidya Sagar Negi**

This chapter is an insider's story—a glimpse of the pastoral life as experienced by a person who is from Kanaor. The author, is not only a person whose family still follows pastoral life style, he himself has been tending his herds of sheep and goats. In this article, one would find appropriate technical terms used in pastoralism and a succinct description of its two prominent modes—the migratory and the household (see Negi, 2007). *This gains more credibility due to his twin efficiencies, as a pastoralist and as a teacher of Bhoti (the Tibetan language).*

The primary objective of this chapter is to describe the life of people rearing sheep and goats in Kanaor, and its services to the society. This is an introduction to the unique traditional knowledge system preserved by an indigenous community of the Himalayas.

Arung Zet and Kim Zet

There are two kinds of sheep and goats in Kanaor. The *kim zet*, those sheep and goats that always stay at home. The *arung zet*, those sheep and goats that always stay out in forest and pastors. *Kim zet* grazes nearby the village and remains in a small enclosure during winter. However, *arung zet* spends all their life under the open sky, tended by the arung zet sa.

As there are two kinds of sheep and goats in Kanaor, in the same way the people tending these animals also have two names. Those who live mostly out with the sheep and goats are the *arung mi*, and those who live mostly at home are the *kim mi*. The *kim mi* looks after the household chores and agriculture. Besides that, the *kim mi* is responsible to take

---

* Vidya Sagar Negi, Department of Buddhist Studies, Himachal Pradesh University, Shimla

care of the *kim chhunga*, all kinds of domestic animals living at home. The duty of *arung mi* is to look after all the animals that live in the open, the *arung chhunga*. He gives the income coming from *arung chhunga* to the *arung mi*. However, all movable and immovable belongings are the joint property of the *arung mi* and *kim mi*.

Besides that, each member of the joint family keeps a part of the earning for him separately; this kind of property is *khechang*. It is for the personal use. The *khechang* may be a common property of two or more members of the family. Generally those women members own such common property who are either nuns or bachelors. Those members of the family are called *khechang-pa*. For her livelihood the *khechang pa* has fields to sow crops, house to live, store or *urach* to keep cereals, and few sheep and goats. The girls have in fact right to keep *khechang* before their marriage. The parents give them *changch* (fields) and *kotich* (box) to keep their goods. The fields remain the property of the women even after marriage till they are alive. All members of the family, other than *khechang pa*, are the *kim pa*.

Talang-sa and Talang-se

The *kim pa*, the person who takes up the responsibility of the main family, is *talang sa* and his spouse *talang se*. Although, the word *talang sa* means a person with keys, the idea behind this is a person who takes over the responsibility of the home. The duty of the *talang sa* and *talang se* is to accomplish all affairs pertaining to house and the village. The other members of the family cooperate with them. The custom forbids entry of all other members of the family in the granary except the two. Both of them take care of any matter related to reciprocity within the community; the other members do not involve themselves in it. The day parents hand over the *talang* to son and daughter-in-law, a record of all necessary house hold things is made. After this, the parents spend most of their time in religious activities. The villagers also do not invite them to their community functions.

The *kim mi* keeps only those animals that are essential to meet daily needs and in the agriculture. They keep cows, bullocks and *kim zet*. All cattle reared at home are called the *kim chhunga* and all the cattle reared out side home is the *arung chhunga*. *Kim chhunga* grazes out only in summer months but for remaining period they remain at home. Therefore, *kim mi* collects fodder during summer for the *kim chhunga*. The *arung mi* keeps the *arung zet*, the horses and ponies for carrying luggage, the dogs for looking after the *arung zet* and the camp.

Why does the arung zet move out of the Kanaor? As mentioned earlier the *arung zet* are those sheep and goats that always stay outside the home. People graze them in the low altitude forests in winter and at high altitude pastures in summer. During winter, the snow envelops everything at high altitudes and there is nothing out to graze for the animals, till the snow melts. In this situation, the *arung zet sa* moves out with his *arung zet* to the lower altitude forests of the Shivalik hills. They return to their *phayuls* or villages at high altitude when summer sets in at the low altitude areas.

Jagni in Fields

Generally, the *arung zet sa* reaches his village at the high altitude in Kanaor around 15 to 20 Jayeshta from the winter pasture. They keep their *arung zet* in the fields at night. To keep the sheep and goats at night, is called *jagni shennu* in the local dialect. Those fields where people grow local crops such as *phaphra* are the *bras saring* but the other fields where people grow crops that ripe later than *phaphra* like wheat, barley, pea and potato, are the *kar bu saring*. The fields having *kar bu* crops one year, they have *bras* the following year. Each year, all villagers keep all the fields on one side of the village for *kar bu* and the fields of the other side as *bras*. It helps in the protection of the crops from cattle, particularly from the *arung zet* during the *jagni shenun*. The *kim mi* plows his *bras saring* without sowing seeds before the arrival of the *arung zet* sa from winter pasture. It is *pal thanglnnu* in local dialect. The sheep and goats rest in these fields at night, and these fields do not need cow dung the following year. Only those fields need cow dung where intentionally people do not allow the sheep and goats to rest due to its proximity to village. These fields are the *kim saring*. The cultivated land distant from the village has two names, the higher one is *rang saring* and lower one is the *nugalang saring*. The people sow *kar bu* and *bras* crops alternatively at *rang saring*. Only the *nugalang saring* and *kim saring* are suitable for horticulture.

Separate Lives of Arung Zet and Kim Zet

The *kim zet* unites with the *arung zet* when the latter arrives in village from its winter pasture. However, the *kim zet* is not so alert as *arung zet*. The pastoralist, *phual* or *zet palas*, takes extra care to look after them while the flock grazes. Often, *kim zet* forms a separate group in the flock and due to slow movement remain behind during grazing from the *arung zet*. The *arung zet* dislikes the *kim zet* in its flock. When the *kim zet* approaches *arung zet*, the latter, while constantly smelling, chase them away. The *kim zet* and *arung zet*, sleep in separate groups at night. If the *phual* takes them to the winter pasture generally they are lost on the way. The *kim zet* mostly grazes in proximity of the village, except in summer months when it goes to higher altitudes with the *arung zet*. Sheep and goats stay in the village *bras saring* for a stipulated period. The reason is that it is also a time for sowing in the *bras saring*. Crops remain unripe if people delay sowing and by that time the snow starts. Therefore, the people sow the seed in *bras saring* before 15 *Ashad. Kim mi* sows the *kim saring* according to their ease. The early crop is *she chhawa*; the late crop is *kal chhawa*. The *kal chhawa* is unreliable bacause snow may cover it at any time. In this high altitude region of Kanaor there is only one crop in a year.

Towards Summer Pasture—the Shol Papang

The total stay of the *arung zet sa* in the village during the resting of the sheep and goats is only for about 15-20 days. After that they move towards summer pasture of the village, *papang*, with their sheep and goats and other cattle. Another name for *shol papang* is *dok sa*. The main summer pastures in Kanaor are Baldar, Lid-fu, Hangrang, Kunu-charang, Chhitkul kanda, Rani kanda and Shelkhar Pungyu. Before the usurpation of Tibet by the Chinese, many pastoralists from Kanaor, those who have insufficient summer pastures, took their sheep and goats to Tibet. The Tibetan plateau was deficient in shrubs and trees, however, the pastors of Kanaor had sparse vegetation of *shur-pa* tree and shrubs of *dama* and *theli*. The leaves of *shug-pa* and *theli* have very pleasant fragrance. Local people use these leaves before or after drying as a herbal incense. In the high altitude pastures, the *kanda*, there are several kinds of precious medicinal herbs. The pastoralists collect these herbs for their use. Some common medicinal herbs are *jimbu-chora*, *rattan jot*, *som lata*, *patis*, etc. While moving towards the *shol papang* with their *arung zet* and *kim zet*, the pastoralists follow the time schedule predetermined by the village community about their traditional *papang* or *dok sa*. The *zet sa* cannot leave before the time schedule. Due to this restriction the *zet sa* cannot afford their sheep and goats to graze in other's *papang*. *Talang se* manages the ample supply of food items for the *zet palas* living with his sheep and goats in the *papang*. *Zet palas* carries the food items provided by the *talang se* on the back of male goats and rams. They also take a sufficient supply of salt for the sheep and goats. At high altitude pastures the *zet palas* live in a permanent small stone hut to escape from biting cold of night and chilly winds. They stay up to 20 *Bhado* in the *papang* with their sheep and goats. Their stay in the summer pasture is the comfortable period in the yearly migratory cycle of a *zet palas*.

Duties of Zet palas at Shol Papang

Besides the herding of sheep and goats during grazing, the *zet palas* performs many other tasks. Some important duties of *zet palas* are: milking of goats and cows, to make curd, to mash curd to make butter, to process butter milk for extraction of cheese, to dry up small pieces of cheese in the sun, to make rope from the goat hairs, to process the sheep and goat hide, and to make small pieces of the meat of the dead sheep and goat and dry it in the sun. The *zet palas* take the sheep and goats in separate herds for grazing around ten in the morning. At about sunset, the *zet palas* directs the sheep and goats towards his camp and reaches his hut with a load of *theli* wood. The sheep and goats slowly grazing on the way reach the hut before it is dark. It is easy to locate the sheep and goats in the *papang* as there are no trees. In the *papang* it is easier to herd the sheep and goat in comparison to the winter forest pasture. Furthermore, the *zet palas* need not stay all the time with the flock. The grass and shrubs in the *papang* are short; the sheep and goats eat upon it. The vegetation in the *papang* is scanty but it is very nutritious. Most of the vegetation in this region contains precious medicinal herbs. The sheep and goats are very healthy after consuming it. The hawk, known as "*ae*" in the local dialect, preys on tiny lambs and kids. The hawk carries away the prey in his powerful claws, and drops them down from a height from the sky, kills and then eats it. Therefore, for the *zet palas* it is essential to keep the tiny lambs and kids away from the sharp preying vision of the hawks.

The Zet sa from Shol Papang Towards his Village

Around 20 *Bhado*, when the rain does not cease in the plains, the vegetation in the *papang* starts yellowing. Soon after the yellowing of grass in his *shol papang*, the *zet sa* starts towards the pastures near the village. To bring the sheep and goats from the *shol papang* to the vicinity of the village is known as *zet-khayan-nu* in the local dialect. At this time the *zet sa* camps near the village. The sheep and goats do not have that kind of grazing facility around the village pasture and in the fields as they have while returning from the winter pastures. The other cattle do not accompany the *arung zet* from *shol papang*; they arrive later. The fodder scarcity and increasing cold in the *shol papang* drive them towards home. No body dares to graze his cattle in the village pasture reserved for the *kim chhunga* before the stipulated period. The villagers let their cattle free in these pastures after a stipulated period until the snow starts. They bring them home as the snow starts. After coming from the *shol papang*, the *zet sa* stays around the village for about 10-15 days with his sheep and goats. During this period, the *zet sa* brings his sheep to his *gora* or a ranch at his house to shear the wool with the help of his friends. He gives a part of wool to meet the needs of the family and sells the rest of it. The wool of sky blue, black, brown and dark shades fetch more money than the white shades. The *zet sa* hands over all the dried cheese, meat, butter and other items brought from the *shol papang* to the *talang se*.

Towards the Winter Pasture

After the shearing of wool, the *zet sa* separates the *kim zet* from the *arung zet*. Then he takes food materials for half of the way from the *talang se*. On an auspicious day, the *zet sa* loads them on the male sheep and goats and starts his lone jouney downwards to the winter pasture. The winter pasture is called *gun chat*.

The *arung zet sa* take their sheep and goats for grazing in the Sirmour, Bilaspur, Solan and Shimla districts of Himachal Pradesh. Earlier they used to take their flocks of sheep and goats to the adjacent areas of the Uttar Pradesh (presently Uttarakhand) and Haryana for grazing. The *arung zet sa* cannot graze his sheep and goats in the government land without a permit. The permission of grazing pertains to a specific patch of forest and for specified number of sheep and goats. A *zet sa* pays the grazing tax every winter, 20 paise per head for sheep and 40 paise per head for goats. But the local villagers charge heavy grazing fee from the *zet sa* for leasing out their pasture land.

Arung Zet sa on the Way

The *zet sa* moves with his flock about five to six kilometers daily. Each *arung zet sa* knows the daily night resting sites from his village to the winter pasture. In the local dialect the *pontang* means a night resting site. The goods carrying bucks and rams follow a straight pathway or a road; however, the main flock moves while grazing along the sides. All the members of flock arrive at the common night stay daily. The *zet sa* wakes up early in the morning and loads their luggage on the goods carrying bucks and rams. *Rubals*, the special kind of bags prepared from wool that fits to back of sheep and goat, contain the essential goods in them. A *rubal* has two pockets in it hanging on the lateral sides of an animal over the back. Goat's hide reinforces the bottom of *rubal* externally on both sides. The rainwater cannot penetrate inside a rubal. The *zet sa* loads the largest rubal, the *dagal*, on the largest buck and contains all the small daily need items in it.

The *zet sa* allows copulation among the animals of the flock during a specific period so that the peak birth coincides with the month of *Ashwin* when he is on his migratory route to winter pasture. Thus the copulation of *bolu* (stud goat) with the goats and *gulas* (stud ram) with the sheep takes place during *Chaitra* to *Jayeshta*. The breeding starts from *Ashwin* and continues up to *Mangshir*. The young ones, *lakhara*, need special care on the way. The newborn goat kids cannot walk efficiently for about fifteen days since birth. During this period, the *zet sa* carries them on his back. At times he loads the kids on goods carrying animals in the rubals. *Zet sa* keeps two kids facing each other in the two pockets of the *rubal*. The heads of the kids remain out and *zet sa* stitches the rest of the upper portion of the *rubal*. Thus, the kids can take fresh air but side-by-side they cannot jump out of the rubal. If *zet sa* has the horses or ponies, they also carry the kids. On reaching the camp, the *zet sa* immediately takes the kids out of the *rubals*. Later on, when the kids are able to walk, the *zet sa* herds them with the goods carrying bucks and rams. However, this problem does not arise with the lambs. A lamb starts following its mother after a day or two of its birth.

On reaching the destination every day, the first task of the person accompanying goods carrying animals is to unload them. Then they take out the *lakhara* from the rubals. Next, the *zet sa* keeps the unloaded items in a pile, called *kharoo*. He also prepares a barn or *khuranch* for the *lakhara*. After enclosing the *lakhara* inside the *khuranch*, he then closes it from all sides so that there is no scope of kids going stray. The barn has dry grass matting to keep it warm. During rain, *zet sa* makes special arrangement to ensure that water does not enter the barn.

After enclosing the *lakhara* carefully, the *zet sa* herds the goods carrying animals as they graze in the nearby area. Simultaneously he collects firewood for cooking. By the time *shai zet*, sheep and goats not carrying loads reaches, the meals are ready. When the *shai zet* arrives, they graze them in the surrounding area and then brings them near the camp. The *zet sa* milks the goats and then allows the kids to settle with their mothers. The *zet sa* takes only some amount of milk so that the rest is sufficient for the kids.

Measures to Make the Mother Accept her Young Ones

Occasionally the mothers refuse to accept their own young ones. She runs here and there to look for her infant among the young ones. She smells every young one below the tail but in vain. Probably such a female confuses the olfactory and gustatory sensation of her lamb with other lambs. Since the lamb mixes with several other young ones and rubs against their bodies due to which the olfactory stimuli originating from the infant's hind portion dilutes or mixes with other's stimuli. The same may occur when carrying the lamb in the rubal. First, the *zet sa*, takes the lamb over the fire place, so that the smoke neutralises the smell. If the mother does not accept the lamb through this procedure, the *zet sa* massages the hind portion of the lamb and the mouth of the mother with her milk. In case this method is also unsuccessful, the *zet sa* inserts his fingers in the vagina of the mother and then rubs with those fingers below the hind portion of the lamb and mouth of the mother. He then allows the mother to smell the lamb. In most of the cases the mother allows the lamb to suck her nipples. Sometimes all these methods fail, the *zet sa* then takes the mother and her lamb to a lonely place. He ties the fore limbs of the mother with a tree or a peg and leaves the lamb under her. The lamb attempts several times to approach the nipples. The mother moves side to side but simultaneously smells the hind portion of the lamb and finally allows him to suckle her nipples.

The *zet palas* takes special precaution while goats suckle their kids. Since he has to attend to several mother-infant pairs simultaneously there are chances that some young ones may suck more milk while the others may remain hungry. It is also possible that the kid in exchange or some times a kid sucks milk of two goats. If a female does not have sufficient milk for her kid, the *zet sa* allows him to suck other female's nipples. The *zet sa* handles those females that do not allow their kids to suck nipples. Sometimes the infants run after the *zet sa* vocalizing continuously until they suckle the nipple of the mother.

The goat gives more milk than the sheep. An ewe has milk enough only for her lamb. Therefore the *zet sa* does not milk the sheep. At times he gives goat's milk to a lamb whose mother does not have enough milk. At night the lambs do not stay in the barn. They remain with their mothers. The kids, however, remain with their mothers only at the time of suckling. Otherwise the *zet sa* cannot get milk from the goats because the kids suckle their mothers.

Generally sheep or goats have only one infant each. A goat occasionally gives birth to twins or *chhema*. In such cases the goat does not have milk for *zet sa*. It is just enough for her twins who drink from one nipple each. The *zet sa* looks that only one kid does not suck milk from both the nipples. Generally, the sheep do not give birth to twins. If a sheep gives birth to twin lambs, people consider it inauspicious. It is a bad omen for *zet sa*. On the other hand, there is no such folk belief about the birth of twins by goats. Rather, the twins are auspicious among goats.

Duties of Person Living at the Camp

After attending to the task of *lakhara*, the *zet sa* takes food. The *zet sa* seldom eats more than two times. After taking meal in the evening, he stuffs all his utensils in a special bag, the *chikoo*. The process of stuffing utensils in the *chikoo* is called *khazangk sang-mu*. Then he encloses the *lakhara* in the barn. The *zet sa* take *mol zet* (sheep) and *bakharang zet* (goats) in separate groups for grazing. The *bakharang zet* grazes in all kind of terrain whereas the *mol zet* prefer reasonably open plains. The *mol zet* herder is the *molas palas* and the *bakharang zet* herder is the *bakharang palas*. Each *palas* carefully looks after their grazing flocks.

The person who remains in the camp takes out the *lakhara* from the barn in the sunlight. If the *lakhara* are older, the *zet sa* brings fodder for them. He gives water and fodder to the horses and ponies if any. He also brings firewood, leaves and grass from the forest. At sun set he encloses the lakhara in their barn. Then he stores water for cooking and drinking. If there is nobody to remain in the camp, the *zet palas* puts a log of wood in the fireplace, which burns slowly and gives smoke all over the period. The reason being that some person coming with wrong intention thinks that somebody is around. He keeps the *lakhara* in the barn and ties his dog nearby the *kharoo* and leaves the sheep and goats for grazing.

It is the daily routine of a *zet sa* while on the migratory way. Wherever he finds a good forest for grazing his sheep and goats, he stops for a day or two. A stop for more than one day on the route is *bethi toshim*. On *bethi toshim*, when the sheep and goats rest in the camp, the *zet sa* finds time for bathing and cleaning his clothes. On that day he gives salt to his sheep and goats. If they do not receive salt they lose their appetite. The sheep and goats graze a lot in the forest after licking the salt. The *zet sa* do not give water to the sheep and goats after the salt. The sheep and goats receive water only the next day; if it is summer they receive it on the same day in the evening. The sheep and goats start licking the salt immediately. While giving salt to his sheep and goats, the *zet sa* spreads it on clean rocks and calls them by whistling. On hearing the sound of whistle the whole flock runs to *zet sa's* direction. Wherever the *zet sa* finds shops on the way he replenishes his supply of food items and salt. A *zet sa* keeps account of his expenditure.

The Zet sa at his Gun Chat

In this way bearing all the hurdles of the migratory pathway, the *zet sa* reaches his *gun chat* or winter pasture at the beginning of *Mangshir*. On reaching there the *zet sa* camps at the higher altitudes in the beginning. Then slowly he descends to warmer areas of his pasture in coming cold days. The *zet sa* and his companions clean a place where they camp. They make the earth plain and enclose it by temporary fence. The fencing of camp saves the sheep and goats straying away during moonlight. It particularly helps a *zet palas* who is alone. He can attend to his other duties after enclosing the sheep and goats inside the enclosure. When the weather gets colder in the higher areas of his pasture the *zet sa* moves downward to lower altitudes with his goats and sheep. In winter pasture the *zet sa* selects such a place for his camp where sunlight remains for the whole day and is safe from cold winds. Mostly a *zet sa* prefers open area. During rains he takes shelter in a nearby *duar* or cave to protect himself and his luggage from drenching. Very occasionally he prepares a shelter or *chhanich*. It has four poles on four corners and a roof of grass or hay.

The *zet sa* grazes *mol zet* and *bakharang zet* separately in the winter pasture also. If the number of *zet palas* is more, the camps of herders for *mol zet* and *bakharang zet* are separate. The *bakhrang zet* graze first in the areas that have many shrubs and steep terrain. The *mol zet* prefer herbs. It is only under compulsion that the *bakharang zet* graze on ground. Moreover sheep cannot stand on the hind legs and thus unable to pull down the leaves of high branches, like a goat. If the sheep and goats graze simultaneously in an area, the goats being faster and more movable crush the grass on the ground. The sheep do not eat crushed grass. Therefore, the sheep remain hungry.

In the month of Chait, when it is greenery everywhere, the *zet sa* takes his sheep and goats to higher area of the winter pasture. They remain in those areas until the start of the *Baishakh*. By that time the *zet sa* yearns for the cold breeze of his native area. At the end of the Chait or in the beginning of the *Baishakh*, *zet sa* starts his arduous migratory journey towards Kanaor with the flocks of sheep and goats.

In longer days and in the forested habitat, the *zet sa* grazes his sheep and goats in two shifts. In the early morning, with the first ray of sun he takes his sheep and goats for grazing and brings them back to the camp around eleven. After finishing his lunch, he takes his flocks again for grazing and brings them to the camp before it is dark.

Shearing Wool and Romang

The *zet sa* starts shearing the sheep wool in the beginning of the month of *Magh*. The winter wool is not as dense and long as the summer wool. In winter pasture the wool on the body of the sheep tears while moving among the shrubs during grazing. In the summer pasture, however, there are no shrubs therefore, the wool is long and dense. The summer wool is *shol cham* and the winter wool is *gun cham*. After shearing of wool, the *zet sa* shears goat hair (*romang*). Unlike the sheep, the shearing of goat hair takes place only once, in the winter. The *zet sa* shears the hair of the ventral side of a goat. He never shears goats kept for selling or in the name of deities.

The *zet sa* thoroughly cleans a portion near his camp where he wants to shear the goat hair. Then he hammers down into ground two wooden pegs about ten feet apart. He ties a rope to each peg. After that he brings a goat for shearing, the *zet sa* pulls her down to the ground. As the goat falls on the ground he ties her hind legs with a rope of the lower peg and then ties the horns with the second rope to the upper peg. In this situation the goat is lying on lateral side and she is unable to move. Then the *zet palas* shears all the hairs on the ventral side of the goat, from the throat to the hind limbs. However, for shearing the wool of the sheep the *zet sa* do not tie them like the goat. He spreads matting on the ground and makes the sheep lie on the mat ventrally. He presses sheep's hind limbs by his feet and presses down her neck and fore limbs by the left side of the body. The *zet sa* then shears the wool of the ventral side of the sheep. After tying together the fore limbs of the sheep, he then shears the wool from other parts of the body. The *zet sa* keeps some wool to his needs; the remaining he sells to the local people or the traders.

A *zet sa* may sell sheep wool, but keeps *romang* to meet his needs. He prepares mattress (*khayarcha*) for sitting and sleeping and other daily use items made from goat hairs are ropes and bags.

Dag Po and his Palas

There is also a system of hiring a person as *zet sa*. This person is called *palas*. This palas respectfully calls his *zet sa* the owner of the flocks, his *dag po*. A person who grazes other's *kim zet* is *kim zet palas* and the one who grazes other's *arung zet* is the *arung zet palas*. Whether one herds his sheep and goats or the others' he is called a *zet palas*. The *dag po* gives the *palas* a fixed salary, food and shoes. The tradition of giving clothes to *palas* is rare. Only that person becomes a *palas* of other's flocks, the one who wants to become *zet sa* one day. Therefore, the *palas* of a *zet sa* never takes cash for his services, but he always takes sheep and goats, the *sar unnu*. The *sar* of a *palas* depends upon his services. According to the custom, the *dag po* gives about eight pregnant goat and sheep to the *palas* as a *sar*. There was a system of giving *pangrang* in place of *sar* to a new *palas*. In *pangrang* tradition, the *palas* gets only the kids for his services but not the mothers.

In case the sheep or goats, that the *palas* receives as *sar* or *pangrang* dies or goes stray, the *dag po* does not give him any compensation. The *dag po* bears all the expenses of rearing goats given to *palas* as *sar* or *pangrang*. A *palas* sometimes takes his *sar* of several years together at the very beginning. A *palas* performs all the duties of a *zet sa*. The superior *palas* is the one where the *dag po's* interference is minimum. A *dag po* may not remain with the sheep and goats. In this case the *palas* keeps all account of the income and expenditure about the sheep and goats. The honesty and efficiency of a *palas* are crucial for his prosperous future. A good *palas* always strives for his bright future and therefore pleases his *dag po* by his honesty and efficiency. A *dag po* always wishes the bright future of his *palas*, besides that he praises the good qualities of his *palas* everywhere. The praise of the *palas* by his *dag po* increases the value of a *palas* among the *zet sa*. A *dag po* always longs for such a *palas*. An honest *palas* is a source of inspiration for the other *palas* in the pastoral community. The dream of a *palas* is to become one day a *dag po*.

A superior *dag po* is one who remains always with his sheep and goats. He at times goes with his *palas* to graze the sheep and goats. A superior *dag po* is one who considers his *palas* a member of the family and takes care of his good and bad, equally. He is the one who is always ready to give directions for the improvement of the business of sheep and goats. A good *dag po* always goes to settle the disputes of damage done to villager's orchards and crops by sheep and goats. Although, the *palas* performs the main task of grazing sheep and goats, the *dag po* looks after several other duties. A *dag po* maintains dynamic relationships with the forest officials, local administrators and the local village community in winter pasture. He arranges ration for the *palas*, procures a grazing permit, manages extra pasture for the winter from local people, and negotiates with buyers of wool, sheep and goats. The maintenance of cordial relations with the local community around the winter pasture is an important task of a *dag po*. The pastoralism requires maintenance of dynamic relationships with all kinds of people. The *palas* of a superior *dag po* never deserts him.

Zet sa's Faithful Dogs

A *zet palas* takes special care at night to avoid the attacks on sheep and goats by predators such as leopard, bear and wolf. He is always alert. The faithful dogs of the *zet sa* help him in protecting the sheep and goats from predatory animals. These good dogs move around the camp during whole night. They do not allow any animal to approach the camp. These dogs even challenge the leopards. The *zet sa* ties a wide and thorny iron belt around the dog's neck so that it is not easy for the predators to bite it in the neck and kill. While moving on roads, the dogs are intelligent enough not to attack unknown persons. If somebody attempts to pick up his master's luggage, he can never escape from these ferocious dogs. Some dogs always accompany the sheep and goats. The *zet sa* ties them in the camp only under compulsion. A dog is like a *zet palas*. In the forest, the dog keeps an eye on the predators that may pick up sheep or goat. Whenever a *zet sa* buys a dog pup from another *zet sa*, a thorough checking takes place. First, he ascertains the strain of the pup's mother. If she is of a good variety, the *zet sa* continues to test the pup. The *zet sa* picks up the pup by the ear. If the pup cries due to pain, it is a disqualification. However, if the pup starts growling instead of crying, he buys that pup. A *zet sa* cuts the tip of pup's tail so that it becomes fluffy with long and dense hair. The pup receives toilet training so that the camp is clean and the pup goes for toilet away from the camp. To achieve it, the *zet sa* brings soil from a distant place or from a hillock and feeds it to the pup with milk. This takes place only once when the pup is given food for the first time after birth. He believes that by doing so the dog never spoils the camp. To make his dog ferocious or *chikhul*, the *zet sa* keeps it all the time tied by the chain. The *zet sa* never forgets to tie the mouth of such a *chikhul* dog while moving on the road so that it does not bite an unknown passer by.

The *zet sa* never feeds his dogs by the legs, limbs and other parts of a dead goat or sheep without roasting it. He gives the other viscera of the sheep and goat to the dog only after some roasting. After such an experience the dog even refuse to smell a fresh hide of sheep or goat. A *zet sa* never gives his dog the *peechh*, the starchy residue extracted from cooked rice. If a dog drinks the *peechh* his hairs fall and he may develop some disease.

Identification of Sheep and Goats

A *zet palas* keeps an account of the total number of sheep and goats. He classifies them into sheep, goats, rams, bucks, young ones, pregnant sheep and goats, and the non-pregnant sheep and goats. He counts his sheep and goats at regular intervals to see if any animal is missing from the flock. If some sheep or goat is missing, the *zet sa* immediately does not start a search for it. First, he finds out who is missing? He ascertains the identity of missing animal by its external features, particularly the shape, size, face, colour, and horns. This method of identification is *bal-shes-mu* in the local dialect. A *zet palas* who is unable to identify his sheep and goats, falls down in the eyes of the *zet sa*.

In Kanaor each *zet sa* has hundreds of sheep and goats. Therefore, it is difficult even for the experienced people to differentiate the animals of a flock, particularly when they get mixed with animals of other flock. Each family has its own identification mark for his flock members. A *zet sa* tattoos this mark on the ears of his sheep and goats and the other animals at the age of about six months. The tattooing of ear of animals is called *sar-shan-nu*.

A *zet sa* is able to tell the age of his animals with great accuracy. He does not assess the age of a sheep or goat by its external features, rather ascertains the age of an animal from its teeth. It is important for a *zet sa* for keeping the age wise record of the sheep and goats. The knowledge of age of his sheep and goats is also essential for a *zet sa* from his business viewpoint, that is when he has to sell or buy a sheep or goat. For regulating the size of his flock a *zet sa* needs to know the age of his sheep and goats so that he can discard the aged members.

Strong Belief in his Deity

There is hardly any village in Kanaor, where people do not have faith in the family deity, village deity, monastery and the monks. However, the belief of a *zet sa* in his deity is a thing of admiration. Early in the morning after cleaning himself, the *zet palas* remembers the names of his deities and prays to them for the safety and good of his sheep and goats as well as his home and family. They also pay respect to other village's deities. When he recalls the gods and goddesses of Kanaor and prays to them, the *zet sa* also recalls the gods and goddesses that are from other areas outside the Kanaor. He firmly believes that his prosperity and happiness lies in the blessings of gods and goddesses. Therefore, every *zet sa* has three to four male goats in the name of his deities.

In local tradition, keeping male goats in the names of deities is *shoo-pang-thapana-ran-nu*. One of the male goats, black in colour, is in the name of *Kali*. The other two male goats are white in colour; one is for the family deity and other for the monastery. A *zet sa* may keep a white male goat in the name of *Kali*, if the black male goat is not in his flock. There may be difference among the *zet sa* for keeping male goats in the name of local deities. Some *zet sa* keep two but may keep more also. However, each *zet sa* keeps at least two male goats in the name of their deities, one for the *Kali* and the other for the family deity.

The *zet sa* neither cuts the hair of these male goats nor does he sell them. When the *zet sa* replaces those male goats kept in the name of his deities by new ones, he can then sell the earlier ones. On the special occasions, the *zet sa* worships these male goats kept in the name of his deities with full honour, complete devotion as if the original gods and goddesses were present. He prepares the necessary items of worship in separate plates according to the requirements of different deities. The main items necessary for the worship of deities is *por-sat*, *loochee* and *kaleeu rot*. He puts small amount of butter on all these items. Then he takes *dhoopang khoningch*, puts some pieces of burning charcoal in it, and over it he places some dhoop and butter. He keeps these worshipping items at a place that he prepares and cleans for this occasion. Then he brings the deity goats to that place. The *zet sa* washes the hoofs, ears and horns with clean water. He puts the symbol of purity, the butter, on their forehead and horns. He prays before them, giving smell of dhoop, for the prosperity and good of his sheep and goats and his family and the home. After sprinkling water on the deity goats, he leaves them. If the deity goats shake themselves, the *zet sa* feels extremely happy. It symbolizes that all the prayers of the *zet sa* are accepted by the deities and they are happy with him. After that with extreme happiness the *zet sa* performs the worship of each deity by taking respective plate in hand. He performs a similar ritual when he wants to sell the deity's goat. He brings a new male goat to replace the former deity goat and worships him. In the end, he sprinkles water on the new male goat. If the new male goat shakes his body, it symbolizes particular deity's acceptance of the new male goat.

After overcoming the fear of the unknown, the *zet sa* embarks upon his journey with the sheep and goats under the open sky. In the lonely forests among predatory animals, and in the high altitude pastures where weather is always uncertain, the only companion of a *zet sa* is his belief in the gods and goddesses. At any uncertain situation where he does not find a solution to cope up with the problem, the *zet sa* keeps a coin in the name of a deity. Finally, it is the inner self that provides him strength and courage. The *zet sa* never forgets to obey his words given to his deities. On reaching his village it is his first task to accomplish such vows by paying visit to the village deity in his temple. He longs for the glance of his deity.

An Arung Zet Sa's Place in the Society

The people of Kanaor address the *zet sa* by *shalang-sa*, a symbolic word for prosperity. These people who always live with their flocks of sheep and goats are the *shala-pa*. The return of *shala-pa* from the winter pasture is an auspicious occasion. The *kim mi* become extremely happy on the arrival of these people in the village. This wave of joy engulfs the whole society to which the *zet sa* belongs. Some members of *arung zet sa* family and relatives may come far away from their village with delicious edibles to receive the *zet sa*. The *talang sa* and other *kim mi* go in the fields to look after the *arung zet* and at night, the *arung* family comes to meet the *kim* family at their home. The *talang se* tries everything to serve the *arung* family in her traditional way. The comfortable arrival of *arung* members of the family, after about eight months, makes everybody in the family fill with a unique happiness.

On return from the winter pasture the *arung* members bring shoes and clothes for the *kim* members of the family and various other essential household items. An *arung* husband brings for his spouse things of her choice. It is hard to imagine the happiness of an *arung* family in the modern luxurious life of people.

There are several festivals such as *bhos* and *kangyur jalen* that villagers celebrate to welcome the arrival of *shala-pa* at home with the sheep and goats. The *bhos* (*bhoj*) means a communal feast. The villagers of Asrang organize it on 20 *Jayeshta*, when all the *shala-pa* arrives home with their *arung zet*. If the winter is longer, the grass also grows later at the village pasture. When the *shala-pa* reach after 20 *Jayeshta* in village, in such case the villagers delay the *bhos* also. Although the date of *bhos* shifts under certain circumstances, the festival takes place in *Jayeshta* only. Therefore, the local people call it "*Jayeshtang Bhos*." In this *bhos* festival all village families bring the flour of *phaphra* in a prescribed amount to the *santang*, the special place of village festival. In the evening the people used to prepare *badi* from the flour collected from all the families in *lamathu*, a big copper vessel. Then, they distribute the *badi* to all villagers. The people take out the village deity from the *shu-koti* (temple) to the *santang* for worship. The village deity expresses his happiness on the comfortable return of the *shala-pa* of his village and blesses them. After that all the people dance in the *santang*. The *shala-pa* expresses their happiness on the *bhos* organized in their welcome by dancing throughout the night.

There are different beliefs about the *kangyur jalen* festival in different villages of Kanaor. In Lippa village people take out the one hundred eight scriptures containing the Buddha's teachings from the monastery. All people carry the scriptures one each on their back with great devotion; take a round of the village and nearby land. In the evening they keep the *kangyur* in the courtyard of the monastery and all the villagers pay visits to it and bow down in respect. After that, they place the *kangyur* again in the monastery. In the night people perform dances in santang.

Besides this, the folk singers convey the people's respect and honour towards *shalang* or *shalang-sa* through their folk songs. Today also one can see that the people sing with great enthusiasm the folk songs composed in honour of the *shalang-sa*. Day by day as the time of the *arung zet sa's* movement to winter pasture approaches, the expressions of sorrow starts appearing on the faces of the *kim mi*. The departure of the *arung zet sa* coincides with the onset of fall in Kanaor. It is strange that on one side the *arung zet sa* leaves the village, the fall also sets in at the same time. The whole village looks as if it has withdrawn in itself after the departure of the *zet sa*. The hustle and bustle of the village goes away with the *zet sa* and his sheep and goats. The charm of the village vanishes. The sounds of the hundreds of sheep and goats and the melodious folk tunes that comes from the flute of the *zet palas* give way to silence. The only sound the *kim mi* hear is the cold wind blowing past the naked trees that increase their misery many folds.

The *talang-se* calls the tailor to prepare warm clothes for the *arung* members, a few days before they start for winter pasture. It is the responsibility of *talang-se* to see that the *arung* members have sufficient blankets and shawls for themselves. Along with it she visits the astrologer to find out an auspicious day for the departure of the *arung* members. On the day of the departure both the *arung* and the *kim* members of the family are very sad. The *talang se* gives new clothes to the arung members for wearing on that day. She tucks flowers in their caps. She fills their pockets with *moodi* (fried cereals) mixed with kernels of walnut, almond and *chilgoza*, some of the *moodi* she packs in the bag also. She visits the temples and monastery of the village early in the morning after taking bath and burns incense and lights lamp for the peace and protection of her *arung* members. The *talang sa* and *talang se* perform the worship of village deity and the *kim-shu* (family deity). She invites the lama or *jomo* (Buddhist nun) to perform a ritual by reading the scriptures to avoid any future bad omen. She prepares delicious food for the *arung* members of her family on that morning. When the *arung* members start from home, she keeps a vessel filled with water, a symbol of happy journey in Indian culture, at the side of the main gate of the house. She herself wears new clothes to see off the *arung* members. In her one hand, she takes a bronze plate with *tsogas* (conical shaped worshipping item) having butter on it for the *sauni*, the protectors of mountains. In her other hand, she takes a *dhoopdani* (a vessel for burning incense) for worship. With the other family members and the relatives she carries some luggage in the *shawl* on her back and walks ahead of the *zet sa* to see them off on an established spot. After some distance, she performs the prayer of the *sauni*. She quickly breaks a small pebble and then puts three stones in a pile. Then, she takes a small part of the *tsogas* and circling it over the heads of the arung members and the sheep and goats walking in front, throws it in three directions. This appeases the ghosts and witches so that they return to their places and do not follow the *arung* members. All members present at the spot distribute among themselves the remaining portion of the *tsogas* and eat it with heavy heart. It is natural because the next moment is of separation from each other. The separation is not for a few days or a month but it is for about eight months. This long separation is painful. After this, with tears in their eyes, the *arung mi* says *dam-toshirach* (take care) to the *kim mi* and other relatives. The *kim mi* and their relatives say *dam birach* (take care on the journey) to the *arung* members. With these departing words the *arung mi* and *kim mi* separate for a long period.

There is snow everywhere in winter in Kanaor. Furthermore, the snowy storms force the *kim* members within the four walls of their home. During this period all the time they remember their *arung* members. Some members who live at home may go to meet the *arung* members at *gun tsat* during the winter. The *talang se* cannot leave her responsibility to any other member, and go to meet the *arung* members. She has to stay at home and spin wool for the clothes of *arung* and *kim* members. The social structure never knows the agony of the heart of a *talang se*. She has to console herself, to habituate, and to surrender her to the responsibilities of the social system. Her social prestige and propriety lie in it.

If a crow caws, in winter, by sitting on the top of *darchhod* (flag) or some other part of the roof of the house, the *kim* members believe that a person may come from far or they may receive a letter. The only source of knowing about their *arung* members is through their letter or by the arrival of some person from *gun chat*. If a postman brings a letter, they verify if it is intact from all sides. Because, people believe that a letter intentionally torn from a corner indicates a bad news. If the letter is intact, a member of *kim-mi* reads it and other members sit around him to listen its contents. If no member knows reading, they take it to some other person in the village. (The reader may find in Chapter 4 and 5 more material about the patterns of attachment and separation.)

In winter, the *kim* members send *moodi* mixed with kernels of walnut, almonds, and *chilgoza*, if they find a person going towards the *guntsat* of their *arung* members. When half of the family members are in *guntsat*, the cawing by a crow in distasteful voice makes the *kim* members fearful. Especially the *talang se* becomes apprehensive and shivers in distress. The cawing of crow in an unusual voice signals a bad news. People call it "*tsang kag bashado*," a bad crow is cawing. If a jackal calls in the night near a house it is also a bad omen. All this narrates the story of the separation anxiety of the *kim mi*, especially the *talang se*. Besides that, the love and respect of the *talang se* and *kim mi* towards *arung* members are visible on the religious, social and cultural functions. Wherever the presence of arung members is essential, the *talang se* and *kim mi* keeps a sword to symbolize them and performs the functions. In the same way, on the occasion of religious and cultural ceremonies, the *kim* members put some butter on their forehead as symbol of goodwill. The *kim* members do not forget to put the butter on the *tagus* (a pole in the middle of the room) in the name of their *arung* members.

For an *arung zet sa*, the sky is the roof and the towering mountains are the walls. He always wants to roam freely in the bright sun and in the dense forest in the company of his sheep and goats. During heavy rain or snow, he takes shelter in natural caves and enjoys the warmth of his animals. Wherever he finds a green pasture for his sheep and goats, he stops. He digs a little in the ground, puts three stones around it and the kitchen is ready. After cooking whatever is in his *rubals*, the *arung zet sa* eats with great satisfaction. There is no animal in the forest that remains hidden from the keen senses of the *arung zet sa*. The wild animal has coexisted with the *arung zet sa's* sheep and goats. A forest gives him solace, inspires him to sing songs and arouses curiosity in him. The *arung zet sa* inculcates this thinking about the forest in his children also through his company and religious ceremonies.

7

Biological Aspects of Pastoralism

Chhaya Pirta and *Sonia Pakhretia**

The biological sciences have significantly contributed to the lives of pastoralists and their animals. Above all, it kindles a hope for the survival of this dying profession, even at this juncture when the once proud arung zet sa are on the verge of leaving it. For they are looked upon as 'tribals' or 'primitives' though serving the society with the provision of everyday needs. As if it is not enough, the champions of wildlife consider herds of sheep and goats as major hurdles for setting up preserves of wilderness. These issues may be resolved by conscientious biologists who adopt these mobile herds of sheep and goats as open-air laboratories.

The favourable environmental conditions, during early Holocene (10,000-7,000 cal years BP) probably facilitated the domestication of plants and animals, which in turn stimulated societies to engage in technical innovations (Gupta, 2004). Even though the domestication of livestock took place in prehistoric times, it is a recent event in the long history of man. Rees (1959) had earlier concluded that goats were probably domesticated 8,000 to 9,000 years ago, and cattle, sheep, and pigs some time thereafter around 5,000 to 6,000 years ago. The movement of human groups along with their flocks, due to seasonal changes in grazing areas, led to pastoral nomadism. The herds of sheep and goats provided milk, meat and wool. The relationship between humans and animals in India has been complementary and diverse. The various communities in India follow different patterns of subsistence, for example, there are hunter-gatherers, fishing communities, nomadic and sedentary pastorals, non pastoral nomads and agriculturalists (Gadgil and Malhotra, 1981). In Himachal Pradesh the density of livestock in the various districts is shown in Table 7.1.

* Chhaya Pirta, Department of Biosciences, and Sonia Pakhretia, Department of Psychology, Himachal Pradesh University, Shimla.

Taxonomy

Schaller (1977) has classified *Capra* (goat) and *Ovis* (sheep) genera under Subfamily Caprinae, and together with oxen they include most of the domesticated livestock. While describing the ecology and behaviour of these ungulates in the Himalayan region, Schaller observes that there must be striking ecological separation between *Ovis* and *Capra.* Where the two species occur together, the sheep occupy mainly the undulating terrain and the goats the precipices. In the domestic herds of sheep and goat, the herder is always conscious of grazing sheep and goats separately due to differences in their food preferences. They are also aware of the different terrains preferred by the sheep and goats.

All oxen, sheep and goats, domestic or wild, forms the Bondate (Prater 1960), a group of hoofed animals. It seems that the behaviour, and utility for human needs were the factors responsible for their domestication. The wild ancestors of sheep and goats in the Himalayan region are shapu or urial, nayan or Great Tibetan sheep, Marco Polo's sheep, bharal, ibex, wild goat, markhor and Himalayan tahr. According to taxonomists (Simpson, 1945) the sheep and goat belong to the Subfamily Caprinae, under the Family Bovidae. It is divided into fourteen genera, grouped under four tribes, one tribe Caprini has five genera (Figure 7.1).

Table 7.1: Area, Forests, Livestock and Human Population in Himachal Pradesh (Census of India 2001; Livestock Census in Himachal Pradesh 2003)

District	*Area (sq km)*	*Density of Humans Per sq km*	*Density of Livestock Per sq km*	*Tree Cover (sq km)*	*Density of Sheep Per sq km*	*Density of Goats Per sq km*
Hamirpur	1118	369	172.38	242	16.02	26.51
Bilaspur	1167	292	179.03	358	2.56	45.26
Una	1540	291	132.82	518	0.10	14.04
Solan	1936	258	165.23	819	2.22	34.85
Kangra	5739	233	154.29	1867	18.75	36.43
Mandi	3950	228	215.05	1648	32.87	48.03
Sirmour	2825	162	162.83	1379	6.28	49.14
Shimla	5131	141	102.82	2383	19.17	19.14
Chamba	6528	71	123.31	2413	43.10	28.31
Kullu	5503	69	70.23	1933	23.59	14.19
Kanaor	6401	13	21.28	613	11.62	5.41
Lahaul & Spiti	13835	2	5.53	180	2.99	0.76

The common ancestor of sheep and goat is the Barbary sheep, *Ammotragus lervia.* Both goats (genus *Capra*) and sheep (genus *Ovis*) share a series of characteristics with *Ammotragus*. Some authors suggest that Barbary sheep should be included in one of these genera. Barbary sheep does not have a goatee and like some sheep species they have a

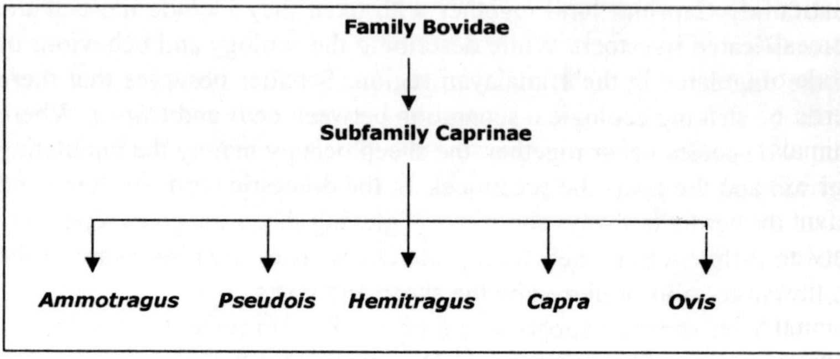

Fig. 7.1: The Classification of Family Bovidae

haired chin. But unlike sheep it lacks pre-orbital, inter-digital and flank glands. Therefore, morphologically Barbary sheep show intermediate characteristics of sheep and goats (Cassinello, 1998; Table 7.2).

Table 7.2: Differences between Sheep, Barbary Sheep and Goats

Phenotypic Character	*Ovis*	*Ammotragus*	*Capra*
Preorbital gland	Present	Absent	Absent
Foot glands	Present	Absent	Absent
Inguinal glands	Present	Absent	Absent
Sub caudal glands	Absent	Absent	Present
Chin beard	Absent	Absent	Present
No. of chromosomes	52 to 58	58	60

The two genera, *Ovis* and *Capra*, fall under the Suborder Ruminata, Family Bovidae and Subfamily Caprinae. *Ovis* can be distinguished from *Capra* by the presence of preorbital glands, inguinal glands and pedal glands on all feet. *Ovis* lacks callus on the knee, a potent body odour and a beard in males. The enamel folds on the molars of sheep bifurcate whereas those of goats do not. Goats have flat and rather long tails bare underneath in contrast to sheep. The horns of female goats tend to be proportionately larger than those of female sheep. In the genus *Capra*, horns provide the basic taxonomic character used in the classification of goats. On this basis Genus *Capra* is divided into six species, which are *Capra aegarus*, *Capra ibex*, *Capra falconeri*, *Capra pyrenaica*, *Capra cylindericornis*, *Capra hircus* (Schaller, 1977). In the Genus *Ovis*, there are six species: *Ovis canadensis*, *Ovis dalli*, *Ovis nivicola*, *Ovis ammon*, *Ovis orientalis* and *Ovis aries*.

Behavioural Taxonomy

Behaviour is a key to understand the life of living animals. This is particularly true for the moving herds of sheep and goats, though domesticated by man, but they live under naturalistic conditions. This mode of pastoralism is known as transhumance. For the management of herds of sheep and goats scientific studies on the behaviour of these animals are as much important as are physiological and anatomical studies. For example, the survival of a lamb or kid is dependent upon mother-infant affectionate relationship. Simultaneously interaction takes place between physiological states and behavioural states.

Investigators have found that the sense of smell is an important means of communication among sheep. Sheep have a scent gland situated in a shallow depression on the skull, just below the eye on the face. They also have a pair of glands in the groin known as inguinal glands, and a gland between the two main toes of the feet. The secretion of these foot glands by scenting the ground over which sheep and goats pass enables members of a scattered flocks to ascertain the whereabouts of their herd members. In the like manner groin glands of sheep are brought in contact of ground when they sit down to rest and their scent serves as a guide. Moreover, it is during this period that the infant becomes the part of social organization where different patterns of behaviour, innate or learned, mature to form normal social relationships. These patterns are important during interactions with age mates or adult members of the group. They are needed for escape from predators. It is through these behaviour patterns that the effective heterosexual relationships develop among adult males and females during mating season.

The objective recording of behaviour under natural and semi-natural conditions was pioneered by the ethologists. The measurement in each ethological investigation involves the ethogram, the precise catalogue of all the behaviour patterns of an animal (Eibl-Eibesfeldt, 1975). This is known as behavioural taxonomy. It consists of macro-units and micro-units of behaviour depending on the objectives of the study. These units of behaviour are recorded on observation sheets following different sampling techniques. A sample is a record of behaviour according to predefined rules. Each macro- or micro-unit of behaviour is defined on the basis of preliminary observations on particular species, on a group of identified individuals.

Some important categories of behaviour observed in sheep and goats by various investigators (McFarland, 1987; Smith, 1971; Stolba *et al.*, 1990) were used in some of our field work in the Himalayas. In our ethological study on sheep and goats we have used the following taxonomy of behaviour, (a) to make comparisons on general patterns of social and non social behaviours (Table 7.3), and, (b) to understand the maternal behaviour in these two species (Table 7.4).

(a) Macro-units of Behaviour to Record General Behavior patterns: 1. Grazing on hind legs. 2. Grazing at shoulder level. 3. Grazing head down. 4. Exploration. 5. Sheltering. 6. Moving alone. 7. Moving in contact/ proximity. 8. Resting alone. 9. Resting in contact/proximity. 10. Dominance. 11. Sexual behavior. 12. Mother-infant behavior. 13. Any other behavior.

(b) Micro-units of Behaviour to Record the Maternal Behaviour: 1. Approach. 2. Departure. 3. Social-grooming. 4. Suckling. 5. Aggressive. 6 Bleats Low Pitched. 7. Bleats High Pitched. 8. Smelling. 9. Tongue manipulation of palate. 10. Udder acceptance. 11. Udder rejection. 12. Resting in contact/proximity. 13. Any other social beahviour.

Table 7.3: Comparison of Goats and Sheep having Females in Each Group 10 Adult Males and 10 Adult

Macro-units of Behaviour	*Goats(Mean±SD)*	*Sheep (Mean±SD)*	*t-ratios (p)*
Grazing on Hind Legs	24.65±12.82	00.20±00.41	08.52 (.01)
Grazing at Shoulder Level	63.00±18.73	00.45±00.94	14.92 (.01)
Grazing Head Down	00.20±00.52	89.70±13.80	29.10 (.01)
Exploration	11.70±05.95	07.15±03.92	02.90 (.01)
Sheltering	01.80±05.53	00.65±01.50	00.90 (.50)
Moving Alone	07.25±05.23	03.35±02.90	02.90 (.01)
Moving in Contact/Proximity	05.15±02.90	08.60±03.12	03.64 (.01)
Resting Alone	02.55±05.45	00.75±03.12	01.28 (.50)
Mother-Infant Behaviour	00.70±01.22	02.05±03.72	01.54 (.50)
Any Other Behaviour	02.50±02.37	02.30±01.55	00.31 (n.s.)

Table 7.4: Comparison of the Maternal Behaviour in Goats and Sheep, Each Group having 10 Mother-Infant Pairs for Observation

Micro-units of Behaviour	*Goats (Mean±SD)*	*Sheep (Mean±SD)*	*t-ratios (p)*
Approach	02.70±01.70	05.30±02.62	2.62 (.05)
Departure	06.00±02.53	02.60±01.50	3.64 (.01)
Social Grooming	00.50±01.51	00.60±01.57	0.18 (n.s.)
Suckling	45.70±08.53	47.20±11.35	0.33 (n.s.)
Bleats Low Pitched	03.60±10.00	00.60±01.07	3.77 (.01)
Bleats High Pitched	00.20±00.67	04.30±03.77	3.41 (.01)
Smelling	02.00±05.51	03.10±01.37	2.01 (.10)
Tongue Manipulation of Palate	01.60±04.57	03.70±03.16	1.89 (.10)
Udder Acceptance	03.40±09.31	05.60±02.17	2.72 (.01)
Udder Rejection	04.70±13.00	01.60±00.96	3.45 (.01)
Resting in Contact/Proximity	31.30±12.17	19.50±12.32	2.15 (.05)
Any Other Social Behaviour	10.00±27.90	20.80±12.10	2.45 (.05)

These observations are on feral herds of transhumant sheep and goats in the Bharmour region of Himachal Pradesh. The data were collected over a period of one month while the herds were moving towards summer pastures along the Ravi river. On general patterns of behaviour, sheep and goats show significant differences on 9 macro-units. There are no observations on three behavior units in goats and sheep since they require observations over a long period. For example, sheep graze head down where as the goats graze at shoulder level. These two behavior units have the highest frequencies. It is only goats who graze on hind legs. The sheep and goats differ in maternal behaviour on 10 micro-units. For example, sheep show more udder acceptance than the goats. Though suckling is most frequent behavior but the two species do not differ in it. In social grooming also the two species are similar but the frequency is very low. The aggressive behavior is rare.

Reproduction and Lamb or Kid Rearing

The Female Reproductive Organs

The structure of the female reproductive system is shown in the Figure 7.2. There is a pair of ovaries where the female gametes, the eggs or ova, are

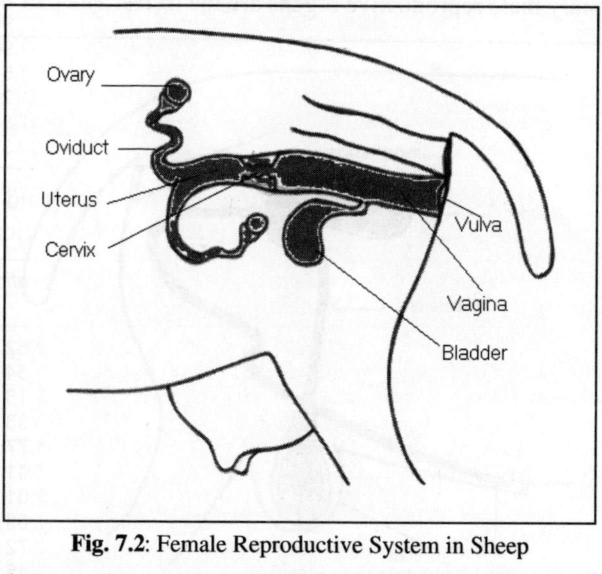

Fig. 7.2: Female Reproductive System in Sheep

produced. From the ovaries they move down the oviduct or fallopian tube and reach the uterus. If fertilization occurs, the embryo implants in the wall of the uterus and grows there until birth. Uterus is joined to the vagina by a narrow region called cervix. Vagina opens to the exterior by the vulva, which is the common opening for the excretory and the reproductive systems.

The females mate when they are in oestrus or heat. Ewes, which are not pregnant, come into oestrus on an average every seventeen days, however the cycle may vary in different regions. The does on the other hand come into oestrus at about 21-day intervals. During oestrus the vulva gets swollen and reddish and there is discharge of mucus. Ram (or a buck) notices the signs of oestrus by smell. The non-pregnant females, which do not show oestrus cycle, are said to be anoestrus. The ewe lamb reaches the stage of puberty at the time when oestrus cycle begins. In the well-fed lambs puberty comes at nine months. In the females the reproductive cycle and pregnancy are controlled by hormones principally estrogen, progesterone, FSH or follicle stimulating hormone, LH or lutenizing hormone, prolactin and prostaglandin. These hormones are produced in the ovaries, pituitary glands and uterus.

The Male Reproductive Organs

The structure of male reproductive system is shown in the Figure 7.3. The primary male reproductive organs are the testes. The pair of testis

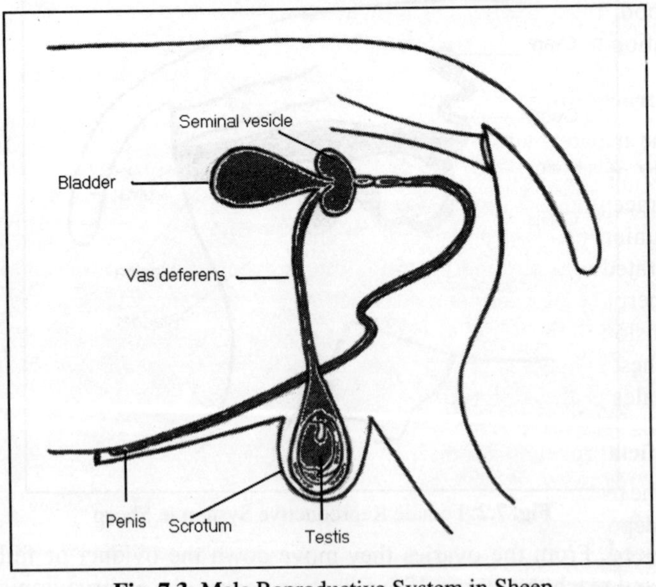

Fig. 7.3: Male Reproductive System in Sheep

lies in the scrotal sac, which hangs beneath the abdomen. Male gametes, the sperms, are produced in the testes and stored in the epididymis. At the time of mating, sperms are propelled with fluids, the semen, and the penis ejaculates it into the reproductive tract of the ewe. The age when the ram lamb is ready to mate is known as puberty. Primary and secondary sexual organs are fully developed at this stage. The puberty occurs at about four months under intensive management and at about two years in the extensive systems. The testosterone is the major hormone responsible for sperm production and sexual behaviour of male sheep and goats.

Mating

Characteristic mating behaviour patterns are seen in both males and females. The female sheep or goat encourages its male counterpart by shaking her tail, urinating, and looking back over her shoulder, nuzzling his scrotum and standing still for mating. The male responds to the urination of the oestrous female by sniffing, extending the lip and curling the lip. The tongue goes in and out and the male may bite the female's wool and raise the lower part of the front leg. If the female is receptive she will stand for copulation. The ram or a buck finally mounts the female and ejaculates into the vagina. Mating efficiency is affected by the shortage of food, thus making the females disperse into small groups. In this situation the females are difficult to locate (Ortman, 2000).

Contraception

In the management of sheep and goat herd size as well as to keep the purity of stock intact, the herders are very particular in using various contraceptive techniques. Contraception is the prevention of conception, the union of male and female gametes. Either males and female are separated or traditional method of contraception is used. In this method the perpuce of male animal is tied to the scrotum, which prevents the extension of the penis. A leather or plastic apron can also be tied under the chest of males to prevent copulation. Permanent method like castration of males is also followed.

Artificial Insemination

It is the technique in which semen is collected from a male and after dilution it is deposited in the vaginal canal of the female. The major advantage of this technique is that semen from selected males is collected and is used for a large number of females in the widely dispersed regions of the world. It is easier and cheaper to import frozen semen than to import live animals.

Semen is collected when the male mounts a dummy animal and ejaculates into an artificial vagina. After that semen is evaluated in terms of volume, concentration, motility and morphology of sperm. Semen is then diluted ten times and used to inseminate large number of females.

Pregnancy

The average duration of pregnancy in sheep is about 150 days. Pregnant sheep or goat must be given enough food so that proper development of fetus takes place. Generally sheep or goats give birth to one young one each. However, sometimes they may give birth to twins or triplets; in certain areas, such as Kanaor, birth of twins to sheep is inauspicious. Energy requirements for those bearing twins and triplets are greater than those bearing single fetus. Poor diet of female animal leads to low birth weight of kids or lambs and low milk yield. It can also lead to a fatal disease known as pregnancy toxemia.

Lambing or Kidding

At the time towards the end of pregnancy the udder swells. It is seen that two days before lambing the concentration of progesterone hormone falls in the blood and the concentration of estrogen rises. Once close to giving birth to the young one the pregnant doe or ewe retires to isolated place, away from the rest of the group. The flock should be moved as little as possible during the time of lambing or kidding. After few seconds of birth the mother begins to lick and smell the placenta and then the young one. This phenomenon is called 'bonding' and helps her identify her kid or lamb (Oltenacu, 1999). After the newborn kid is strong enough to stand it immediately searches for doe's udder. While suckling, the kid wags its tail and the doe intermittently sniffs under the kid's tail. This strengthens the bonding. In the same way, the lamb also locates the teats of its mother within 1-2 hours of birth, and visual cues are important in this process (Bareham, 1975).

Maternal Behaviour

A healthy lamb or kid is large and has enough colostrum to feed upon. The digestive system of a newborn functions differently from that of the adults. The newborn digests food in the abomasum not in the rumen. For this reason the young ones are unable to digest fibrous food such as grass and therefore must have highly digestible food such as milk. The growth rate of the young one increases with the milk intake. For similar reason, the single lamb or kid grows faster than the twins. As the lambs get older their capacity to drink milk also increases however after 2-3 weeks the mothers are not able to produce enough milk to fill the needs of growing lambs. After reaching two weeks of age the lamb begins to nibble solid food and its rumen begins to develop. So to satisfy its food requirement lamb is provided grass or fodder. And once the lamb starts eating solid food it needs water. But the doe automatically weans her kid at six months to an year of age. She accomplishes this by actively rejecting the suckling attempts of her grown up kid (Oltenacu, 1999).

The herders are very careful about the formation of mother's attachment with the new born infant. They even carry the new born infant in their bodices to keep them warm while the herd is on the move. Biologists have found that hybridisation between different local populations can sometimes destroy the locally adapted gene complex. For example, Grieg (1979) observed that in an attempt to raise hybrids of two ibex species, the kids of hybrids were born in February which is the coldest month of the year in Czechoslovakia and as a consequence the entire population went extinct. In such cases behavioural technology is useful.

It involves the objective recording of behaviour under natural and seminatural conditions (see Table 7.4). The basis for such ethological investigation is the ethogram, the precise catalogue of all the behaviour patterns of an animal (Eibl-Eibesfeldt, 1975). Investigators have prepared ethograms for naturalistic observations on sheep and goats (McFarland, 1987; Smith, 1971; Stolba *et al.*, 1990).

Lambe, Conington, Bishop, Waterhouse and Simm (2001) studied maternal behaviour in Scottish black face sheep. The ewe behaviour was quantified by maternal behaviour score (MBS). It was found that MBS is a heritable trait in the Scottish black face ewe. On the basis of the MBS certain ewes can be separated who do not take care of their lambs. These lambs perhaps die due to the deficiency in maternal behaviour. In another study Hernandez, Delgadillo, Serafin, Rodriguez and Poindron (2004) observed olfactory recognition of young in nursing goats. They also found a period of postpartum anoestrous whose duration depended on the presence of kid.

The nose of sheep consists of two blind ending, epithelial-lined tubes. The tubes are situated on either side of the base of the nasal septum and each is enclosed in a "C" shaped cartilage. The rostral portion of each tube opens into the nasoincisive duct, which communicates with both the nasal and oral cavities. This forms the vomeronasal organ. According to Booth and Katz (2000), offspring recognition via olfaction in most female animals is believed to be based upon the offsprings' individual olfactory signature, which emanates from its body coat, but more specifically from the anal region.

Physiology of Wool

Wool fibers and hair grow in the follicles of the skin. Follicles are the saccular tube like structures present in the outer layer of sheep's skin. There are two types of follicles in the skin of sheep and goats. These are the primary follicles and the secondary follicles. Primary follicles are those, which produce hair and coarse wool. Secondary follicles are those, which are smaller and produce wool (Figure 7.4). These follicles mostly develop before a lamb is born and after the birth the number of follicles remain constant. However, it is seen that the wool production increases in the first few years because both the wool fibre diameter and the growth rate increases. The pre-wool cells are similar to the other body cells.

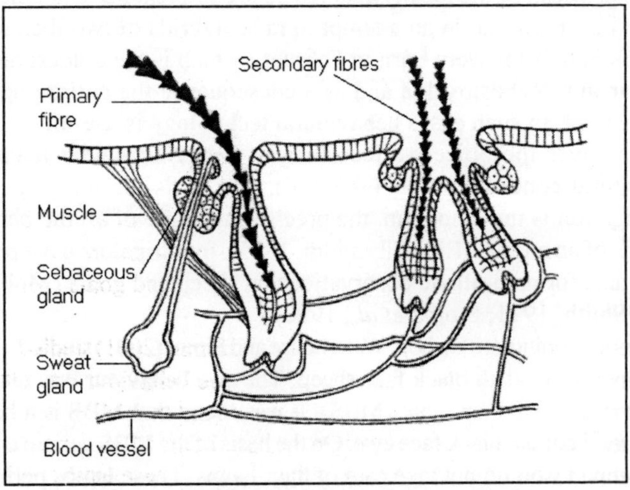

Fig. 7.4: Vertical Section of the Skin of Sheep

They form new cells near the follicle and the older cells are forced outwards through the follicle channels. During this passage the cells die, some of them elongate and form the core of the fibre, whereas others flatten to form the cover of the fibre. The outer covering made up of flattened cells are commonly called scales. They are associated with a very important property of the wool fibres known as felting, which means entanglement of fibres with each other (Lundgren, 1966).

The elastic and soft nature of the wool depends upon the architecture of the cortex of the fibre. The cortex or the heart of the wool fibre consists of spindle like cells or fibrils, made up of the coiled, threadlike keratin molecules. Similar keratin molecules are the building blocks from which hair, feathers, nails, skin, horns and hoofs are made. The fibrils are embedded in amorphous cementing material, which has higher sulphur content. This architecture of the heart of the wool is important to understand the quality of wool—its crimp—the softness of the fibre. The hydrogen bridges cement the coils together back to back. Groups of cells are tied together by two sulphur atoms of a disulphide bridge (Figure 7.5). Wool products are improved through the modification of the physical and molecular structure of the fibre.

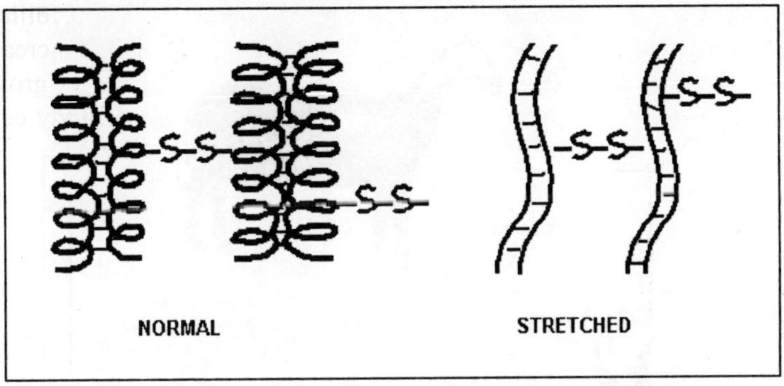

Fig. 7.5: The Heart of Wool Fibre: Internal Structure of a Wool Fibre

Health and Diseases

Disease usually results from a combination of factors including inadequate feeding and a low standard of management. The productivity of sheep or goats is lowered if they are not healthy. A sick animal behaves in a different manner from the rest of the flock and good shepherds notice such changes in sheep or goats. The most important symptoms are that the sick animal often stays alone, lies down while the others are grazing, and usually stops foraging. Other symptoms are thinness, low productivity, rough coat and diarrhoea. There are many diseases that affect sheep and goats. Generally the internal parasites cause maximum economic loss. The characteristics and life cycles of the internal parasites are described here to introduce pastoralists to these worms that affect their livestock.

Internal Parasites

Helminths, which include round worms, liver flukes, schistosomes and tapeworms, are the major internal parasites of sheep and goats.

Nematodes or roundworms, which live in the digestive tract of sheep and goats, are a major cause of poor productivity and sometimes mortality. Acute cases often lead to death. The life cycle of nematodes in infected animals is shown in Figure 7.6. The adult worms reside in the digestive tract of the infected animal. They lay eggs in the abomasum. The eggs are passed out of the body along with the faeces. The eggs hatch and develop through three larval stages on the pasture. Sheep and goats grazing infected pastures ingest the larvae along with the vegetation. The larvae then develop into egg laying adults in the digestive tract and the cycle goes on.

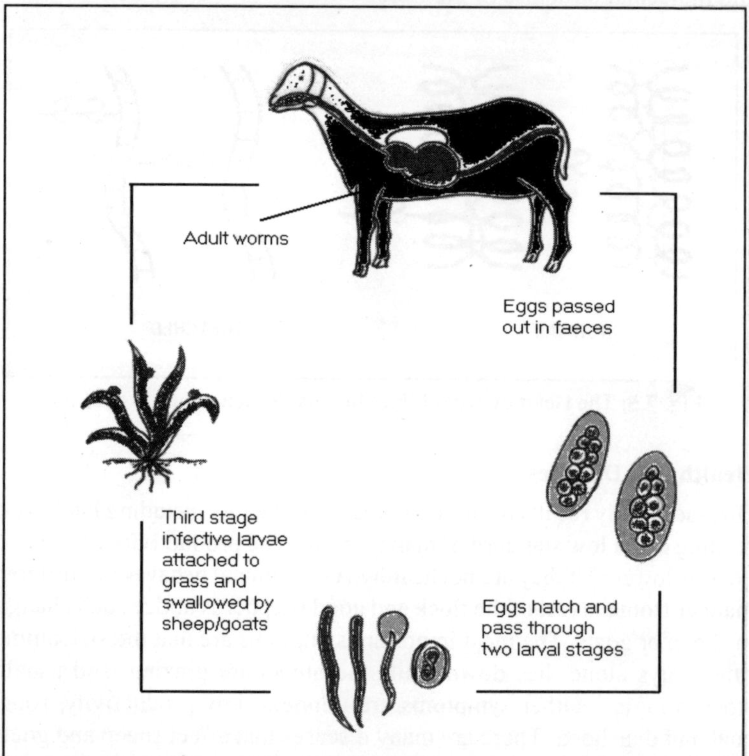

Fig. 7.6: Life Cycle of Roundworms in Sheep

Young sheep or goats are more susceptible than older animals. The infection is low in the migratory flocks, and pastures grazed by cattle are notably safe for sheep and goats.

Liver flukes, *Fasciola gigantica* and *Fasciola hepatica* are the common flatworms present in herbivorous animals like sheep, goats and cattle. Stages of life cycle of liver fluke are shown in Figure 7.7. They live in the biliary passages of the liver. They are occasionally found in man. Sheep and goats with acute infection die soon and chronic infections result in poor body condition. They are the definitive or primary hosts in which the parasite reproduces sexually. Whereas snail of genus *Lymnaea* acts as the intermediate host in which the larval stages of the parasite takes shelter. The adult liver fluke lays eggs in the body of the animal from where these eggs pass out along with the faeces. The egg hatches outside in the open and miracidium larva comes out. Then the miracidium larva

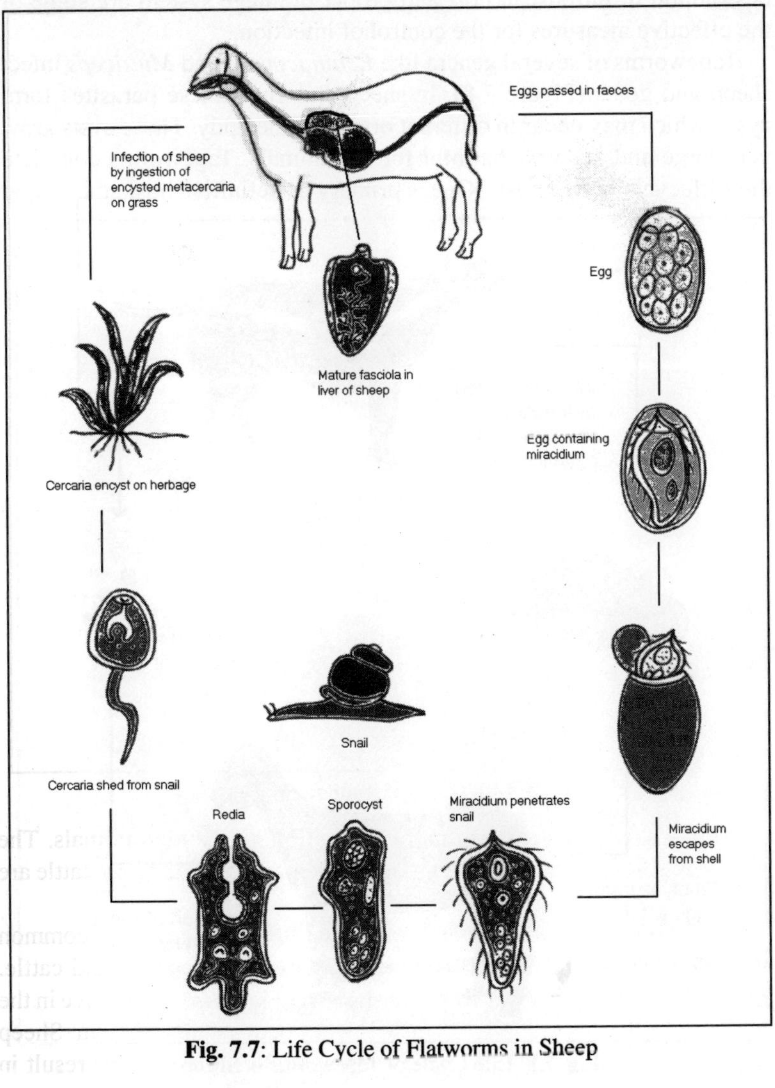

Fig. 7.7: Life Cycle of Flatworms in Sheep

penetrates the body of a snail where it undergoes further transformation through sporocyst, redia and cercaria larval stages. Cercaria larvae are then shed from snail's body and they encyst in the form of metacercaria on the herbage. Encysted metacercaria reaches inside the body of sheep or goat when they feed on infected herbage. Inside the body of animal metacercaria transforms into adult and starts laying eggs. Prevention by destruction of molluscan host and proper drainage system are some of the effective measures for the control of infection.

Tapeworms of several genera like *Echinococcus* and *Multiceps* infect sheep and goats (Figure 7.8). In sheep and goats these parasites form cysts, which may occur in different organs of the body. These cysts grow very large and are very harmful for the animals. Tapeworms complete their lifecycle in two hosts. One is primary or definitive host and second

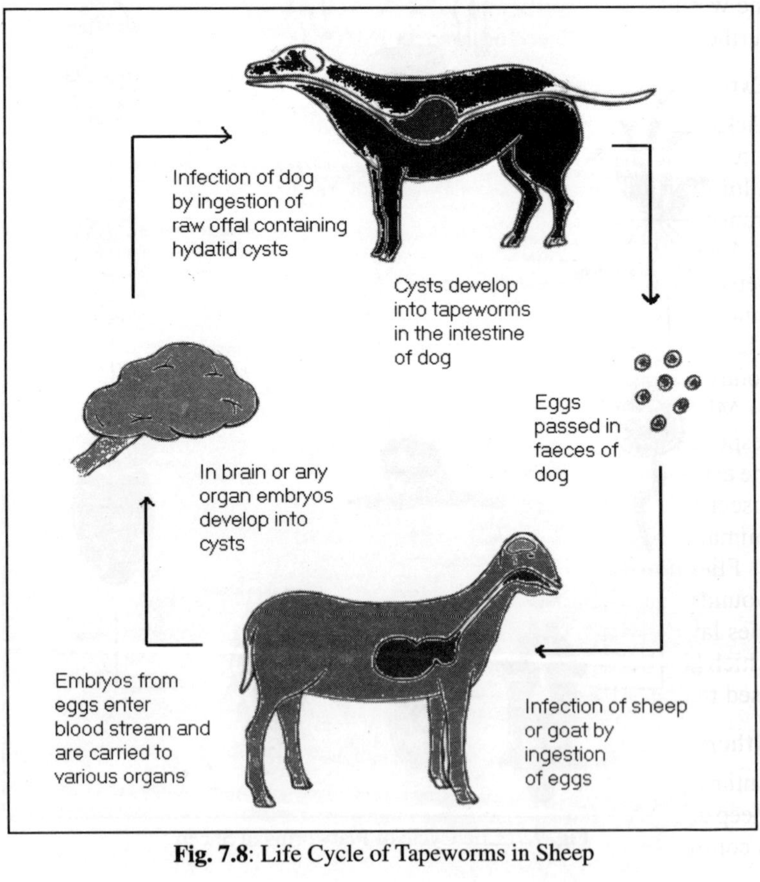

Fig. 7.8: Life Cycle of Tapeworms in Sheep

is secondary or intermediate host. Dog acts as the definitive host in the parasite's lifecycle whereas sheep or goat acts as intermediate host in the lifecycle of tapeworms. Adult worms reside in the small intestine of the dogs and lay eggs there. Eggs pass out of the body in dog's faeces. Infection in sheep and goats occur when they ingest eggs orally while grazing in the fields where dogs have defecated. Eggs hatch inside their body and embryos migrate into different regions of the body where they change into hydatid cysts. Hydatid cysts can be seen in the various organs like lungs, liver, kidney, muscles and brain of the infected animal. Dogs get infection by eating the dead carcasses of these animals. Therefore, to break the lifecycle dogs should be prevented from eating the dead carcasses of infected livestock.

Lungworms are also roundworms, which reside in the lungs of sheep. *Dictyocaulus filaria* is the most damaging lungworm. Sheep lose most of the worms within two months of infection and thereafter are resistant to further infection. Therefore, most problems are seen in the young ones.

External Parasites

Ticks are a serious problem for sheep, goats and other livestock. They bite the animal usually in the ears and between the hind legs. This causes a lot of irritation and loss of blood. Besides this many species of ticks transmit various diseases. Insecticides destroy the ticks.

Lice is a small wingless insect. It resides on the skin of the animal in between the hair. Lice bites on the skin and suck the blood. It causes so much irritation that a sheep or a goat rubs its body against solid objects. Lice develop under unhygienic and overcrowded rearing. It can be controlled by insecticide dust, which penetrates down to the skin of animal.

Mites are other very serious parasites of the farm animals. They are responsible for a condition known as mange in the livestock animals. In the arid regions head mange is a very serious problem in sheep. Applying insecticide as dust or spraying on the body of animal, or dipping the animal in insecticide solution can control it.

Flies bite the skin of animal and also feed on mucous membranes and wounds. Various flies also act as carriers of several diseases. Several flies lay their eggs on the animal's body. These eggs develop into larvae which later feed on the animal causing much damage. Insecticides can be used to control them.

Other Diseases

Anthrax is an acute disease, symptoms include fever, and then death in sheep and goats. It is caused by the bacteria *Bacillus anthracis*. The disease is controlled by vaccination.

Brucellosis disease affects both sheep and goats and is caused by the bacteria *Brucella melitensis*. This disease can spread to humans and cause undulant fever. In sheep it causes abortions. Vaccination is useful in the prevention of the disease.

Pneumonia is the inflammation of the lungs caused by bacteria, viruses or other factors. It is seen that goats are more susceptible to pneumonia than sheep.

Sheep pox is a disease caused by a virus, which affects only sheep and goats. The other animals suffer from other poxes. In acute cases there is fever and discharge from nose and eyes. Blisters appear on the mouth, nose, udder and between the legs. Young ones and imported breeds are most seriously affected.

Tetanus, also known as lockjaw, affects many animals including man. It is caused by the bacterium *Clostridium tetani*. This bacterium infects wounds and produces toxin, which affects the muscles. Control includes hygienic management to prevent infection of wounds.

Foot and mouth disease is caused by a virus. Although it is not a serious problem in the local breeds of sheep and goats, but when imported breeds are infected they suffer from fever, lesions on mouth and feet, loss of appetite, abortion and sometimes death in young animals. Vaccination against the appropriate strain of virus can give immunity for up to six months.

Blue tongue is a viral disease that spreads by an insect called *Culicoides vector*. This insect bites some carrier animal usually a cow and then transmits the virus to sheep. The sheep develops symptoms of the disease, starting with an increase in temperature, boils on the gums/tongue and later redness and watering of eyes. Accumulation of venous blood in tongue gives the disease its name. Blue tongue is controlled by vaccination.

Enterotoxaemia are disorders caused by *Clostridium perfringens* in the digestive tract of the animal. They include pulpy kidney and lamb dysentery. Great losses occur in the flocks due to the rapid death of animals.

Biotechnology

Biotechnology is broadly defined as technologies, which involve the use of living organisms or products from living organisms for the benefit of humans. Basically there are two techniques, which are used for the genetic manipulation of the livestock animals. These techniques include the recombinant DNA technology used in the production of transgenic animals and the controversial technique of mammalian cloning.

Transgenic Animals

Transgenic organism contains recombinant DNA that has been integrated into their genome (Brooker, 2005). The gene is introduced into the genome by transfection method. This genetic modification of livestock animals, particularly sheep and goats, aims at improving their milk, meat and wool production. Human growth hormone gene has been introduced in sheep in order to promote growth and meat production. The transgenic animals show improvements in body weight gain, feed efficiency, lean meat/fat ratio, fat composition etc. Several bacterial genes like *cysE* and *cysM* (genes concerned with cysteine) have also been introduced in sheep for the improvement of wool production and quality. Molecular farming or gene farming is a new avenue of research that involves the production of medically important proteins in the mammary glands of livestock (Table 7.3).

Table 7.5: Proteins Obtained from Milk of Sheep and Goats by Molecular Farming

Protein	*Host*	*Use*
Tissue Plasminogen Activator (TPA)	Goat	Dissolves blood clot
Alpha-1-antitrypsin	Sheep	Treatment of emphysema
Factor IX	Sheep	Treatment of certain inherited forms of hemophilia

Several human proteins have been successfully produced in the milk of domestic animals of sheep and goat. To introduce a human gene into an animal so that encoded protein will be secreted into its milk, the strategy is to clone the gene next to a milk-specific promoter. In mammals certain genes express themselves only in mammary glands and thus their protein product goes directly into milk. They include genes encoding for â-lactoglobulin, casein and whey acidic proteins. To express a human gene that encodes a protein hormone into a domestic animal's milk, the promoter and regulatory sequences for a milk-specific gene are linked to coding sequences for human gene. In this way protein hormone can then be isolated from the milk obtained from the animal (Figure 7.9A).

Mammalian Cloning

Organism cloning refers to methods that produce two or more genetically identical individuals. In nature this happens in the case of identical twins, which develop from the same fertilized egg. Ian Wilmut and his colleagues at the Roslin Institute near Edinburgh created 'Dolly,' the first genetically cloned sheep. Figure 7.9B shows the procedure of Dolly's creation. The researchers removed mammary cells from an adult female sheep and then grew them in the laboratory. The researchers

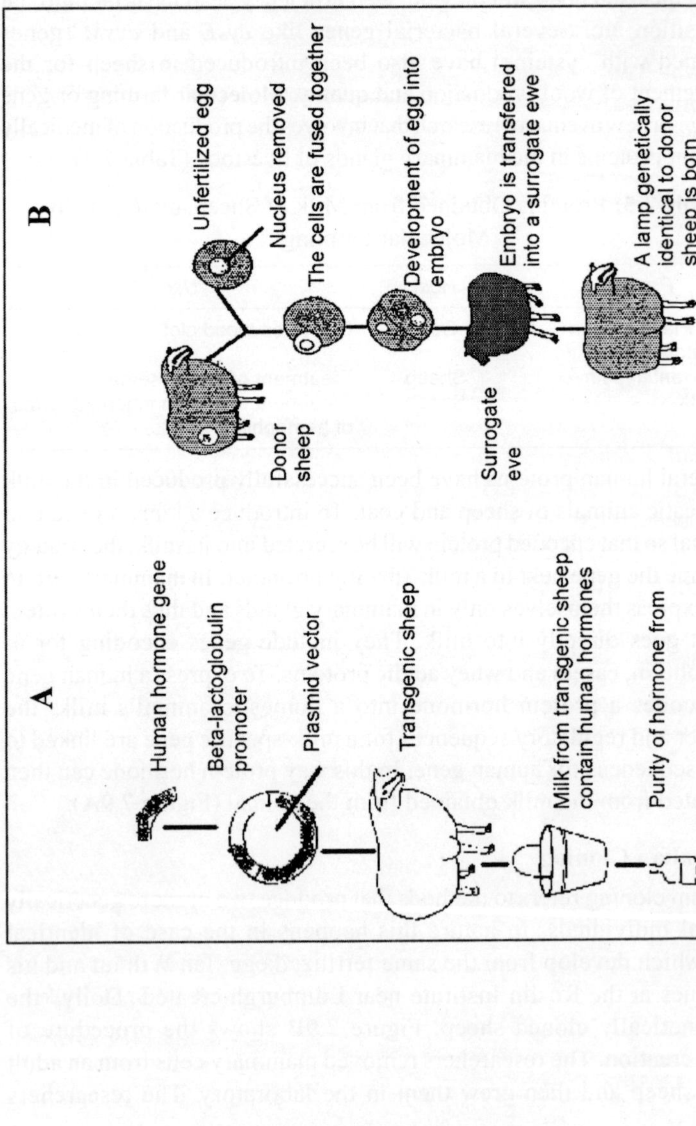

Figure 7.9: Incorporation of Selected Protein (A) and Cloning (B)

then removed the nucleus from a sheep oocyte and then fused it with the diploid mammary cell. After fusion the zygote was implanted into the uterus of an adult sheep. 140 days later the surrogate ewe 'July' gave birth to the first genetically cloned sheep 'Dolly'. Dolly was genetically identical to the sheep that donated the mammary cell to create her. The mammalian cloning is still at an early stage of development. It was considered to be the major breakthrough as clones of those animals could be made which are good at producing meat, milk or wool (Kolata, 1997). Another unique feature of Wilmut's experiment is that a carbon copy of an individual was produced without involvement of the male genetic material, which indicates that sperms are not necessary for the progeny (Joshi, 1998).

Conclusion

Human beings use living and non-living resources for their survival. Livestock is one such animal resource. It includes sheep, goat, cow, buffalo, horse etc. The common uses of livestock for the human beings are milk, meat, transport, draught power, clothes and manure. Although technology has provided alternatives for some of these items, the livestock is still the main source of milk and meat. Since the consumption of these two items show an increasing trend in recent years, the developmental schemes need radical orientation towards pastoral activities. The chapter has summarized the knowledge base of biology for improving traditional scenarios of pastoralism.

8

Traditional Institutions of Pastoral Well-being

*Randhir Singh Ranta**

The chapter recounts some socio-cultural and cognitive structures for the well-being of pastoral and agro-pastoral populations. Human beings perceive the surrounding physical and social systems through their cognitive and mental processes, their views have variability, as we find in this article. Though the article does not measure the matter assimilated and kept in deeper recesses of brain and mind, yet it is an attempt in a direction that may later be modified and strengthened with the experiential methodologies which may penetrate into deeper recesses of mind, where the holy lamas and the volatile malis or gurs of local deities take us. His comparative study of the three villages, selected from the three areas where pastoralism is still in practice, may help us in developing an alternative understanding of the life of these agro-pastoral communities.

An archeologist in Australia, Pardoe narrated interesting stories of human behaviour to Leslie (2005), as the visitors poured in to see the Aboriginal burials, "one visitor took a look at the graves, started 'weeping like a baby, 'and immediately produced his chequebook, asking, 'How much money do you need?' And when Purdoe uncovered a burial that showed signs of being associated with sorcery, an aboriginal colleague grew fearful and asked him to close it up without carrying out an intended analysis." (Page 294) How do we explain such behaviours? It would be a gross error to ignore such issues for the well-being of people. Though the father of modern psychology William James (1902) placed such phenomena before the scientific community, psychologists did not follow it up. At the dawn of twenty first century some signs are there to move in this direction.

---

* Randhir Singh Ranta, Department of Psychology, Himachal Pradesh University, Shimla.

The data collected during 1985-1990 by Anthropological Survey of India under the People of India Project (Singh, 2002) shows that great majority of Indian population follows six major religions: Hinduism, Islam, Christianity, Sikhism, Buddhism and Jainism. A few follow traditional tribal religions or other faiths. The POI data indicated that all religious identities are being consolidated. The deities were worshipped at the family, local and village level, regional level and national, even transnational level. As many as 61.2 percent of Hindu communities worship a family deity. Singh further mentioned that for their well-being the communities sought protection from the evil spirits and curing diseases through the medium of Shamans.

In Himachal Pradesh, the majority of population is of Hindus, and the pastoralism is the main occupation. But some population living in Lahaul and Spiti and Kanaor districts, along with Hinduism also follow Tibetan Buddhism. Although most of the investigators still consider the majority of people, mainly pastoral communities follow animistic beliefs. It is only in Sharma's (1976) pioneer work that an attempt has been made to explore the institution of local deity in a particular region—the Kanaor. He has also analysed the motifs in folk songs and folk tales, one way of exploring the mind of people in these remote regions. These local institutions of deities with their linkages with political, social and other institutions affect the day to day life of people and their social interactions.

The global forum of scientists in its Millennium Ecosystem Assessment (MA, 2005) has recognized the dependence of human well-being on material welfare, health, good social relations, security, and freedom. This particular recognition in the MA 2005 and its thrust on gearing the ecosystem services for human well-being, will change the scenario in near future where ecological principles guide the path of sustainability. Even though globalization brings new opportunities, the transition can be wrenching (Bardhan, 2006). Rural communities need to strengthen the local social institutions to enhance their inner resources to meet these challenges effectively.

For the people of Himalayan region an important area of participation at global level is the sustainable development and human well-being. In this endeavor, psychologists can contribute through the traditional institutions of mental health at grassroots level. The rich cultural diversity of India derives from its folk traditions or little traditions. Our aim here is to draw the attention of academic psychology to the contribution of little tradition in the well-being of rural masses in Himachal Pradesh who are largely pastoralists. Of particular interest are the institutions of deities.

It is through them that individuals, households, villages and regions live as cooperative units. These deities in Kanaor, behave like living organisms; they become happy, live family life, engage in squabble, show cleverness, have polyandry and keep high self-esteem.

Village Deities

All households (*ghar*) living in a village are members of the institution of deity and participate in its activities. These activities involve physical, social, psychological and spiritual aspects of human life. In the following section we introduce various concepts with their social and psychological relevance for the mental health of people. These observations are based on the institutions of Deo Boindra, Shadi ra Deo, and Narainu Deo (Pirta, 2005; 2006; Pirta and Ranta, 2007; Ranta and Pirta, 2007; Figure 8.1). These concepts are used with the institution of deity by the pastoral communities of Kanaor also.

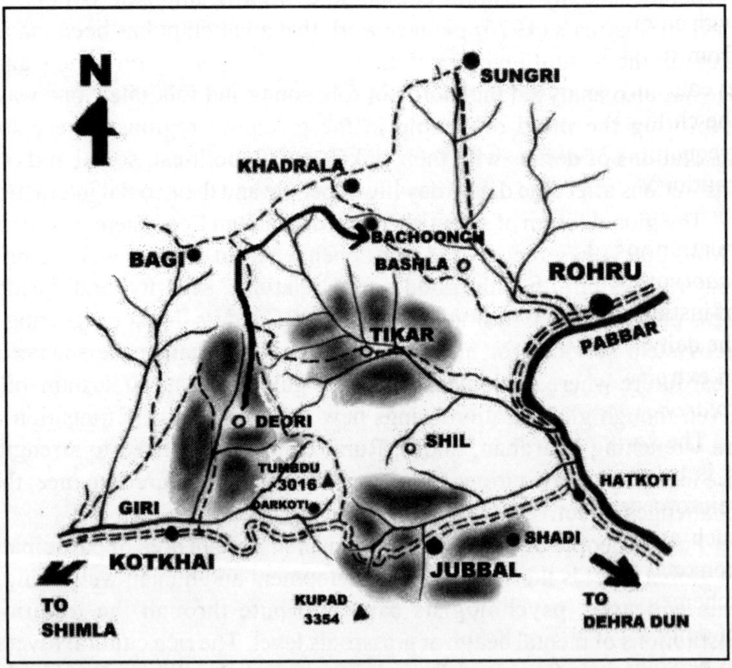

Fig. 8.1: Institutions (Dark Areas) of *Deo Boindra* (Kotkhai), *Shadi ra Deo* (Jubbal) and *Narainu Deo* (Rohru) in District Shimla. The Areas under These Institutions are not Confined by the Political Boundaries (Pirta, Ranta and Vashisht, 2008)

The typical system of healing in the institution of deity involves the deity (physical), the abode of the deity, the space around it, the territory of the deity, the people who worship the deity, the property belonging to people and the natural happenings (e.g., rain, snow, drought, forest, etc.). The most distinctive characteristic of this institution, however, is the assumed presence of divine in the temple and a number of concepts associated with it, forming non-terrestrial elements in the system. An individual and his family or household (the *ghar*) interacts with these terrestrial and non-terrestrial elements. One learns these ways of behaving, thinking and feeling while growing as a member of the institution of deity. This process may start even before birth of child, for example, the deity may have fulfilled the parent's wish for a child. After birth of child it is customary to visit the institution of deity or to invite the deity at home.

These learning experiences, though taking place when the child's cognitive abilities are not well developed, occur in an atmosphere charged with emotion. There is a longing in parent's mind for the security of child from the deity and they express it in a socially sanctioned way. These events may form part of child's emotional and procedural memories. As the child grows up in the family and in the company of age mates, he is frequently prompted to seek blessings of the deity. Along with this he is cautioned about the rules and regulations of the institution. He receives instructions about the concepts and their pragmatic implications with relation to sacred space, social structure of institution, and divineness (*saot*) of the deity. Furthermore, it is through the internalization of roles of institution that an individual not only develops stronger attachment to the deity, he is likely to become deity's functionary (*kardar* or *thani*) and in extreme case a spokesperson (*mali*) of the deity. The *mali* in trance (*otarana*) speaks on behalf of the deity.

The *kara*, the rules of the institution of deity, are supreme. To disobey it is to invite trouble for the family. These cognitions receive further reinforcement from oral and written prescriptions in the greater tradition such as the *Bhagvat Katha*. Life histories of saints, numerous myths, personal experiences of people, all provide rich material for cognitive schemes where variety of positive and negative expectations become part of deity's image. Concept of *dosh* (or annoyance of the deity) has a basis in person's own perceptions and expectations from the deity. Therefore irrespective of whether a person is actually wrong and right in his actions, it is self-perception (about himself and his deity) that has greater significance. If a person is right in his action and the deity also blesses him, there is likely to be a positive effect. However, conflict arises when a person is wrong but he does not receive punishment from the deity. Similarly, somebody may be wrong and escapes punishment from the deity. The deity's decisions (or the orations of the *mali*), overcome this difficulty by following a course where the client has freedom for other options. However, the most significant point is, the decisions largely confine to modifications in behaviour. Although there are suggestions about causes, the remedies have only superficial relation with it.

Narainu Deo of Tikar

The institution of Narainu Deo belongs to Tikar sub-tehsil of Shimla district (Table 8.1). Historically, this area was part of Bushahr State, and Kanaor was also a part of this State. All in all ten villages worship Narainu Deo and all households in these villages along with their physical terrain come under the protective fold of the deity (Pirta, Ranta and Vashisht, 2008). There were 872 households, with an average of five members per household. The literacy rate (percentage of literates to the total population aged 7 years and above) ranged from 65 to 80. Largely people belong to three castes: Brahmin (bhat), rajput (khoshia) and others (koli, dhaki, barhi). All are engaged in agriculture and horticulture, previously they were pastoralists (Table 8.2).

Table 8.1: Sociological Data of Villages in the Territory of Institution of Narainu Deo (Census of India 2001)

Village	*Number of Households*	*Population*	*Literacy Rate*	*Proportion of Scheduled Caste*
1. Sharonta*	151	717	72.0	81.2
2. Shekal	44	254	69.5	16.1
3. Narain	47	247	65.0	48.1
4. Kashaini	104	618	73.6	40.9
5. Thana	105	470	74.6	15.9
6. Khangta	202	849	80.1	29.7
7. Daroti	118	575	68.7	47.5
8. Gujandli	101	482	79.3	16.8

* Also includes two villages Breshtu and Gharla.

However a few are in government services or have private business. In the adjacent Dodra Kwar tehsil people still rear large number of sheep and goats (Table 8.3).

To organize the institution of Narainu Deo a committee of 35 informally nominated members meet from time to time (Table 8.4). Some of these members are assigned special tasks, which include the *pradhan* (president)

Table 8.2: Number of Sheep and Goats in Different Villages in Tikar Sub-tehsil during the Year 2003-04

	2003-04	
	Sheep	*Goats*
Kuthari	200	45
Kadiun	131	121
Khalgar	15	1
Khelai	79	0
Dheral	46	50
Pharog	120	17
Bathara	16	18
Hanstari	6	0
Pujarli-3	0	4
Khulawan	20	45
Koti	26	0
Khangta	2	0
Gujandli	80	0
Narain	7	0

Table 8.3: Number of Sheep and Goats in Different Villages in Dodra Kwar Tehsil during the Year 2003-04

Dodra Kwar Tehsil (Name of Villages)	*2003-04*	
	Sheep	*Goats*
Jakha	1760	1108
Jiskun	789	404
Pandar	389	115
Kiterwari	3483	948
Dhandarwari	4767	2948
Asandha	37	5
Dodra	2654	1468

Source: 17th Livestock Census, Government of Himachal Pradesh, Directorate of Animal Husbandry, Shimla, 2003.

up-pradhan (vice-president), *bhandari* (store-keeper), *khazanchi* (cashier), *halmandi* (messenger), *pujari* (priest) and *mali* (medium or spokesperson). The main temple of the deity is located in Narain village. Most of the year the deity remains in this temple, however it spends around three months out of the temple spending few nights in each of its ten villages (Table 8.5). During this period, known as *khalatra*, all households in a village worship the deity and share their happiness and sorrow with the deity. At nights, in *khalatra*, people gather around the temple where the deity stays, they sing songs and participate in dance. The deity also accepts invitations from households.

The organizational activities of the institution of deity become conspicuous on festivals, religious ceremonies and pilgrimages. For example, an important activity is to organize a pilgrimage of the deity to Yamunotri, Gangotri, Badrinath and Kedarnath (Char Dham Yatra in the Himalayas) that usually occurs at an interval of ten to twenty years. In this journey, besides Narainu Deo, his elder brothers, the Golinag and the Roother also accompany the deity. In 2002 one such pilgrimage took place, 105 persons traveled together carrying the *moharas* (facemasks) of the three deities to the four religious places of the greater tradition of Hindus in the Himalaya. During each pilgrimage, the devotees walk through the traditional path via Haridwar, the famous religious place

Table 8.4: Committee Members of the Institution of Narainu Deo for 2005-2006

Names of Members		
1. Bhajan Das Janartha, **Pradhan**	13. Ranveer	25. Ratan Chand
2. Mehar Singh, **Bhandari**	14. Purshotam	26. Liaq Ram
3. Parmeshwar Das, **Khajanchi**	15. Shamsher	27. Shamu Ram, **Halmandi**
4. Manmohan, **Up-Pradhan**	16. Mohan Lal	28. Prabhu Nand
5. Amolak Ram, **Bhandari**	17. Tulsi Ram	29. Durga Chand
6. Prem Chand	18. Pyare Lal	30. Daya Nand
7. Bhadur Singh	19. Ram Das	31. Kamla Nand
8. Narain Singh Ranta	20. Thapu	32. Durgu Ram
9. Keshri Nand	21. Banshi Lal	33. Keshru, **Pujari**
10. Durga Singh	22. Dewan Chand	34. Jagdish, **Pujari**
11. Amar Chand	23. Karam Chand	35. Rajesh, **Mali**
12. Veeru Ram	24. Mast Ram	

Table 8.5: Days Spent by Narainu Deo in Khalatra (Visits to the Territorial Villages)

Village	*Days*	*Village*	*Days*
1. Sharonta	10	6. Kashaini	6
2. Shekal	5	7. Thana	11
3. Breshtu	3	8. Khangta	12
4. Gharla	4	9. Daroti	9
5. Narain	5	10.Gujandli	9
		Total	**74**

in the north India and from here they take traditional routes along the Yamuna and Ganga rivers. During the pilgrimage, which includes male members from various villages, the travelers eat only one meal a day, stay in the open, and observe several other norms. For this journey approximately three hundred rupees per household was collected, however some may have donated even more (Table 8.6).

Table 8.6: Contribution Received for Char Dham Yatra of Narainu Deo in 2002. Some Households are Exempted as They Serve the Institution in Various Other Ways

Village	*Households*	*Amount*	*Households Exempted*
1. Sharonta	108	53,148	Nil
2. Shekal	37	11,104	Nil
3. Breshtu	22	11,234	2
4. Gharla	27	10,933	6
5. Narain	50	6,676	36
6. Kashaini	135	81,763	25
7. Thana	70	58,014	Nil
8. Khangta	102	99,747	Nil
9. Daroti	81	62,233	Nil
10. Gujandli	76	36,776	Nil
Total	**708**	**4,31,628**	**69**

There is a function at the beginning of the pilgrimage but even more elaborate function takes place when the deity returns from the pilgrimage. In the process of the pilgrimage the deity rejuvenates (gains *saot*, the divine power) and purifies itself. It is an occasion when the little tradition goes to pay obeisance to the greater tradition, or the part merges with its whole. In recent times the pioneer environment movement, the Chipko, made an effort to recapitulate the spirit of these pilgrimages to save the holistic image of the Himalayas (Pirta, 2003).

Pilgrimages provide a glimpse of the enormous organizational ability of peasantry in these Himalayan regions at the village level aiming at the well being of all. There is a collective effort for social integration at physical, social and mental level. In the above region, a grand religious ceremony took place from 24 to 26 December 2005 when more than seventy thousand people participated in Bhoonda Mahayajna on the 25th of December for material prosperity as well as to develop a feeling of affection and brotherhood in the region. All arrangements of boarding and lodging of such a mammoth population were made under the institution of Boindra Devata of Bachoonch. Several deities were invited; his brother (also Deo Boindra) traveled the longest distance among the invited deities, from the village Deori in Kotkhai tehsil to Bachoonch (see Figure 8.1). More than one thousand villagers from the Ghayaal area, the territory of Deo Boindra, walked in snow and rain carrying Deo Boindra in palanquin for three days to reach Bachoonch. The Ghayaal is an economically prosperous apple belt with high literacy, however people have strong faith in the institution of Deo Boindra. Similarly two brothers, Deo Bakralu from Dalgaon and Deo Maheshwar from Pujarali also joined him at Bachoonch. In a three day long religious ceremony about one crore rupees were spent. What people remembered after the ceremony was the peace that prevailed over three days, hospitality of local people, organizational skills of the committee of the institution of Boindra Devata, and the rare religious and cultural peculiarities.

Possession or Trance

Possession of mali by the deity plays central role in healing of vast variety of cases brought to the institution of deity. When mali gets possessed by deity during the course of therapeutic ritual or during the festivals, a unique change occurs in his body and mind. The socio-cognitive explanation of dissociation is getting credence in psychology (Spanos, 1994). Moreover there is suggestion to explore possession as a form of indigenous psychiatry (Crook, 1997). In developing countries, the continuing existence of healing (Singh, 2003) in the institution of deity questions the value of Western psychiatry for a wide range of conditions.

Social learning and training make the *mali* of the deity perform this task according to the norms of institution. In beginning the preparation (*tyari*) takes place during festivals of deity when the atmosphere is charged with devotion. The person may experience very high affective arousal accompanied by seemingly irrelevant motor activities and verbalizations. Content of his memories during these verbalizations is emotional and procedural. But on later occasions the person goes into the state of possession only during social and therapeutic rituals where the aim is to sort out the individual and social problems. However, as a person gains experience of possession he is socially accepted spokesperson of the deity. He shows control on behaviour and above all his speech is coherent. The socio-ecological study of Ladakhis by Crook (1997) provides an analysis of the phenomenon of possession among young females in that region in the light of several contemporary theories. The prime mover, both in the initiatory illness and in the promotion of the possessed to the status of village oracles, appeared to involve psychological pressure (within gender, family or social relations) requiring an adjustment in an individual's sense of identity. According to Crook (1998) the dissociative possession has remained poorly understood by the therapists as well as the psychologists though possession was not uncommon in the western medical and psychiatric consulting rooms.

Reconciliation Process

After a person or party accepts deity's decision, he is absolved from the assumed annoyance (dosh) of the deity. But he may have to do something for the appeasement of the deity and on some occasions to satisfy the demands of other good or bad spirits. In case the other party refuses to abide the *kara*, a unilateral sanction is enforced, and the other party or individual may then be liable for further annoyance of deity. Occasionally, the deity suggests severing (*chhuan*) of all physical and social relations with the disobeying party, even if one is a close kin.

There is another concept, the sin (*paap*). It is culturally general as well as specific. We provide here a case to illustrate the point. In a particular family, one of the three brothers developed strained relations with other members of the family due to non-cooperative nature of his wife for the common good. He was finally given a separate house and a share of land; still his wife did not change her indifferent attitude to work and was neglectful in her chores. For instance, to clean the child she would use wool ('*oon*'). An elderly neighbour pointed out this to her husband, who was by that time disgusted with his wife's behaviours. The neighbour told him "Oon, soon hai," meaning that the wool is like gold, but his wife was throwing it out after cleaning the fecal matter of the child. This proved the last straw for a highly depressed person to end his life.

But while committing suicide, he might have spoken in the name of deity "here I am ending my life due to rejection from my brothers and also due to the misbehaviour of my wife, you are witness to it." Some time later, trouble started in the family of his brothers. The remedy suggested by the local deity was to worship the '*paap*' of the deceased. It is a small silver plate cut to resemble the person, and enclosed by pieces of cloth. Since then, four generations have passed and the family has grown considerably, but the '*paap*' is still worshipped. If the family members do not worship the '*paap*' some misery may fall upon the family.

Sometimes, allergy of the skin (*oshta*) is associated with the annoyance of the '*paap*'. It is also possible that the local deity takes the '*paap*' in its fold and along with the deity the 'paap' is also worshipped daily. There are two ways of diagnosing as well as suggesting therapeutic measures in association with the '*paap*.' One is known as *bharoon*, where several *malies*, the mediums, go into the state of possession, sound of beating a brass plate (*thali*) accompanies, finally one of the family members or their kin gets possessed by the '*paap*' (the deceased person). In the other process, a person with special powers to communicate with the dead persons, the *mashania*, is called for and this person speaks about the problems, desires and feelings of the particular deceased person. They may also suggest some remedial measures.

The little traditions are adaptations to local needs, beliefs and environmental conditions. For example, in the higher regions of the Indian Himalaya, from west to east, where Tibetan Buddhism has influenced local traditions, elaborate rituals exist to monitor this intermediate stage of life, from the physical death to entry into another womb (maximum period is 49 days). These rituals are described in *Antarabhav Shrutvimukti* (*bar-do tho-dol*), written by Acharya Padmasambhava (Bisht, 1996 has translated it into Hindi for the government of Himachal Pradesh). The aim is to get rid of the attachment, anxiety and fear of the *chitta*, so that the state of nirvana or true state of mind is achieved.

Three Himalayan Villages

This section explores the socio-ecological characteristics (Table 8.7) of three Himalayan villages with relation to the religious affiliations of people that may have consequences for their mental health. The investigator collected relevant data from the three areas, Malana in Kullu, Chhitkul in Kanaor and Bachoonch in Shimla of Himachal Pradesh (Ranta and Pirta, 2007).

In each area, 20 adult males and females were selected through purposive sampling, and eight statements were orally spoken to each subject, one by one, to know his/her religious affiliations. Each statement has a main stem that elicited great information on one specific aspect of religious affiliation (Table 8.8). For each statement there was a four-point scale to quantify the subject's involvement in that religious aspect. The score varied from zero to three, the higher the score, higher the religious affiliation. Statistical analyses involved applying one-way analysis of variance (ANOVA) on the scores obtained for each of the eight statements for the three groups having 60 participants in all.

Table 8.7: Socio-ecological Characteristics of Malana, Chhitkul and Bachoonch (Ranta and Pirta, 2007)

S. No.	Characteristics	Study Areas		
		Malana	Chhitkul	Bachoonch
1.	Himalayan Zone (Degree Celsius)	Temperate (–5 to +25)	Temperate (–10 to +15)	Temperate (–7 to +25)
2.	Altitude	>2000m	>3000m	>1500m
3.	District/Tehsil	Kullu/Kullu	Kinnaur/Sangla	Shimla/Rohru
4.	Rural/Urban (Literacy)	Rural (14.3 %)	Rural (81.9%)	Rural (69.8%)
5.	Households (Household Size)	214 (5.0)	111 (6.0)	100 (6.0)
6.	Population (Male/Female)	1101 (544/557)	563 (270/293)	607 (317/290)
7.	Livelihood	Cultivators	Cultivators	Cultivators
8.	Transhumance	Prevalent (Indirect)	Prevalent	Vanishing
9.	Special Status	None	Scheduled Tribe	None
10.	Trade relations	Tourism	Apples	Apples
11.	Religion	Hinduism	Hinduism & Buddhism	Hinduism
12.	Social isolation	Extreme (cultural)	Extreme (natural)	None
13.	Local Deity	Jamlu Devata	Mathi Devi	Boindra Devata

Table 8.8: The Differences on Various Aspects of Religious Affiliation among the Villagers of Three Socio-ecological Habitats (Ranta and Pirta, 2007)

Aspects of Religious affiliation	Means			F-ratios (df 2/57) (n = 60)
	Malana (n = 20)	Chhitkul (n = 20)	Bachoonch (n = 20)	
A. Extent of spirituality	2.75 ± .44	1.8 ± .41	2.95 ± .22	54.47**
B. Visits to temple of deity	3.00 ± 0	2.05 ± .75	1.45 ± .76	31.79**
C. Visits to religious places	1.75 ± .44	2.05 ± .76	3.0 ± 0	33.02**
D. Extent of religiousness	2.75 ± .44	1.85 ± .58	2.85 ± .36	26.91**
E. Relationship with other beings	2.4 ± .5	2.0 ± 0	2.85 ± .36	28.04**
F. Meaningfulness of spirituality	2.4 ± .5	2.0 ± 0	2.25 ± .44	5.44*
G. Importance of religion	2.45 ± .51	2.25 ± .44	2.1 ± .3	3.34
H. Joining religious activities	2.9 ± .3	2.8 ± .41	2.91 ± .3	55

* p <.01; ** p <.001

Our purpose was to understand the implications of the socio-ecological characteristics of the three villages situated in three habitats along with the religious affiliations of people as revealed through self-reports, for social psychiatry or community mental health. Another term used for it in recent years is the rural psychiatry (Srinivasa Murthy, 1998; 2004). We will deal here with some broad aspects of the community's mental health. Although it involves the state structure supporting community services at national level, the local level structures can also contribute through various ways, such as finances, manpower and basic necessities. At both levels, it is the power structure that is an integral part of the social psychiatric analysis. In psychology the absence of power structure in the analysis of behaviour is rather conspicuous. Though the power is confined to a few in a society, it has tremendous influences in controlling the Behaviour of a submissive majority that do not have power. There are two aspects of this power structure that has significance here. It is controlled through two parallel institutions: the socio-political and the religious. For the three agro-pastoral villages discussed here, though the political entity at present was one, the government of India, the religious institutions were predominantly specific to each village. The latter included, the Jamlu Devata in Malana, the Mathi Devi in Chhitkul and Devata Boindra in Bachoonch. An elected body of members governed the institution of deity, the latter played important role in the physical, social and mental aspects of the community.

Before the independence of India the political entity was different for each of these villages, and at that time the institution of deity and the institution of Raja has operated side by side, often interacting with each other in complex ways (Thapar, 2002). One such example is given here that has relationship with the territorial conflict and to the acquisition of a position in the political power structure.

In fact territorial conflicts represent among the few social conflicts that have close relationship with survival of social groups and may involve co-evolution of biological and cultural traits. In such cases, the significant thing is the involvement of some higher cognitive processes (the representations of divine factor) with regard to movement and occupancy over a territory. One such case is the institution of Mathi Devi in Chhitkul that has some relation with the two erstwhile adjacent states, the Bushahr (now in Himachal Pradesh) and the Garhwal (now in Uttaranchal). The evidence comes from the *chironing* (history of deity) narrated by the *grokch* (the spokes person) of the Badri Nath of Kamru in the Baspa valley (Mamgain, 1971; page 362). Note that the old capital of Bushahr state was at Kamru. The Mathi Devi of Chhitkul is the wife of the Badri Nath of Kamru, and both have relationship with the Garhwal state. These relations of deities are in myths and beliefs. They perhaps indicate territorial relations of the Bushahr and Garhwal states before the independence of India.

More recent documentary evidence comes from the tussle for occupying the throne of Bushahr state in the beginning of the twentieth century. The Raja of Tehri Garhwal tried to install his brother on the throne of Bushahr. But the attempts were unsuccessful due to the resentment of local elite families, who succeeded in installing Padam Singh on the throne of Bushahr. The contribution of Gopi Chand of Rohru (from Naor valley) is significant in this case. He was the *mukhtyar* or attorney on behalf of the minor Padam Singh and took up the case with British authorities. After about four years the case was decided in favour of Padam Singh keeping in view the sentiments of local populations (Mamgain, 1971; Page 65). It is significant to note that the local deities from these areas go to pay obeisance to Lord Badrinath in Garhwal (Himalaya). One such visit took place in early 2006 when Davata Boindra from Bachoonch (one of the study villages) visited the shrines of greater deities in Garhwal Himalya. Before this pilgrimage, the institution of Boindra Devata organized a Bhunda *yajna* for the well-being and prosperity of its subjects, a unique show of solidarity between villages over a large area. To summarize, until the case was decided there was turmoil in the Bushahr state and the well-being of its people was at stake. Moreover, there are indications of the involvement of the local institutions of deities in this conflict for power through the *dhoom*, a socially accepted way of registering protest to the authority in power.

Whereas Chhitkul has remained a physically isolated terrain, Malana people have isolated themselves through social fencing, following some religious and cultural practices. Bachoonch is comparatively open to the outside world. Social fencing of Malana community is so complete that in association with the institution of Jamlu Devata it does not even expose its members to education; for communication they use *Kanashi*, a local dialect, they keep sheep and goats and hire herders to take them to winter and summer pastures. The literacy rate according to 2001 census is 14.3 per cent. Chhitkul people, taking advantage of the scheduled tribe status and faith in Buddhist teachings, besides the other Hindu religious affiliations, have achieved a remarkable literacy rate of 81.9 per cent. They keep big herds of sheep and goat and follow transhumance. It is followed by physically and socially more accessible Bachoonch community with a literacy rate of 69.8 per cent. In this village of Naor valley the transhumance is now non-existent.

Now consider some aspects of religious affiliations revealed through the self-perception measure. People from all the three communities, pay equal and high importance to spirituality and religion (see results of ANOVA on aspects F, G and H in Table 8.8) in their lives, however, the socio-cultural sanctions are different. Jamlu Devata of Malana does not allow its subjects access to other religious places (see aspects B and C). This last aspect of religious affiliations and other sanctions of social fencing in Malana, contradicts some stark realities of the World's oldest democracy. The third case is associated with the social psychiatric implications of abusing a local resource, traditionally used for entirely different purposes (e.g., fibres of Cannabis plant were used for making ropes, shoes and stitching), for earning quick money illegally even flouting the religious and cultural practices. For example, the villagers of Malana are getting deeply entrenched in the illicit trade of *charas* (*bhang* or *ganja*) extracted from leaves of Cannabis plant. Now the important question is, does the village deity sanction such transactions for illicit trade? Drug addiction was ruining the health of the younger generation, in addition it was exposing them to extremely hazardous relationships. Although one would expect the openness of Chhitkul community, its comparatively lower religiousness (see mean scores on aspects A and D), and high literacy as facilitators to drug addiction, it has not happened in this physically remote village of Sangla valley, though the Cannabis plant grows there. The people of this village follow the Hindu goddess Mathi Devi and they also strongly believe in Buddhism. This village is on the Kinner Kailash pilgrimage path of the people of Kinnaur district in Himachal Pradesh. Such drug addiction is almost negligible in more open (see aspect E) Bachoonch village near Shimla. Perhaps the social fencing in the Malana village, the flux of tourists in Kullu and Manali, and the high monetary incentive have combined together and put Malana on a path where the physical, social and mental well-being of an ancient democratic community was in danger.

Conclusion

The main objective in this article was to recount some socio-cultural and cognitive structures for the well-being of pastoral and agro-pastoral populations. Since human beings perceive the surrounding physical and social systems through their cognitive and mental processes, their views have subjective noise. But establishment of the criterion to rectify this noise depends upon the human agency itself. This is a dilemma in ecology and sustainability debate. Where ecology refers to life-supporting relationships among the elements of ecosystems, sustainability is the human constraint to maintain these relationships for present and future generations (Box 8.1).

Box 8.1: Environmental Consciousness of the *Arung Zet Sa*

Vidya Sagar Negi (pers. comm.) described the environmental consciousness among the pastoralists, the *arung zet sa* of Kanaor, as follows. On reaching his village, the *arung zet sa* invites the deity to his house on an auspicious day. The *arung zet sa* makes all preparations for the worship of the deity and decorates the necessary items of prayer in different plates. The *grokch* of his deity comes to *arung zet sa's* house with the *kro*, a symbol of the deity. Then the *zet sa* makes a request before the *grokch* for the invocation of the deity. The deity speaks through the *grokch* and listens to the prayer of the *arung zet sa*. His prayer is for the safety of his family and home, sheep and goats and the yearly crops. The *arung zet sa* visits the *thanang* (abode or village temple) of the deity, once after returning from summer pasture and once after returning from winter pasture. On these two visits he offers some money or *deedun* to the deity according to his will. If the village deity accepts animal's sacrifice, *zet sa* may offer a male goat to seek the deity's blessings. Before ascending for the summer pasture, *arung zet sa* worships his deity goats to seek their blessings for the welfare of his family and the sheep and goats. When the *arung zet sa* reaches in his summer pasture, he prepares special dishes for the worship of the protector goddesses of the mountains, the *sauni*. He worships the *sauni* and seeks their blessings for his safety and the safety of his sheep and goats throughout the stay in winter pasture. While returning from the winter pasture, the *arung zet sa* performs a prayer to thank the *sauni* and worships his deity goats. On reaching his village from the summer pasture, he burns a lamp from the fresh butter prepared by him. On descending towards the winter pasture he again presents *korang* to his village deity. He seeks the blessings of all the gods and goddesses for the removal of the ill omens on his route. Only then the *arung zet sa* embarks upon his arduous migration towards the winter pasture. An *arung zet sa* hardly takes education in a school; for him the nature is the school as well as the teacher.

The former Secretary General of the United Nations Conference on Environment and Development (Strong, 2001), has also referred to this dilemma. He pointed out that even political leaders, who were strongly committed to sustainable development, could not impose it upon people who did not understand or appreciate its importance. Conversely, even the most reluctant of political leaders could not fail to pursue sustainability when their people demanded it. Thus the problem lies in cognitive domain since mental faculties alone apprehend interactions between society and nature.

It is being realized that if local communities, for example the people of Himachal Pradesh, remain aloof from global issues, the cost may be very high. Not only that, the minds of the people will be colonized (Gergen, 2005). Chances of combating any such colonization, in particular, and avoidance of subjugation in general, would increase if people of Himachal Pradesh participate actively in the global cognitive revolution. However, this participation in the global cognitive revolution, which is likely to benefit the people of this state as well as the entire humanity, further depends on choosing between the two options. The first is to leave behind the traditional cultural base and adopt the western individualistic ideology, having its associated losses and gains. The alternative is to build upon the existing traditional base and incorporate and assimilate the new information according to contextual elements (Misra and Gergen, 2002; Pirta, 2007).

Our social problems generally include conflicts between individual and collective preferences embedded in the environmental milieu. An ecologist, Madhav Gadgil, has explored social conflicts along this dimension in the institution of local deities in the villages. He writes, "*One often finds associated with such deities a rich body of folklore which can illuminate the history of human groups that worship these deities. Such folklore can be particularly fascinating when it appears to have its origin in conflicts of interests amongst the different human groups.*" (Gadgil, 2001)

The above issues have significance for understanding the mental health of pastoral people. They include the power structure of the deity, the high religious affiliations, and using social fencing for the acquisition of wrong practices of resource use. Religious institutions of deities are the traditional community mental health centers in the hills (Singh, 2003). They provide the basis to explore mental health of people and have been noticed by other investigators as well. A major change observed in recent times is in the area of power relations. The government is taking over the administrative control of these institutions of deities, presumably for the well-being of people. We suggest that such changes should harmonize with the traditional role of these institutions and this is possible by developing the institutions of deities as community mental health centers.

Epilogue

More than twenty million self-dependent households engaged in pastoralism meet the basic needs of milk, meat and clothing of the society to a considerable extent. In India, they even today live a classic pastoral life, spending most of their time under extremely inhospitable conditions. The public attitude towards these people is charaterised by apathy and utter neglect of their life and culture. Their future seems bleak. Though the livestock caters to the primary human needs from its products, the curiosity in animals nourishes the mental complexity. While the former is more obvious and visible, the latter is largely hidden from planners, public and users. In fact, the curiosity about other life forms is more fundamental to human nature, and is reflected in the animal science, specially the techniques of livestock management and development. The present volume has drawn attention to this hidden aspect of man-animal relationship.

Though it is not known whether plant domestication started earlier to, simultaneously with or later than the animal domestication, the most common pattern is the practice of animal husbandry with agriculture. The other two patterns, only agriculture or animal rearing, are less common. How people use herds of sheep and goats in the rugged Himalayan mountains is a key to understanding their social life and environmental adaptations and is the focus of present study. The Gaddis and Kanaoras of Himachal Pradesh moving with the herds of sheep and goats exemplify this mutual relationship. It also provides a contrast to understand the impact of modern agriculture and horticulture development in the fragile ecosystem of the Himalayas.

The present volume has in focus the pastoral system of Kanaor for two reasons. First, the people of Kanaor have been engaged in two systems of pastoralism. The less intensive *kim zet* system where the sheep and goats are daily brought to house after grazing in nearby areas of village, and the more intensive *arung zet* system where the sheep and goats always remain in the open in large herds and range over vast area. In addition, they were also involved in trade with Tibet. Second, the complexity of the social systems that evolved in Kanaor needs attention. The people of Kanaor not only incorporated an element of Mahayani Buddhism through pastoral trade, spanning from the Tibetan plateau to the Indian planes, there is readiness to adopt the modern horticulture to supplement their livelihood. It has relationship with unexplored cognitive complexity characterizing this pastoral region.

Learning Avenues: An important task is to create learning avenues for the pastoralists engaged in traditional mode of sheep and goat rearing. This would (a) increase the self-esteem among pastoralists; (b) expose them to advanced scenarios of pastoralism. This is to be achieved through mutual exchange between the pastoral groups of developed and developing countries. Observational learning is an efficient method to acquire and disseminate information, whereas individual training by experts is more expensive and takes longer time. For example, if a pastoralist from Kanaor or Chamba visits a group of pastoralists in some European country or Australia, he will quickly assimilate some of the techniques essential for improvement in his profession and use them on return. A successful use of these techniques in Himachal Pradesh will then be an observational learning experience for other pastoralists, and the newly learned techniques will spread all over the area. On the other hand, if an expert is sent abroad for training, though he may come equipped with various techniques, they may or may not be adopted by the pastoral community due to communication gap. The visit of the pastoralists from other countries may also be useful, as they would encounter the problems *in situ* and give their suggestions. There will be, we-feeling, between the two groups of pastoralists and communication would take place in a friendly atmosphere.

The exposure to modern pastoral systems in developed nations will create an interest among the younger generation, which seems indifferent to the traditional mode of pastoralism. Moreover the opportunity would motivate the pastoral community in general to improve their lot, since they would come to know that even developed countries are engaged in this profession. This new experience would not be limited to enhancement of their professional competence, but positively affect their archetypal living.

The research programmes need orientation towards understanding the problems of shepherds and their needs. They may be locality specific, for example, the ecosystem of the *arung zet sa* of Kanaor is different from the shepherds of Rajasthan. Even within the same ecosystem, Gaddis did not engage in trade with Tibet whereas Kanaoras suffered a lot due to India's conflict with China as they were engaged in trade with Tibet. The research on varieties of sheep and their products is second important area of consideration. This has to do with the local population, the consumers. It may be the preference for the colour of wool and its texture, the varieties of meat, and the general attitude towards sheep and goats of different age-sex classes.

Development of Pastoral Organization/Union: The pastoralists have expressed feelings of isolation as rapid urbanisation and homogenization are eroding their community feeling. Pastoralism is becoming an occupation about which nobody cares. Moreover, there is a feeling among shepherds that their job is of low dignity or social prestige, though their produce serves the community with essential commodities of food and clothing.

Pastoralists think that their voice remains unheard because pastoralists do not have strong organization. But at the same time there are difficulties to bring together a large group of pastoralists, which is spread spatially over a large area. These people are always busy in their tedious work, and cannot spare time to meet each other regularly. They live in remote areas where the communication is difficult. There is no system of enrollment. The educated among the pastoral community prefer to break away with the profession. Though politicians empathize with the pastoralists, the solutions to their problems are, however, overshadowed by preference for hydroelectric schemes, industries, forestry and mining. In fact these developmental schemes have eaten up large pastoral areas but there is not even an inch of grazing land that has been developed for sheep and goats.

The formation of a pastoral union is considered as a viable alternative to solve the problems of these people. They have, however, shown eagerness to participate in this process. This, however, needs dynamic leadership, which cuts across the communities of shepherds, such as Gaddis and Kanaoras. Once such organisation takes its roots, irrespective of regional and political affiliations, each pastoral family may become its member. This large organization can raise various policy matters about the pastoralism as an occupation and resolve grassroots problems, for example, the scarcity of winter pastures. It may have local units at the level of village and block. These units will be instrumental in social welfare activities such as provision of daily needs, sale of the produce, insurance of the livestock, education of children and other activities.

The development is a holistic effort of the local population according to its needs. Instead we find that experts of different hues enter in the developmental process who are not only alien to the local community, they are alien to each other's goals and ways of work. They have little or no knowledge of the intricate processes taking place in the milieu; they even do not have patience to see the effects of their interventions. Nowhere is an attempt to see the things holistically—the animals, the pastures, the lake, the monastery, the history, and the people. These people are perceived as belonging to an alien race, lacking necessary wisdom and will to take charge of their affairs. Only experts can solve their problems and bring them in the mainstream of development. In this drive for homogenization, the creative work of individual or community has no scope.

In the high altitude Himalayan ranges, transhumance along with trade has played significant role in the life of people due to lesser scope for agriculture. Interaction with diverse ways of life becomes necessary while moving with herds of sheep and goats, an essential aspect of transhumance. With this the people moving with the *arung zet sa* assimilated various aspects of culture from other groups in whose contact they came. During this process, they assimilated those skills, which enhanced survival in the harsh environment. Instead of huge temples, that needed masonry work and huge amount of wood, they preferred simple mud walls but very intricate mural paintings and stuccos.

One consequence of developmental changes in the Himalayas is associated with the psychological dimension of the allostatic systems of those people who have been displaced due to large-scale interventions from their native habitat. A psychologist would like to integrate the vulnerability and resiliency approach with the cognitive viewpoint of native people to understand the mental health of such displaced populations. Whereas, on one hand, displaced populations face problems that are highly specific, on the other hand, there are certain common behavioural issues faced by migrants. These issues can be probed in the light of affection systems or theory of attachment. The flocks of sheep and goats are not only naturalistic laboratories to study the affectionate relationships, they are more economical than the laboratory studies. Social psychiatrists engaged in community mental health, especially with the lost homes, have applied the biological model based upon separation studies on various animal species. It may be appropriate to use it to understand the effects of displacement among human beings. One may feel separation anxiety from her age mates, boys and girls in the village, and mother, father and other elders, or from the village environs itself. It may happen for an *arung zet sa* or *zet palas* moving with the flocks of sheep and goats to winter and summer pastures.

Feeling of Hope: The hope that one is going to survive tomorrow, keeps a person and his survival mechanisms alive. But the feeling of hopelessness reduces the zeal of individual and impairs his survival mechanisms. It is this latter attitude that is engulfing the psyche of pastoralists. The harshness of physical environment inculcated feeling of conquest in them. Though the Kanaoras and Gaddis are able to cope with the extreme physical conditions, the challenge from the fellow human beings is threatening their survival. The rich culture, which developed over a long period, and assimilated biology of pastoralism in it, selected those who contributed to the pastoral institution. But cooperativeness can increase in a system when the benefits of its members are met to a certain level of satisfaction. The present social structure around the pastoralists has changed those levels of satisfaction in the first instance. Secondly, it has increased the social problems manifold in comparison to physical problems. Thirdly, the indifference of contemporary economic and political system toward pastoral system has further aggravated the problems of people who are engaged in it. Lastly, the incentives and entitlements as a result of 'tribal' designation to some pastoral communities are perceived by other pastoralists, who are non-tribal, as further deprivation.

Considering this scenario, a suspicion is engulfing the minds of pastoral communities, that sooner or later the transhumant mode of pastoralism was destined to vanish under the present unfavourable circumstances. The tragedy is that humanists seem ignorant in comprehending the dynamics of transhumance, and they strongly advocate sedentarisation of those engaged in it. They are not able to grasp the fact that this system of production can be modernised in various ways to reduce the miseries of man and animal, and to serve the society in a much better way. Moreover, pastoralists feel that the contribution of the state to pastoral produce, in comparison to horticulture development is discriminatory, though their contribution to the society has greater significance. Since milk, meat and wool meet the primary needs of the society. Pastoralists think that forestry should be geared to develop good pastures. However, the mining industry, which destroys the pastures of sheep and goat, receives scientific and political support. The prudent pastoralist guarding the borderland and producing essential items suffer from utter neglect. Demolition and neglect of the traditional institutions have created a chasm. On one hand are people in the space age, but on the other hand, pastoral groups are at the nomadic stage. The challenge is to bridge this gap by improving the pastures of sheep and goats and creating social structure where those who tend to these animals receive respect from the society and live a dignified life.

The process of conservation needs a new perspective. It has to develop as an interspecies interaction where human beings express pro-social behaviour toward other fellow creatures. However, this pro-social interspecies interaction between animal world and humankind must have an objective basis. Therefore, it is imperative to re-evaluate the subjective protectionism considering the adequate demographic and Behavioural data from long-term field studies. Apathy towards damage to sheep, goats and crops by animals engenders protests from local people in urban as well as rural areas. A re-evaluation of man-nature relationship is key to this new conservation approach. We are exploiting our natural resources increasingly faster, the rich consuming more than the poor. The inequality among human beings is cause and consequence of this disparity in our manipulation of the material, trans-material and nonmaterial worlds. It does not disturb most of us led by the modern way of life.

The biological aspects of pastoralism have been largely ignored, they seldom find place even in the modern dairy development programmes. In other words, the developments in animal behaviour (comparative psychology, ethology or sociobiology) are altogether overlooked in efforts to improve pastoralism in a holistic way. Furthermore, the adaptations acquired by pastoralists over a long period, their knowledge about particular animal species, its behaviour and utilitarian aspects go almost in vain. This is a significant social neglect. There is an interesting relationship between biodiversity and bio-productivity. It is ironic that some major centers of diversity and the origin of crop plants and domesticated animals fall in tropical-subtropical-hot-temperate belt where people are still dependent upon sustainable agriculture, animal husbandry and forestry. It has been suggested that biotechnology may help these developing nations, including India, increase their productivity without the loss of biodiversity. There is need to incorporate modern biological and behavioural research in the traditional pastoral systems, especially to revolutionise the transhumant systems. In fact, there is evidence, which shows that farm output from livestock can exceed output from crop production.

The supernatural beliefs of people arouse academicians in variety of ways. Some evolutionary theorists call it 'misfiring,' which takes place in highly intricate ways, and may require higher level of cognitive awareness for its understanding, which is still confined to a minority of scientific specialists. The 'misfiring' of sexual urges entangles even the most talented minds. They need to understand the finer motherly emotions, so important for the survival of an infant, be it sheep, goat, monkey or human infant. Secondly, the humanistic enterprise requires deeper knowledge of the cohesive forces, so that the attachment to mother or mother figure remains intact and proliferates, whether they are flocks of sheep and goats or the human social groups does not matter.

The FAO (2001) report suggests four major policy orientations for the protection and support of pastoralism in the twenty-first century. They suggest integration of pastoralism with the new world order in such a way that the supply of traditional needs of meat, milk and wool becomes secondary and certain other needs take precedence. Some of the essential ingredients of these new world order needs are: (a) advertisement and sale of products produced in unique ecosystems, from unique species, and free from contaminants, (b) exploring new symbiotic relations with horticulture farming—the sheep and goats grazing in well-grown orchards where they reduce weeds, eat grass and provide manure fertilizer to the soil, (c) acceptance of the damage done to biodiversity, and take it as a challenge to involve in conservation activity, and (d) using the rich cultural complexity in various ways to ecologically sensitive, low volume but financially remunerative tourism.

Traditionally pastoralists have evolved ways and means to cope up with uncertainties that surround them. Though it is difficult to predict the consequences of the large-scale developmental interventions in the fragile Himalayan landscape on life of people in general, the transhumance is prone to restriction on the area available for grazing sheep and goats. The overall survival or extinction of pastoralism is associated with economic and cultural factors. Whether the institutions of deity would continue to solace them, or not is an issue related to the threat to the identity of these communities. Pastoralists in the Himalayas already encounter enormous environmental uncertainties, which require biological adaptations, but the present populations have to face the ever-increasing environment of man made uncertainties. It is challenging for these pastoralists to adapt to these uncertainties along with their sheep, goats and the institutions of deities. The great challenge for a cognitive scientist is to help pastoralists in this endeavor, particularly in preparing them for the new world order.

References

Abdul Kalam, A.P.J. and Rajan, Y.S. 1998. *India 2020: A Vision for the New Millenium.* New Delhi: VIKING Penguin Books India.

Acharya, R.M. 1982. *Sheep and Goat Breeds of India.* Rome: Food and Agriculture Organization of the United Nations.

Adair, J.G., Pandey, J., Begum, H.A., Puhan, B.N. and Vohra, N. 1995. Indigenization and development of the discipline: perceptions and opinions of Indian and Bangladeshi psychologists. *Journal of Cross-cultural Psychology, 26*(4), 392-407.

Adams, M. 1988. *Agriculture, Livestock and Forestry: An Environmental Strategy for Semi-arid Areas.* International Institute for Environment and Development, London, Drylands Paper No. 1.

Agrawal, A. 1992. *The Grass is Greener on the Other Side: A Study of Raikas, Migrant Pastoralists of Rajasthan.* International Institute for Environment and Development, London, Paper No. 36.

Anand, M.R. 1990. "The Term 'Classical' as a Misnomer in the Critique of Pahari Painting: A Note. In N.K. Rustomji and C. Ramble (Eds.), *Himalayan Environment and Culture* (pp. 245-247). Shimla: IIAS and New Delhi: Indus Publishing Company.

Anandalakshmy, S. 1982. There's a Method to the Measurement. In D. Sinha, R.C. Tripathi and G. Misra (Eds.) *Deprivation: Its Social Roots and Psychological Consequences* (pp. 37-47). New Delhi: Concept Publishing Company.

Anonymous 1904/1996. *Gazetteer of the Chamba State 1904.* Punjab State Gazetteer Volume XXII A. New Delhi: Indus Publishing Company.

Anonymous 1986. HP-UP Grazing Issue Hits Shepherds. *The Tribune*, October 10.

Anonymous 1995. *His Holiness the XIV Dalai Lama on the environment.* Department of Information and International Relations (Environment and Development Desk), Central Tibetan Administration of His Holiness the XIV Dalai Lama, Gangechen Kyishong, Dharamsala.

Aris, M. 1993. "Man and nature in the Buddhist Himalayas". In N.K. Rustomji and C. Ramble (Eds.), *Himalayan Environment and Culture* (pp. 85-101). Shimla: IIAS and New Delhi: Indus Publishing Company.

Bagla, P. and Menon, S. 1990. "Across Kinnara Country". *Frontline*, July 21-August 3.

Bahuguna, S. 1968. *Madhaya Himalaya. Vikas Ki Smasyain*. Silyara: Parvatiya Navjeevan Mandal. (in Hindi)

Bahuguna, S. 1987. Chipko: The People's Movement with a Hope for the survival of Humankind (pp. 9-20). In *The Chipko Message*. Silyara, Tehri-Garhwal: Chipko Information Centre.

Bahuguna, S.L. 1987-88. "Planting Wisdom to Restore the Eroded Earth: A Cultural Response to a Crisis of Civilization". *Future*, Winter.

Bahuguna, S. 1993. (*Bhartiyon se adhik Bhartiya thi Meera.*) *Amrit Sandesh*, January. (In Hindi)

Bahuguna, S. 1997. *Chipko Message. Development, Environment and Survival*. Ganga Himalaya Kuti, Tehri: Save Himalaya movement/Chipko Information Centre.

Bajaj, J. and Srinivas, M.D. 1996. *Annam bahu kurveeta*. Madrass: Centre for Policy Studies.

Baker, R. St. B. 1989. "Reverence for Life-reverence for Trees". In I. Ramesh and N.D. Jayal (Eds.), *Richard St. Barbe Baker: Man of the Trees* (pp. 75-87). NewDelhi: INTACH and Silyara: Chipko Information Center.

Balland, D. 1991. "Nomadism and Politics: The Case of Afghan Nomads in the Indian Subcontinent". *Studies in History*, 7(2), 204-229.

Bardhan, P. 2006. "Does Globalization Help or Hurt the World's Poor?" *Scientific American India*, 1(11), 68-75.

Batchelor, M. 1994. Even the Stones Smile. Selections from Scriptures. In: Batchelor, M. and Brown, K. (Eds.). *Buddhism and Ecology* (pp. 2-17). Delhi: Motilal Banarsidass.

Bareham, J.R. 1975. "The Effect of Lack of Vision on Suckling Behaviour of Lambs". *Applied Animal Ethology*, 1, 245-250.

Bedi, J.S. 1991. "Nomads of the Hills". *Indian Express*, March 30.

Behl, B. 2003. "Murals of India". *Frontline*, October 24.

Bell, C. 1928. *The People of Tibet*. London: Oxford University Press.

Bennett, J.W., Lawry, S.W. and Riddell, J.C. 1986. "Land Tenure and Livestock Development in Sub-Saharan Africa". AID Evaluation Study 39. Washington: USAID.

Bhasin, V. 1996. *Transhumants of Himalayas. Changpas of Ladakh, Gaddis of Himachal Pradesh and Bhutiyas of Sikkim*. Delhi: Kamla-Raj Enterprises.

Bhatt, C.P. 1992. *The Future of Large Projects in the Himalaya*. Nainital: PAHAR.

Bhattacharjji, C. 1993. Troubled Waters: Laying a Leh Lake Open to Waste. *Frontline*, December 31.

Bisht, R.N. 1996. *Antarabhav Shrutvimukti*. Shimla: Himachal Academy of Arts Culture & Languages. (A Hindi translation of *Bar-do tho-dol* by Acharya Padmasambhava).

Booth, K.K. and Katz, L.S. 2000. "Role of the Vomeronasal Organ in the Neonatal Offspring Recognition in Sheep". *Biology of Reproduction*, 63, 953-958.

Boyd, R. and Mathew, S. 2007. "A Narrow Road to Cooperation". *Science*, 316, 1858-1859.

Bowlby, J. 1969. *Attachment and Loss. Vol. 1: Attachment*. New York: Basic books.

Bowlby, J. 1973. *Attachment and Loss: Vol. 2. Separation*. New York: Basic Books.

Brandon-Jones, D.D. 2004. A Taxonomic Revision of the Langurs and Leaf Monkeys (PRIMATES: COLOBINAE) of South Asia. *Zoos' Print Journal*, 19(8), 1552-1594.

Bronfenbrenner, U. 1977. "Towards an Experimental Ecology of Human development". *American Psychologist*, 32, 513-531.

Brooker, R.J. 2005. *Genetics: Analysis and Principles. Part II*. New York: McGraw-Hill.

Bueva, L.P. 1981. *Man: His Behaviour and Social Relations*. Moscow Progress Publishers.

Bunyard, P. (Ed.) 1996. *Gaia in Action: Science of Living Earth*. Edinburgh: Floris Books.

Cairns, R.B. 1979. *Social Development: The Origins and Plasticity of Interchanges*. San Francisco: W.H. Freeman and Company.

Campbell, D.T. 1975. On Conflicts between Biological and Social Evolution and between Psychology and Moral Tradition. *American Psychologist*, 30 (12), 1103-1126.

Carter, O.L., Presti, D.E., Callistemon, C., Ungerer, Y., Liu, G.B. and Pettigrew, J.D. 2005. "Meditation Alters Perceptual Rivalry in Tibetan Buddhist Monks". *Current Biology*, 15 (11), R412-413.

Chadwick-Jones, J.K. 1987. Social Psychology and Primatology: Proximate Explanations. *Ethology*, 74, 164-169.

Chaitanya, K. (2000). "Man, Nature and Cosmos in Vedic India". *The Ecologist*, 30, 21-24.

Charney, D.S. (2004). "Psychobiological Mechanisms of Resilience and Vulnerability: Implications for Successful Adaptation to Extreme Stress". *American Journal of Psychiatry*, *161*, 195-216.

Charak, S.S. 1980. "History and Culture of Himalayan States", Vol. 5. Jammu Kingdom, Part II. New Delhi: Light and Life Publishers.

Chaudhuri, K. 1993. "Gateway to China: Kalimpong and the Silk Route Option". *Frontline*, December 17.

Chavan, S.A. 1989. "Effect of Grazing on the Feeding Behaviour of Ungulates in Gir Forest, Gujrat, India". In B.J. Patel (Ed.), *The Behaviour* (pp. 44-48). Bhavnagar: Sir P.P. Institute of Science.

Chetwode, P. 1975. "Traditional Hindu Architecture in the Western Himalaya". In V.C. Ohri (Ed.), *Arts of Himachal* (pp. 116-123). Shimla: State Museum.

Chhabra, T. 1994. "Forgotten Culture: Todas, Their Life and Times". *Frontline*, September 23.

Chhogdup, T. (Ed.) 1986. *Pratityasamutpada*. Varanasi: Central Institute of Higher Tibetan Studies.

Chitkara, M.G. 1999. *World Government and Thakur Sen Negi*. New Delhi: APH Publishing Corporation.

Choudhary, S. (Ed. & Trans.). 1971. *Shrimaryashurvirachit Jatakamala*. Delhi: Motilal Banarasidass. (in Hindi).

Ciechanowski, P.S., Walker, E.A., Katon, W.J. and Russo, J.E. 2002. Attachment theory: A Model for Health Care Utilization and Somatization. *Psychosomatic Medicine*, 64, 660-667.

Clifford, T. 1984. *Tibetan Buddhist Medicine and Psychiatry. The Diamond Healing*. New York: Samuel Weiser.

Courtillot, V.E. 1990. A Volcanic Eruption. *VIGYAN Scientific American*, October.

Crook, J.H. 1995. "Psychological Processes in Cultural and Genetic Coevolution". In E. Jones and V. Reynolds (Eds.), *Survival and Religion: Biological Evolution and Cultural Change* (pp. 45-110). London: John Wiley & Sons.

Crook, J.H. 1997. "The Indigenous Psychiatry of Ladakh, Part I: Practice Theory Approaches to Trance Possession in the Himalayas. *Anthropology and Medicine*, 4, 289-307.

Crook, J.H. 1998. "The Indigenous Psychiatry of Ladakh, Part II: Narrative and Metanarrative in the Cultural Control of Dissociative States in the Himalayas. *Anthropology and Medicine*, 5, 23-42.

Crook, J. and Osmaston, H. (Eds.) 1994. *Himalayan Buddhist Villages*. Delhi: Motilal Banarsidass.

Dalai Lama, "His Holiness The XIV. 1992.Universal Responsibility and Our Global Environment". *Tibetan Bulletin*, May-June, 8-10.

Dalai Lama, 2000. *Karuna Shakti*. Delhi: Full Circle. (in Hindi)

Dandekar, A. 1991. "Landscapes in Conflict: Flocks, Hero-stones, and Cult in Early Medieval Maharashtra". *Studies in History*, 7(2), 301-324.

Dargey, G.N. 1978. *Tibetan Tradition of Mental Development*. Dharamsala: Library of Tibetan Works and Archives, (3rd ed.).

Das, F.H. 1932. *Leap-home and Gentlebrawn*. London: J.M. Dent & Sons.

Das, J.P. 1998. *The Working Mind: An Introduction to Psychology*. New Delhi: Sage Publications.

Davey, G. 1989. *Ecological Learning Theory*. London: Routledge.

Davidar, D. 1990. "Our Man in Maxico". *Indian Express Magazine*, October 28.

Dawkins, R. 2006. *The God Delusion*. London: Bantam Press.

Dawson, J.L.M.B. 1969. "Theoretical and Research Bases of Bio-social Psychology". *University of Hongkong, Supplement to the Gazette*, XVI(3), 1-10.

Dawson, J.L.M.B. 1977. "Theory and Method in Biosocial Psychology: A New Approach to Cross-cultural Psychology". *Annals of New York Academy of Sciences*, 285, 46-65.

Deitz, R.S. and Holden, J.C. 1970. "The Breakup of Pangaea". *Scientific American*, April.

Denniston, D. 1993. "Saving the Himalaya". *World Watch*, November-December, 10-21.

Dev, S. 1997. "Ethnotherapeutics and Modern Drug Development: The Potential of Ayurveda". *Current Science*, 73(11), 909-928.

Deuster, R.H. 1939. *Kanawar (Kinnaur)*. Shimla: H.P. Academy of Arts, Culture and Languages.

de Waal, F. 1989. *Peacemaking among Primates*. London: Penguin Books.

Dharampal 1983/1995. *The Beautiful Tree. Indigenus Indian Education in the Eighteenth Century*. Coimbatore: Keerthi Publishing House; and AVP Printers & Publishers.

Dharampal 1993. *Bharatiya Chitta Manas and Kala*. Madras: Center for Policy Studies.

Dhavalikar, M.K. 1997. "Culture-environment Interface: A Historical Perspective". *Trends in Social Science Research*, 4(1), 11-26.

Diamond, J. 1989. "The Accidental Conqueror". *Discover*, December.

Dolling, C.H.S. 1968. "Informal Technical Report on Methodology of Experiments Concerning Sheep and Wool". *FAO, Rome: LA-SF 68/53*

Dorje, S. 1991a. *Triskandhadharamaparyaya-vayakhaya kusumannjali*. Vidya Bharati,11, 25-59. (in Hindi).

Dorje, S. 1991b. *Kun jom nagakanya. Kinner ki lok kahani. Vidya Bharati*, 11, 75-79. (in Hindi).

Dorje, S. 1993. *Vinaya Vastu main Nirdisht: char mitra bhaion ki kahani. Vidya Bharati*, 13, 79-85. (in Hindi).

Dorjee, P. (Trans.). 1987. *Dammuk Sutra (Tales of the Wise and Fools)*. Ladakh: Central Institute of Buddhist Studies.

Dreze, J. and Sen, A. 2002. *India: Development and Participation*. New Delhi: Oxford.

Drijver, C. 1990. "People's Participation in Environmental Projects in Developing Countries". International Institute for Environment and Development, London, Paper No. 17.

Dummer, T. 1994. *Tibetan Medicine and Other Holistic Health-Care Systems*. New Delhi: Paljor Publications,

Eibl-Eibesfeldt, I. 1975. *Ethology. The Biology of Behaviour*. New York: Holt, Rinehart and Winston.

FAO. 1990. *Proceedings of the International Workshop on Pastoralism and Socio-economic Development*. Food and Agricultural Organisation of the United Nations, Rome.

FAO. 2001. *Pastoralism in the New Millennium*. Food and Agricultural Organisation of the United Nations, Rome.

Feys, J. 1973. *The Philosophy of Evolution in Sri Aurobindo and Teilhard de Chardin*. Calcutta: Firma K.L. Mukhopadhyay.

Fisher, E., Ohri, V.C. and Sharma, V. 2003. *The Temple of Devi-Kothi*. Artibus Asiiae, Spplement, 43.

Gadgil, M. 1991. "Ecological Organization of the Indian Society". *ICSSR News Letter*, XXI(4), 1-9.

Gadgil, M. 1998. "Making of a Naturalist". *Frontline*, March 6.

Gadgil, M. 2001. *Ecological Journeys. The Science and Politics of Conservation in India*. New Delhi: Permanent Black.

Gadgil, M. and Malhotra, K. 1981. "What Prize is Develpment? *Science Today*, February.

Gadgil, M., Joshi, N.V., Shambhu Prasad, U.V., Manoharan, S. and Patil, S. 1998. "Peopling of India". In D. Balasubramanian and N. Appaji Rao (Eds.), *The Indian Human Heritage* (pp. 100-128). Hyderabad: Universities Press.

Gaston, A.J., Hunter, M.L. and Garson, P.J. 1981. The Wildlife of Himachal Pradesh: Western Himalayas. Report of the Himachal Wildlife Project. University of Maine, School of Forest Resources, Technical Note 82.

Gazetteer of the Simla Hill States 1910. (Reprinted 1995) Indus Publishing Company, New Delhi.

Gazzaniga, M.S. 1994. *Nature's Mind: The Biological Roots of Thinking, Emotions, Sexuality, Language and Intelligence*. New York: Penguin.

Geist, V. 1966. "The Evolution of Horn-like Organs". *Behaviour*, 27, 175-214.

Gergen, K.J. 2005. The Self: Colonization in Psychology and Society.

Downloaded from *http://www.swarthmore.edu/SocSci/kgergen1*.

Goldsmith, E. 1993. *The Way: an Ecological World-view*. Boston: Shambhalla.

Goleman, D. and Thurman, R.A.F. (Eds.) 1991. *Mind Science: An East West Dialogue*. Boston: Wisdom Publications.

Goodwin, B. 1996a. *How the Leopard Changed Its Spots*. New York: Touchstone.

Goodwin, B. 1996b. The Evolution of Cooperative Systems. In P. Bunyard (Ed.), *Gaia in Action. Science of the Living Earth* (pp. 135-146). Edinburgh: Floris Books.

Gopinathan, K.P. Hello Dolly. *Current Science*, 72(6), 1997.

Goswamy, B.N. 1975. "On Some Pahari Portraits of 'Ordinary' People". In V.C. Ohri (Ed.), *Arts of Himachal* (pp. 27-36). Shimla: State Museum.

Goswamy, B.N. 2007. "Culture Under Stress". *The Tribune*, January 2007.

Govinda, L.A. 1969. *Foundations of Tibetan Mysticism.* Rider and Company, London.

Greig, J.C. 1979. "Principles of Genetic Conservation in Relation to Wildlife Management is Southern Africa". *South African Journal of Wildlife Research*, 9, 57-78.

Grinewald, J. 1996. "Sketch for a History of the Idea of Biosphere". In P. Bunyard (Ed.) *Gaia in Action. Science of Living Earth* (pp. 34-53). Edinburgh: Floris Books.

Groves, C.P. 1989. *A Theory of Human and Primate Evolution.* Oxford: Clarendon Press.

Guha, S. 1999. *Environment and Ethnicity in India 1200-1991.* New York: Cambridge University Press.

Gupta, A.K. 1991. Pastoral Adaptation to Risk in Dry Regions: A Framework for Analysis. *Studies in History*, 7(2), 324-341.

Gupta, A.K. 2004. "Origin of Agriculture and Domestication of Plants and Animals Liked to Early Holocene Climate Amelioration". *Current Science*, 87(1): 54-59.

Gupta, K.M. 1993. *Mira Behn: Gandhiji ki putri avam shishya.* New Delui: Himalaya Seva Sangh.

Gupta, S.K. 1998. "Tribal Areas and Tribes of Himachal Pradesh: Some Myths and Realities". In S.K. Gupta, V.P. Sharma and N.K. Sharda (Eds.), *Tribal Development: Appraisal and Alternatives* (pp. 44-80). New Delhi: Indus Publishing Company.

Haas, E. and Minke, G. 1978. *Himalayan Pilgrimage* (A Studio Book). New York: The Viking Press.

Handa, O.C. 1998. Role of Rin-chen bZang-po in the Development of Buddhism. In S.K. Gupta, V.P. Sharma and N.K. Sharda (Eds.), *Tribal Development: Appraisal and Alternatives* (pp. 488-507). New Delhi: Indus Publishing Company.

Handa, O.C. 2005. *Gaddi Land in Chamba: Its History, Art and Culture. New Light on the Early Wooden Temples.* New Delhi: Indus publishing Company.

Hardin, G. 1968. The Tragedy of the Commons. *Science*, 162, 1243-1248.

Harlow, H.F. and Mears, C. 1979. *The Human Model: Primate Perspectives.* New York: John Wiley & Sons.

Hayes, N. 1994. *Principles of Comparative Psychology.* Hillsdale, USA: Laurance Earlbaum Associates.

Hernandez, H., Delgadillo, A.J., Serafin, N., Rodriguez, A.D. and Poindron, P. 2004. Prepartum peripherally-induced hyposmia does not reduce postpartum anoestrous duration in nursing goats. *Reproduction, Nutrition and Development*, 44, 251-259.

Hinde, R.A. 1990. The interdependence of the behavioural sciences. *Philosophical Transactions of the Royal Society of London, B, 329*, 217-227.

Hingston, R.W.G. 1988. *A Naturalist in Himalaya*. Pilgrims Book House, Kathmandu, Nepal.

Hoon, V. 1996. *Living on the Move: Bhotias of the Kumaon Himalaya*. New Delhi: Sage.

Hutchison, J. and Vogel, J.Ph. 1933/1982. *History of the Panjab Hill States. Volume 1*. Himachal Pradesh: Department of Language and Culture.

Ivanov-Smolensky, A.G. 1954. *Essays on the Patho-physiology of the Higher Nervous Activity*. Moscow: Foreign Languages Publishing House.

James, W.C. 1902. *The Varieties of Religious Experience: A Study in Human Nature*. New York: The Modern Library.

Jones, J.G. 1979. *Tales and Teachings of the Buddha: The Jataka Stories in Relation to the Pali Canon*. London:George Allen & Unwin.

Joseph, G. 1991. "Changpas, the Pashmina People, An Exploited Lot". *Indian Express*, Novembr 17.

Joshi, L.M. 1967. *Studies in the Buddhistic Culture of India During the Seventh and Eighth Centuries A.D.* Delhi: Motilal Banarsidass.

Joshi, N.V., Gadgil, M. and Patil. S. 1993. "Exploring Cultural Diversity of the People of India". *Current Science*, 64(1), 10-17.

Joshi, P.C. 1998. "From Cell to Cloning". *Science Reporter*, February

Kagitcibasi, C. (1988). "Diversity of Socialization and Social Change". In P.R. Dasen, J.W. Berry and N. Sartorius (Eds.), *Health and Cross-cultural Psychology: Towards Applications* (pp. 25-47). New Delhi: Sage.

Kakar, S. 1995. *The Colours of Violence*. New Delhi: VIKING Penguin India.

Kakar, S. 2001. *The Essential Writings of Sudhir Kakar*. Delhi: Oxford.

Kalin, N.H. 1993. The Neurobiology of Fear. *Scientific American*, May.

Kapoor, S. 1993. *Scheduled Tribes of Himachal Pradesh: Marriage and Divorce Customs*. New Delhi: NAVRANG.

Kavoori, P.S. 1991. "Transhumance in Western Rajasthan: Trends and transformations". *Studies in History*, 7(2), 255-278.

Kendeigh, S.C. 1980. *Ecology with Special Reference to Animals and Man*. New Delhi: Prentice Hall.

Khatana, R.P. 1992. *Tribal Migration in Himalayan Frontiers: Study of Gujjar Bakarwal Transhumance Economy*. Gurgaon: Vintage Books.

Kipling, R. 1894. *The Jungle Book*. New York: Exeter Books (Reprinted 1986).

Kipling, R. 1895. *The Second Jungle Book*. New York: Exeter Books (Reprinted 1986).

Kolata, G. 1997. "A Brave New World? Adult Mammal Cloned". *Frontline*, March 21.

Kothari, A. 2006. "Rights and Promises". *Frontline*, July.

Kropotkin, P. 1914. *Mutual Aid: A Factor in Evolution*. New York: Alfred A. Knoff.

Kumar, P. 1993. "Fairs in Focus: Pushkar, Sonepur Cast a Spell. *Frontline*, December 17.

Kunwar, S.S. (Ed.) 1982. *Hugging the Himalayas. The Chipko Experience*. Gopeshwar (Chamoli), U.P.: Dasholi Gram Swarajya Mandal.

Krumbein, W.E. and Lapo, A.V. 1996. Vernadsky's Biosphere as a Basis of Geophysiology. In P. Bunyard (Ed.), *Gaia in Action. Science of Living Earth* (pp. 115-134). Edinburgh: Floris Books.

Lambe, N.R., Conington, J., Bishop, S.C., Waterhouse, A. and Simm.G. 2001. "A Genetic Analysis of Maternal Behaviour Score in Scottis Blackface Sheep". *Animal Science*, 72, 415-425.

Lafitte, G. 1998. An End to Nomadic Way of Life? *Tibetan Bulletin*, October-December.

Lane, C. and Swift, J. 1989. *East African Pastoralism: Common Land, Common Problem*. International Institute for Environment and Development, London, Paper No. 8.

Leslie, J. 2005. *Deep Water: The Epic Struggle Over Dams, Displaced People, and The Environment*. New York: Farrar, Straus and Giroux.

Levy, G. 1988. Lush Green to Brown Desert. *Indian Express*, October 29.

Lorenz, K. 1952/1976. *King Solomon's Ring*. Great Britain: Cambridge University Press.

Lorenz, K. 1981. *The Foundations of Ethology*. New York: Springer-Verlag.

Losal, J. 1982. *New-sun Self-learning Book on the Art of Tibetan Painting*. Dharamsala: Tibetan Culture Printing Press.

Lovelock, J.E. 1987. *Gaia. A New Look at Life on Earth*. New York: Oxford University Press.

Lovelock, J. 1996. "The Gaia Hypothesis". In P. Bunyard (Ed.), *Gaia in Action. Science of Living Earth* (pp. 15-33). Edinburgh: Floris Books.

Lundgren, H.P. 1966. "Wool and Mohair". In H.H. Cole (Ed.), *Introduction to Livestock Production Including Dairy and Poultry* (pp. 82-99). London: W.H. Freeman and Company.

MA 2005. Millennium Assessment Web site: http://www.ma-secretariat.org [update: http://www.millenniumassessment.org/en/index.aspx]

Mahapatra, L.K. 1993. "Customary Rights in Land and Forest and the State". In M. Miri (Ed.), *Continuity and Change in Tribal Society* (pp. 84-96). Shimla: Indian Institute of Advanced Study.

Mann, R.S. (Ed.) 1981. *Nature-Man-Spirit Complex in Tribal India*. New Delhi: Concept Publishing Company.

Malik, S.C. 1999. Tribal art: A Universal Creative Act. Anadi Seminar, http://www.ignca.nic.in

Mamgain, M.M. (Ed.) 1971. *Himachal Pradesh District Gazetteers. Kinnaur.* Himachal Pradesh.

Mathpal, Y. 1992. "Uttarakhand Ki Adyatihasik Sanskriti Tatha Kala". *PAHAR*, 5/6. 181-190.

Maunder, R.G. and Hunter, J.J. 2001. Attachment and Psychosomatic Medicine: Developmental Contributions to Stress and Disease. *Psychosomatic Medicine*, 63, 556-567.

McEwen, B.S. 1998. Protective and Damaging Effects of Stress Mediators. *The New England Journal of Medicine*, 338 (3), 171-179.

McFarland, D. 1987. *Animal Behaviour. Psychology, Ethology and Evolution.* England: English Language Book Society/Longman

Mearns, R. 1993. *Policy Alternatives for Livestock Development in Mongolia (PALD)*. Institute of Development Studies, University of Sussex, U.K.

Menon, P. 1991. "The Art of Ajanta: The Last Extant Buddhist Monument". *Frontline,* September 28-October 11.

Menon, S., Narasimhan, M.G., Sinha, A. and Sreekantan, B.V. (Eds.) 1999. *Scientific and Philosophical Studies on Consciousness*. Bangalore: National Institute of Advanced Studies.

Miller, D.J. 2008. The World of Tibetan Nomads. *Tibetan Bulletin*, 12(1), 16-26.

Miller, G. 2006. The Asian Future of Evolutionary Psychology. *Evolutionary Psychology*, 4, 107-119.

Mira Behn 1951/1993. "Himalaya Ki Seekh". In B.P. Nautiyal (Ed.), *Mira Behn: Gandhi ji ki putri avam shishya. Janm shatabdi granth* (pp. 115-129). New Delhi: Himalaya Seva Sangh. (originally the article was published in *Harijan Sevak* in 1951) (in Hindi)

Miri, M. 1993. "Identity and Tribesman". In M. Miri (Ed.), *Continuity and Change in Tribal Society* (pp. 165-174). Shimla: Indian Institute of Advanced Study.

Mishra, A. 1995. *Rajasthan ki rajat boonden*. New Delhi: Paryavaran Kaksha, Gandhi Shanti Pratishthan. (in Hindi).

Mishra, L.K. 1996. "MP-Rajasthan Morder is Tense Over Sheep Grazing. *The Times of India*, November 10.

Mishra, R.C., Sinha, D. and Berry, J.W. 1996. *Ecology, Acculturation and Psychological Adaptation: A Study of Adivasis in Bihar.* New Delhi: Sage Publications.

Misra, G. and Gergen, K.J. 2002. "On the Place of Culture in Psychologcal Science". In A.K. Dalal and G. Misra (Eds.), *New Directions in Indian Psychology: Volume 1: Social Psychology* (pp. 405-424). New Delhi: Sage.

Mountain Agenda 1992. *An Appeal for the Mountains*. Switzerland: Institute of Geography, University of Berne.

Mukhopadhyay, R. 1997. "Folk Performing Arts: The Indigenous Channel of Communication. *Trends in Social Science Research*, 4 (1), 55-61.

Naerland, G. 1958. Report to the Government of India on Animal Disease Control and Sheep Husbandry. *FAO Report No. 792.*

Naess, A. 1986. Intrinsic Value: Will the Defenders of Nature Please Rise? In M.E. Soule (Ed.), *Conservation Biology* (pp. 504-515). Massachusetts: Sinauer Associates.

Naess, A. 1989. *Ecology, Community and Lifestyle. Outline of an Ecosophy.* New York: Cambridge University Press.

Nain, R. 1992. Why do cattle fairs desert. *Jansatta*, June 21. (in Hindi)

Narendradeva, A. 1971. *Bodh-Dharma-Darshan.* Patna: Bihar-Rashtra-Bhasha-Parishad. (in Hindi).

Negi, D.S. 1996. (Severing Agriculture and Animal Husbandry Relationship.) In K. Prasun (Ed.) *Heritage of Seeds* (pp. 26-30). Tehri Garhwal: Chipko Prakashan. (in Hindi).

Negi, H.R. and Gadgil, M. 1996. Patterns of Distribution of Macrolichens in Western parts of Nanda Devi Biosphere Reserve. *Current Science*, 71(7), 568-575.

Negi, J.P. 1985. *Developmental Perspectives in the Himalayan Mountain Desert of Spiti (Himachal Predesh)—Greening the Mountain Deserts.* Special lecture delivered at 72nd Session of the Indian Science Congress Association, Lucknow University, Lucknow, January 3-8.

Negi, T.S. 1998. Tribes of Himachal Pradesh: Past, Present and Future. In S.K. Gupta, V.P. Sharma and N.K. Sharda (Eds.), *Tribal Development: Appraisal and Alternatives* (pp. 100-106). New Delhi: Indus publishing Company.

Negi, V.S. 1991. Gyanashri dwara virachit lochava rinchen jangpo ka jeevan vritant. Prathama. *Vidya Bharati*, 10, 30-47. (in Hindi)

Negi, V.S. 1995. Kinner Kailash Prikrama Path Mein Boudhch–Bodhetra Poojasthal. *Somasi*, 78, 17-47.

Negi V.S. 2007. *The Nomadic Shepherds of North-West Himalayas: In the context of Kinnaur* (A socio-cultural Study). Sarnath, Varanasi: Central Institute of Higher Tibetan Studies. (in Hindi)

Noble, C. 1983. Gaddis, Gaddinis and Their Goats: The Migratory Trail of a Hill People. *The India Magazine*, July.

Noble, C. 1987. *Over the High Passes. A Year in the Himalayas with the Migratory Gaddi Shepherds*. London: Collins.

Norberg-Hodge, H. 1994. "May a Hundred Plants Grow from One Seed. The Ecological Tradition of Laddakh Meets the Future". In M. Batchelor and K. Brown (Eds.), *Buddhism and Ecology* (pp. 41-54). Delhi: Motilal Banarsidass.

Nowak, M.A. 2006. "Five Rules for the Evolution of Cooperation". *Science*, 314, 1560-1563.

Oltenacu, E.A.B. 1999. *New York State 4-H Dairy Goat Project*. New York: Cornell University.

Ortman, R. 2000. Monitoring of Oestrous Cycles of Ewes by Ram-seeking Behaviour. *Small Ruminant Research*, 37 (1/2), 73-84.

Padmanabhan, R. 1992. "Dairy Battles: With a Crusader at NDDB". *Frontline*, September 11.

Pagel, M.D. and Harvey, P.H. 1989. Comparative Methods for Examining Adaptation Depend on Evolutionary Models. *Folia Primatologica, 53*, 203-320.

Pal, P. and Fournier, L. 1982. *A Buddhist Paradise: The Murals of Alchi Western Himalaya*. Ravi Kumar, Lilakala Ag Vaduz, Basilius Presse Basel; New Delhi: Kumar Gallery.

Pandey, N. and Tripathi, R.C. 1982. "Scheduled Caste Children in High Caste Schools. In D. Sinha, R.C. Tripathi and G. Misra (Eds.) *Deprivation. Its Social Roots and Psychological Consequences* (pp. 217-34). New Delhi: Concept Publishing Company.

Parkipuny, M.S. 1991. *Pastoralism, Conservation and Development in the Greater Serengiti Region*. International Institute for Environment and Development, London, Paper No. 26.

Parmar, B.S. 1959. *Report on the Grazing Problems and Policy of Himachal Pradesh*. Himachal Pradesh Forest Department, Shimla.

Parmar, Y.S. 1985. "People and Development of Forest in Western Himalaya. *Himalaya: Man and Nature*, 8 (12), 41-43.

Pathak, S. 1994. *Pahar ki aour se Rahul ke nam patra. Pahar*, 7, (no page).

Patton, R.A. 1964. "Abnormal Behaviour in Animals. In C.P. Stone (Ed.), *Comparative Psychology* (pp. 458-513). New Delhi: Prentice-Hall of India.

Pirta, R.S. 1986. "Cooperative Life of Rhesus Monkey". In T.C. Majupuria (Ed.), *Wildlife Wealth of India. Resouces and Management* (pp. 346-365). Bangkok: Tecpress Service.

Pirta, R.S. 1990. "Cooperation in Urban Macaques and Langurs". A Project Report (DST Ref. SP/SO/C-32/85), Department of Science and Technology, Government of India, New Delhi.

Pirta, R.S. 1993. "Imperilled Western Himalaya and Deteriorating Man-Nature Relationship: A Case Study of Hanuman Langur. In V. Singh (Ed.), *Eco-crisis in the Himalaya* (pp. 165-205). Dehra Dun: International Book Distributors.

Pirta, R.S. 2002. "Comparative Psychology: Understanding Behaviour of Non-human Primates. *Psychological Studies, 46*, 25-37.

Pirta, R.S. 2003. Native Cognition of Sustainable Development in the Western Himalaya. *Psychological Studies*, *48*, 30-42.

Pirta, R.S. 2004. Environmental Implications of Biological, Cultural and Humanistic Pathways of Evolution. Part-I. Affectionate Relationships in Primates. *Psychological Studies*, 49(4), 220-226.

Pirta, R.S. 2005. Environmental Implications of Biological, Cultural and Humanistic Pathways of Evolution. Part-II. Transcending from material to non-material. *Psychological Studies*, 50 (1), 16-20.

Pirta, R.S. 2006. "Community-based Approach to Mental Health: The Traditional Healing". *Journal of Community Guidance and Research*, 23 (2), 161-177.

Pirta, R.S. 2007. *Ecology and Human Well-being: Nature and Society in Himachal Pradesh*. Delhi: Shipra Publications.

Pirta, R.S., Gadgil, M. and Kharshikar, A.V. 1997. "Management of the Rhesus Monkey *Macaca mulatta* and Hanuman Langur Presbytis Entellus in Himachal Pradesh, India". *Biological Conservation*, 79: 97-106.

Pirta, R.S. and Negi, V.S. 2000. The Wheel of Life and the Noosphere. In M.G. Chitkara (Ed.), *Encyclopaedia of Buddhism. A World Faith. Volume IV. Buddhism and Environment* (pp. 391-423). New Delhi: A.P.H. Publishing Corporation.

Pirta, R.S. and Ranta, R.S. 2007. "Social Conflicts and Possession: The Role of Reconciliation Processes Mediated by Local Deities". *Journal of Indian Academy of Applied Psychology*, 33, 2, 201-212.

Pirta, R.S. and Singh, M. 1978. "Establishment of Home Range, Intraspecific and Interspecific Relations in Rhesus Monkey (Macaca mulatta) under Infant-infant Rearing Conditions". *Proceedings of Indian Academy of Sciences (Animal Sciences)*, 87, 267-278.

Pirta, R.S. and Singh, M. 1980. "Changes in Home Ranges of Rhesus Monkey (*Macaca mulatta*) Groups Living in Natural Habitats. *Proceedings of Indian Academy of Sciences (Animal Sciences)*, 89, 515-525.

Porges, S.W. 2001. "The Polyvagal Theory: Phylogenetic Substrates of a Social Nervous System". *International Journal of Psychophysiology*, 42, 123-146.

Porges, S.W. 2003. "Social Engagement and Attachment: A Phylogenetic Perspective". *Annals of New York Academy of Sciences*, *1008*, 31-47.

Possehl, G.L. 1982. *Harappan Civilisation: A Contemporary Perspective*. New Delhi and IBH.

Prabhu, R.K. and Rao, U.R. 1967. *The Mind of Mahatma Gandhi*. Ahmadabad: Navajivan Publishing House,.

Prater, S.H. 1980. *The Book of Indian Animals*. Bombay: Bombay Natural History Society and Oxford University Press.

Protsch, R. and Berger, R. 1973. "Earliest Radiocarbon Dates for Domesticated Animals". *Science*, 179(4070), 235-239.

Punalekar, S.P. 1994. "On Dymystification of Methodology in Social Sciences". *The Indian Journal of Social Science, 7*(2), 111-123.

Radhakrishnan, S. 1940. *Indian Philosophy. Volume 1*. Oxford University Press, Delhi. (1997)

Ramakrishanan, P.S. 1993. "Traditional Societies in the Himalaya and their Sustainable Development". In M. Miri (Ed.), *Continuity and Change in Tribal Society* (PP. 314-322). Shimla: Indian Institute of Advanced Study.

Raman, C.V. 1968. *The Physiology of Vision*. Bangalore: The Indian Academy of Sciences.

Ranchan, S.P. 2001. *Aurotherapy: An Alternative Therapy System*. Delhi: Indian Publishers Distributors.

Ranta, R.S. and Pirta, R.S. 2007. "Socio-ecology and Religious Affiliation in Three Himalayan Villages: Implications for Mental Health". *Journal of Indian Academy of Applied Psychology*, 33 (1), 23-30.

Rappaport, R.A. 1979. *Ecology, Meaning, and Religion*. Richmond, California: North Atlantic Books.

Ratnagar, S. 1991. "Pastoralism as an Issue in Historical Research". *Studies in History*, 7(2), 181-193.

Ray, O. 2004. "How the Mind Hurts and Heals Body". *American Psychologist*, *59* (1), 29-40.

Renolds, S.G. 2006. Providing Winter Bases for Transhumant Herders in Altai, Xinjiang China: Some consequences and lessons learned. USDA Forest Service Proceedings RMRS-P-39.

Read, H., Fordham, M., Adler, G. and McGuire, W. (Ed.). 1959. *The Collected Works of C.G. Jung. Vol.9 Part I. The Archetypes and the Collective Unconscious*. London: Routledge & Kegan Paul.

Rees, C.A. 1959. "Animal Domestication in the Prehistoric Near East". *Science*, 130, 1629-1639.

Rhys Davids, C.A.F. 1900. *A Buddhist Manual of Psychological Ethics*. London: Royal Asiatic Society. (Oriental Books Reprint Corporation, New Delhi, 1975).

Richard, C. 2005. Developing Alternatives to Resettlement for Pastoralists on the Tibetan plateau. *Nomadic Peoples*, June 1.

Rock, I. and Palmer, S. 1990. The Legacy of Gestalt Psychology. *VIGYAN Scientific American*, December.

Rodgers, W.A. 1991. Environmental Change and the Evolution of pastoralism in South Asia: A Discussion. *Studies in History*, 7(2), 195-204.

Roonwal, M.L. 1989. "Ecological and Behavioural Appraisal of Tail Carriage in the deity Hanuman and Comparison with the Common Langur, *Presbytis Entellus*: A Problem in Mythozoology". *Uttar Pradesh Journal of Zoology*, 9, 127-139.

Rothenberg, D. 1989. "Introduction: Ecosophy T-from Intuition to System". In A Naess, *Ecology, Community and Lifestyle: Outline of an Ecosophy* (pp. 1-22). New York: Cambridge University Press.

Roy Burman, B.K. 1993. Tribal Population: Interface of Historical Ecology and Political Economy. In M. Miri (Ed.), *Continuity and Change in Tribal Society* (PP. 175-216). Shimla: Indian Institute of Advanced Study.

Runge, C.F. 1986. Common Property and Collective Action in Economic Development. *World Development*, 14 (3), 623-635.

Saberwal, V.K. 1999. *Pastoral Politics: Shepherds, Bureaucrats and Conservation in the Western Himalaya*. Delhi: Oxford University Press.

Sachs, J.D. 2006. "Welfare States, Beyond Ideology". *Scientific American*, November.

Saint, K. 1991. *Development Cooperation and the Development-Environment Crisis*. International Institute for Environment and Development, London, Paper No. 25.

Sankrityayan, R. 1948/1957. *Kinner-desh*. Allahabad: Kitab Mahal.

Sarin, M. 1996. *Joint Forest Management. The Haryana Experience*. Ahmedabad: Center for Environment Education.

Sarala Devi 1978. *Swasth arthvyavastha*. Pattikalyana. Haryana: Gram Bhavana Prakashan. (in Hindi)

Sarala Devi 1980. A blue-print for survival of the hills. *Supplement to Himalaya: Man and Nature*, 4(6), 1-16.

Schaller, G.B. 1977. *Mountain Monarches: Wild Sheep and Goats of the Himalaya*. Chicago: The University of Chicago Press.

Schumacher, E.F. 1973/1993. *Small is Beautiful*. London: Vintage.

Scott, C.A. and Walter, M.E. 1993. "Local Knowledge and Conventional Soil Science Approaches to Erosional Processes in the Shivalik Himalaya". *Mountain Research and Development*, 13 (1), 61-72.

Segall, M.H., Dasen, P.R., Berry, J.W. and Poortinga, Y.H. 1999. *Human Behaviour in Global Perspective. An Introduction to Cross-Cultural Psychology*. London: Allyn and Bacon.

Segerstrom, S.C. and Miller, G.E. 2004. "Psychological Stress and the Human Immune System: A Meta-analytic Study of 30 Years of Inquiry". *Psychological Bulletin*, 130 (4), 601-630.

Sen, A. 1997. "Radical Needs and Moderate Reforms". In J. Dreze and A. Sen (Eds.) *Indian Development: Selected Regional Perspectives* (pp. 1-32). Delhi: Oxford University Press.

Sen, A. 2006. *Identity and Violence: The Illusion of Destiny*. New Delhi: Penguin.

Sen, N.N. 1968. A Historical Introduction to Behaviour Therapy. Paper presented at a Seminar on Behaviour Therapy and Speech Disorders at The All India Institute of Speech and Hearing, Mysore.

Shakspo, N.T. 1990. Notes on Ladakhi popular culture. In N.K. Rustomji and C. Ramble (Eds.), *Himalayan environment and culture* (pp. 273-279). Shimla: IIAS and New Delhi: Indus Publishing Company.

Sharma, A. 1990. "Rampur's Lavi is a Mirror of the Culture". *Jansatta*, October 29. (in Hindi)

Sharma, A. 1994. "In Splendid Isolation". *The Hindustan Times*, August 27.

Sharma, A. 1999. *An American in Khadi: A Definitive Biography of Satyanand Stokes*. New Delhi: Penguin Books.

Sharma, B.D. 1987-89. Report of the Commissioner for Scheduled Castes and Sceduled Tribes, 29th Report.

Sharma, B.R. 1976. *Kinnar Lok Sahitya*. Bilaspur: Lalit Prakashan.

Sharma, R. and Tripathi, R.C. 1988. "Teacher Expectation and Attribution. In A.K. Dalal (Ed.), *Attribution: Theory and Research* (pp.). New Delhi: Wiley Eastern.

Sharma, S. 1983. "Reviving the Kangra Kalm. Chandulal Raina, the Last of the Painters. *The India Magazine*, July.

Sharma, U.N. 1971. Foreword. In M.M. Mamgain (Ed.) *Himachal Pradesh District Gazetteers. Kinnaur (pp. i-ii)*. Himachal Pradesh.

Shantideva, A. 1979. *A Guide to Bodhisattua's Way of Life*. (Translated by Stephen Batchelor). Dharamsala: Library of Tibetan Works and Archives.

Shashi, S.S. 1979. *The Nomads of the Himalayas*. Delhi: Sundeep Prakashan.

Shroder, J.F. Jr. 1989. "Hazards of the Himalaya". *American Scientist*, November-December.

Simpson, G. 1945. Principles of classification and a classification of mammals. *Bullietin of American Museum National History*, 85, 1-350.

Singh, Chetan 1998. *Natural Premises. Ecology and Peasant Life in the Western Himalaya 1800-1950*. Delhi: Oxford University Press.

Singh, Chhatrapati 1987. "Forestry and the Law in India". *The Journal of Law Institute*, 29(1).

Singh, K. and Ballabh, V. 1996. *Cooperative Management of Natural Resources*. New Delhi: Sage Publicatins.

Singh, K.S. 1993. "Tribal Scenarios: 1969-1990". In M. Miri (Ed.), *Continuity and Change in Tribal Society* (pp. 5-10). Shimla: Indian Institute of Advanced Study.

Singh, K.S. 2002. *People of India. Introduction*. New Delhi: Oxford.

Singh, M. 1975. "Mother Infant Separation in Rhesus Monkey Living under Natural Environment". *Primates*, 16, 471-476.

Singh, M. and Pirta, R.S. 1978. "Movement Out of Home Range and Disturbed Behaviour Patterns of a Group of Bonnet Monkeys-*Macaca radiata*". *American Journal of Physical Anthropology*, 49 (2): 265-270.

Singh, M., & Pirta, R.S. 1980. Field experiments on separation effects in rhesus monkeys. *Indian Journal of Clinical Psychology*, 7, 35-41.

Singh, S., Kothari, S. and Pande, P. (Eds.) 1990. *Directory of National Parks and Sanctuaries in Himachal Pradesh. Management Status and Profiles*. New Delhi: Indian institute of Public Administration.

Singh, S.D. 1966. Effect of Human Environment on Cognitive Behaviour in the Rhesus Monkey. *Journal of Comparative and Physiological Psychology*, 61(2), 280-283.

Singh, S.D. 1969. Urban monkeys. *Scientific American*, July.

Singh, S.D. 1977. "Effects of infant-infant Separation of Young Monkeys in a Free-Ranging Natural Environment". *Primates*, 18: 205-214.

Singh, T. 1991. "On Demise of Animal Wealth Neither We Survive nor Our Fields". *Jansatta*, Julai 30. (Hindi)

Singh, U. 2003. *Between Worlds: Travels among Mediums, Shamans and Healers*. New Delhi: Penguin.

Singh, V.P. 1996. "Affirmative Action in India". *Working Group on Alternative Strategies*, New Delhi, Occasional Papers 1.

Sinha, D. 1988. "Basic Indian Values and Behaviour Dispositions in the Context of National Development. An appraisal". In D. Sinha and H.S.R. Kao (Eds.), *Social Values and Development: Asian Perspectives* (pp. 31-55). New Delhi: Sage.

Sinha, D., Tripathi, R.C. and Misra, G. (Eds.) 1982. *Deprivation: Its Social Roots and Psychological Consequences*. New Delhi: Concept Publishing Company.

Sinha, J. 1958 (Reprint, 1986). *Indian Psychology. Vol. 1 Cognition*. Delhi: Motilal Banarasidass.

Sinha, J. 1961 (Reprint 1986). *Indian Psychology: Volume II: Emotion and Will*. Delhi: Motilal Banarsidass.

Smith, F.V. 1971. *Purpose in Animal Behaviour*. London: Hutchinson University Library.

Snellgrove, D.L. 1978. *The Image of the Buddha*. New Delhi: Vikas Publishing House/UNESCO.

Soule, M.E. 1986. "Conservation Biology and the "Real World." In M.E. Soule (Ed.), *Conservation Biology: The Science of Scarcity and Diversity* (pp. 1-12). Sunderland, Massachusetts: Sinauer Associates.

Southwick, C.H. 1972. *Ecology and the Quality of Our Environment*. New York: D. Van Nostrand Company.

Spanos, N.P. 1994. "Multiple Identity Enactments and Multiple Personality Disorder: A Socio-cognitive Perspective". *Psychological Bulletin*, 116(1), 143-165.

Srinivas, K., Kokate, K.D. and Nand, H. 1996. "A New Horizon in Lahoul". *Yojana*, December.

Srinivas, M.N. 2002. Foreword. In K.S. Singh. *People of India. Introduction* (pp. vii-xvi). New Delhi: Oxford.

Srinivasa Murthy, R. 1998. "Rural Psychiatry in Developing Countries". *Psychiatric Services*, *49*, 967-969.

Srinivasa Murthy, R. 2004. Mental Health in the New Millennium: Reseach Strategies for India. *Indian Journal of Medical Research*, 120, 63-66.

Staddon, J.E.R. 1983. *Adaptive Behaviour and Learning*. New York: Cambridge University Press.

Stamps, J.A. 1991. "Why Evolutionary Issues are Reviving Interest in Proximate Behavioural Mechanisms". *American Zoologist*, 3, 338-348.

Stolba, A., Lynch, G.N., Hinch, J.J., Adams, D.B., Munro, R.K. and Davies, H.I. 1990. "Social Organisation of Merino Sheep of Different Ages, Sex and Family Structure". *Applied Animal Behaviour Science*, 27(4), 337-349.

Stone, C.P. 1964. Introduction. In C.P. Stone (Ed.), *Comparative Psychology* (pp. 1-8). New Delhi: Prentice-Hall of India.

Stroebe, M., Gergen, M.M., & Gergen, K.G. 1992. Broken hearts or broken bonds: Love and death in historical perspective. *American Psychologist*, 47, 1205-1212.

Strong, M. 2001. Foreword. In G.G. Marten *Human Ecology. Basic Concepts for Sustainable Development* (pp. xii-xiii). London: Earthscan Publications.

Suman, S.D. 1939. Report of the non-official enquiry into the tragic happenings in Dhami State, (Simla Hills) on 16th July, 1939. Simla.

Super, C.M. and Harkness, S. 1997. "The Cultural Structuring of Child-Development. In J.W. Berry, P.R. Dasen, and T.S. Sarasvathi (Eds.), *Handbook of Cross-cultural Psychology, 2 ed. Vol. 2, Basic Processes and Human Development* (pp. 1-39). Boston, MA: Allyn and Bacon.

Suttie, J.M. and Reynolds, S.G. 2003. *Transhumant Grazing Systems in Temperate Asia*. Rome: Food and Agriculture Organization of the United Nations.

Suzuki, B.L. 1981. *Mahayana Buddhism*. London: George Allen & Unwin.

Swift, J. 1988. *Major Issues in Pastoral Development with Special Emphasis on Selected African Countries*. Food and Agriculture Organization of the United Nations, Rome.

Thakur, L.S. 2001. *Buddhism in the Western Himalaya: A Study of the Tabo Monastery*. New Delhi: Oxford University Press.

Thakur, M.R. 1994. Descendents of Vedic 'Pani': 'Dhani' People. *Vipasha*, 9(59), 72-78. (in Hindi)

Thanavi, S. 1992. "Canal is Becoming a Curse". *Jansatta*, June 4. (In Hindi).

Thapar, R. 2002. *Early India: from the origins to AD 1300*. New Delhi: Allen Lane, Penguin.

Tikekar, I. 1988. *Srimad Bhagavad: Ek yuganukul darshan*. New Delhi: Acharya Kakasaheb Kalelkar Smarak Nidhi.

Tinbergen, N. 1968. On War and Peace in Animals and Man: An Ethologist's Approach to the Biology of Aggression. *Science*, *160*, 1411-1418.

Tripathi, L.B. and Misra, G. 1975. "Cognitive Activities as a Function of Prolonged Deprivation". *Psychological Studies*, 21(2), 54-61.

Tripathi, R.C. 2003. "Culture as a Factor in Community Interventions". In J.W. Berry, R.C. Mishra and R.C. Tripathi (Eds.), *Psychology in Human and Social Development: Lessons from Diverse Cultures: A Festschrift for Durganad Sinha* (pp. 235-259). New Delhi: Sage.

Tripathi, R.S. 1989. *Acharya Shantideva's Bodhicharyavatar* (Bhot-version,

Hindi-translation and commentary). Laddakh: Central Institute of Buddhist Studies.

Trusov, Yu. P. 1983. "The Ecological Approach and Problems of Moulding the Noosphere". In A.D. Ursul (Ed.), *Philosophy and Ecological Problems of Civilisation* (pp. 58-78). Moscow: Progress Publishers.

Trussell, D. 1990. "The Arts and Planetary Survival". *The Ecologist*, 20. 4-8.

Tucci, G. 1988. *The Temples of Western Tibet and Their Artistic Symbolism*. New Delhi: Aditya Prakashan.

Tumurjav, M. 1990. "Economic and Biological Characteristics of Mongolian livestock". In Proceedings of the international workshop on pastoralism and socio-economic development. Food and Agricultural Organisation of the United Nations, Rome, pp. 28-35.

Upadhayay, V.K. 1994. How did green Sahara became a desert. *Jansatta*, March 20.

Valdiya, K.S. 1993. *High Dams in the Himalaya*. Nainital: PAHAR.

Valdiya, K.S. 1996. "Antecedent Rivers: Ganga is Older than Himalaya". *Resonance*, 1: 55-63.

Valdiya, K.S. 1997. "High Dams in Central Himalaya in Context of Active Faults Seismicity and Societal Problems". *Journal Geological Society of India*, 49, 479-494.

Varma, S. 1991. "Village Abandoned: The Case for Mobile Pastoralism in Post-Harrapan Gujarat". *Studies in History*, 7(2), 279-300.

Vaudeville, C. 1986. "Krishna Gopala, Radha, and the Great Goddess". In J.S. Hawley and D.M. Wulff (Eds.), *The Divine Concert: Radha and the Goddesses of India* (pp. 1-12). Boston, Massachusetts: Beacon Press.

Vaughan, H.W. 1950. Breeds of live stock in America. Ohio: Long's College Book Company.

Verma, V. 1996. *Gaddis of Dhauladhar: A Transhumant Tribe of the Himalaya*. New Delhi: Indus Publishing Company.

Verma, V. 1997. *Pangi: A Tribal Habitat in Mid-Himalaya*. New Delhi: K.K. Publishers & Distributors.

Verma, V. 1999. *Ban-Gujars. A Nomadic Tribe in Himachal Pradesh*. Delhi: B.R. Publishing Corporation.

Verma, V. 2002. *Kanauras of Kinnaur. A Scheduled Tribe in Himachal Pradesh*. Delhi: B.R. Publishing Corporation.

Vinoba 1951/1995. *Gita Pravachan*. Varanasi: Sarva Seva Sangh Prakashan.

Vogel, J. Ph. 1972. *Indian Serpent-lore or the Nagas in Hindu Legend and Art*. Varanasi: Indological Book House.

Warren, A. and Agnew, C. 1988. An assessment of desertification and land degredation in arid and semi-arid areas. International Institute for Environment and Development, London, Drylands Paper No. 2.

Warwick, B.L. 1959. "Report to the Government of India on Sheep and Wool Improvement by Breeding". *FAO Report No. 1053.*

Waters, R.H. 1964. "Historical Background of Comparative Psychology." In C.P. Stone (Ed.), *Comparative Psychology* (pp. 9-29). New Delhi: Prentice-Hall of India.

WHO 2001. *The World Health Report: 2001: Mental Health: New Understanding, New Hope*. Geneva: World Health Organization.

Williams, G.R.C. 1874. *Memoir of Dehra Dun: Historical and Statistical.* Roorkee: Thomas Civil Engineering Press.

Wilson E.O. 1975. *Sociobiology: The New Synthesis*. Cambridge, Massachusetts: Harvard University Press.

Wilson, E.O. 2006. *The Future of Life*. London: Abacus Workman, L. and Reader, W. 2004. *Evolutionary Psychology: An Introduction*. London: Cambridge University Press.

Wray, E., Rosenfield, C., Bailey, D. and Wray, J.D. 1979. *Ten Lives of the Buddha: Siamese Temple Paintings and Jataka Tales.* Tokyo: Weatherhill.

Wynne-Edwards, V.C. 1986. *Evolution Through Group Selection.* London: Blackwell Scientific Publications.

Wynne-Edwards, V.C. 1991. Ecology Denies Neo-Darwinism. *The Ecologist*, 21(3), 136-141.

Yadav, K. 1998. Rahul Sankrityayan's '*Kinner Desh Mein'*. In S.K. Gupta, V.P. Sharma and N.K. Sharda (Eds.), *Tribal Development: Appraisal and Alternatives* (pp.). New Delhi: Indus Publishing Company.

Yan, Z., Wu, N., Yeshi, D. and Ru, J. 2005. "A Review of Rangeland Privatisation and its Implications in the Tibetan Plateau, China". *Nomadic Peoples*, June 1.

Young, W.C. 1991. *The Rashaayada Bedouin: Arab Pastoralists of Eastern Sudan*. Florida: Harcourt Brace.

Yonfan, M. 1981. *Tibet: A Distant Horizon*. New Delhi: Vikas Publishing House.

Young, G.L. (ed.). 1983. *Origins of Human Ecology* (Benchmark Papers in Ecology: 12). New York: Hutchinson Ross Publishing Company.

Zhao, Q. and Deng, Z. 1988. "Ranging Behaviour of *Macaca thibetana* at Mt. Emei, China". *International Journal of Primatology,* 9, 37-47.

Zoller, C.P. 1990. Aspects of Traditional Relations between Man and Environment in Bangan (North-western Garhwal). In N.K. Rustomji and C. Ramble (Eds.), *Himalayan Environment and Culture* (pp. 159-172). New Delhi: IIAS, Shimla and Indus.

Zuberbuhler, K., Cheney, D. and Seyfarth, R.M. 1999. Conceptual semantics in a Nonhuman Primate. *Journal of Comparative Psychology*, 113, 33-42.

Index